THE
COOK'S
FISH
GUIDE

The Cook's Fish Guide

JACQUELINE E. KNIGHT

A SUNRISE BOOK

E. P. DUTTON & CO., INC. / NEW YORK / 1973

Published simultaneously in Canada by
Clarke, Irwin & Company Limited, Toronto and Vancouver
ISBN: 0–87690–101–1
Library of Congress Catalog Card Number: 73–79563
Outerbridge & Lazard, a subsidiary of E. P. Dutton & Co., Inc.

For Marion, whose appetite for fish is limited only by capacity

CONTENTS

Introduction

While there have never been more than wild guesses as to the total number of people of all ages who regard fishing and related water activities as a means of relaxation (or perhaps even a way of life), the fact that better than 25,000,000 fishing licenses were issued in 1971 is at least a starting point. This figure, of course, does not take into consideration those who enjoy this segment of the outdoors without the legal need for an official permit.

Many fishermen take their catches home for the table, but often they pass up excellent possibilities because they are unaware of them. It is my hope that this book will help correct that.

Regardless of the fisherman's motive—a day away from problems or a search for an IGFA or ISFA record—frequently the day's catch can present him with major problems in the kitchen or, more realistically, can present these problems to his wife in her position as chief cook. When the fisherman is junior grade and proudly brings in his catch, threatening open rebellion if *his* fish isn't cooked for dinner, and nonfishing mother doesn't even know what kind it is, this is a time to call for help.

In this volume I have tried to present the widest possible range of answers to the question, "What can I do with it?"

One of the first problems in such a project as this is the major one of nomenclature. It seems that for almost every area in which a species of fish is found it acquires its own local name. By way of example, the *Tautoga onitis* (as classified by the 1970 edition of the American Fisheries Society's *A List of Common and Scientific Names of Fishes from the United States and Canada*) is known as the "tautog," which is the Society's recognized common name, as well as blackfish and oysterfish. For another example, if someone says "dogfish" he might mean a freshwater fish also known as bowfish or lake lawyer (among other names) or the saltwater sand shark. The Society, incidentally, is fighting an uphill battle to regularize common names. It would make life much simpler for all of us who talk and write about fish if we would use the agreed-on names.

To eliminate as much confusion as possible, you will find that the recipe sections have been divided into categories based on flesh characteristics. Since the qualities of texture and moisture dictate the methods of preparation, I have grouped together all the recipes that can be used, for example, for firm-fleshed moist fish. As a result, you will find both fresh- and saltwater fish in almost all of the sections. Your eye and sense of touch will tell you which section to use. If you know the recognized common name, you are that much ahead (the common names can be found in the index in the back, along with many strictly local names).

Naturally this method of grouping must of necessity be somewhat arbitrary. Few of the recognized food fishes have been scientifically analyzed as to nutritional value, let alone moisture and fat content. The assignment to groups is the result of my years of personal observation and discussion with fishermen in many parts of the world. The determinations are, of course, relative; your dividing line between moist and oily may differ from mine, but at least mine will give you a reference point.

As a further aide, the recipes within each section are in sequence, ranging from appetizers (and don't forget that these can frequently be used for sandwich fillings) through main courses to the use of leftovers.

One further advantage to this pattern of organization is that I hope it will help you to use this book as the starting point for experimentation. As with any food preparation, there really are no hard and fast rules beyond using the finest and freshest ingredients possible—from the fish itself on down the line. This book will serve its intended purpose if a New England housewife, firm in the tradition of Friday night fishcakes, is tempted by the recipe for Basque stew made from local salt cod—and tries it. To encourage your own exploration, seasonings and sauces have their own section as do basic cooking methods. Recommendations are made, of course, but your own combinations, dictated by your imagination, your family's taste and the contents of your larder are bound to result in treasured family recipes.

Since the condition of the fish when it arrives in your kitchen is of prime consideration for enjoyment and full nutritive value (in which fish and shellfish usually rank high), the first two chapters are for the fisherman to read whether he personally goes on with the recipes or not. Unfortunately, all too few fishermen take the time and trouble after unhooking a fish to care for it properly to assure table excellence, and many just don't know. However, by way of apology, I have noted in the index with an asterisk any sport fish recognized by the International Game Fish Association and with a # any International Spin Fishing Association fish. Perhaps this will help a sport fisherman justify an extra fishing day; after all, it's food for the table as well as one of the major sports.

It is unfortunately true that a few southern fishes have earned the reputation of being poisonous. The puffer, for instance, carries a poison gland that must be removed without breaking lest it contaminate the flesh; otherwise it is not only edible, but considered delicious by some. The barracuda, rabbitfish, and more recently the southern grouper, have all made people painfully and frighteningly ill with a nerve poison. But this is not due to anything inherent in these species; it is, according to marine biologists, a result of the fish eating smaller species down the food chain that have accumulated a toxin from a plant that grows on a virtually barren sea floor near the Bahamas. It is always wise to ask about the edibility of fish taken from any area, particularly in the Caribbean. Keep in mind that many fish, such as the barracuda, are considerable travelers.

The northern blowfish is not only edible, but popular with the restaurant trade. There is some question, however, as to the edibility of the liver and roe; one of the Indo-Pacific subspecies of blowfish is poisonous (flesh as well as organs) during certain stages of the reproductive cycle. Since even scientists are not sure whether the northern and southern blowfish are the same species, it is quite possible that when the southern one becomes tainted, it is because of its diet, as with the barracuda.

Unfortunately, there is no possible way of telling where (nor frequently what) a fish—any kind—has been eating. The safest thing to do is to ask people who are knowledgeable in the local area if you have any doubts about edibility.

As a fishing guide can point out the methods and techniques that make for a successful fishing day, so I hope this book will lead to successful and enjoyable seafood meals. If it helps as I intend it to, it will live up to its name —The Cook's Fish Guide.

CHAPTER ONE

First Things First

CARE
OF THE
CATCH

"Now that I've got 'em, what do I do?" is not a question often asked by any fisherman, good or bad. Rarely does he bother with anything more than getting that lure or bait back in the water, fast, in hopes that the granddaddy of the one just caught is still in the same waters. Unfortunately, this is not the attitude guaranteed to put the finest food on the table—regardless of cooking methods or fancy recipes.

While there is undoubtedly a seasoning of tribal pride when daddy produces dinner from his outing, it's rarely true that his "fresh-caught" fish is better than or even equal to anything available in the local market, whether from Joe the fishdealer or the nearest frozen food cabinet. Unrecognized by some, unknown by others, commercially caught and marketed fish are handled quickly and expertly to provide the highest-quality and best-tasting product.

Since the digestive process in fish is a chemical rather than mechanical one, it continues after death and does damage to the quality of flesh far more quickly than any other factor. When a fish is feeding (which is when the majority of sport fishermen take their catch), his digestive juices are most active. These acids continue working to their saturation point on the stomach and surrounding areas after the mechanical intake of food ceases. A "fishy" odor is the first sign of decomposition; a fresh-from-the-water fish doesn't smell fishy. A touch more acid action leads to a slightly "fishy" taste. If unchecked, this chemical reaction eventually leads to bloat and rupture of the stomach walls. While the *beginning* of this process is not harmful or positively unpleasant, it is the first step leading to rotten fish, unpleasant to handle and unhealthy to eat. If this chemical decomposition has begun, the catch cannot be classified "strictly fresh."

To qualify their catch for a governmental category of "strictly fresh," the majority of commercial fishing vessels have a portion of the crew assigned to handling the fish after they are boated. Also, a portion of the ship's space and weight allowances are sacrificed to maintain the catch in the best possible manner. Why should the sport fisherman who brings home a day's catch with justifiable and often vociferous pride be any less careful of his take?

Since the freshest possible fish is the most delicious and nutritious, whether for immediate use or for preservation for the future (Chapter III), "strictly fresh" fish needs defining. These have certain characteristics which are easily discernible to the senses.

1. The eyes are bright, shiny and clear.
2. Skin colors are relatively bright although fading begins practically immediately upon taking some species from the water.
3. The gills are bright red, covered with clear mucous, and have a fresh odor.
4. Skin mucous is also clear.

5. The flesh is firm and does not retain finger impressions.
6. The belly walls are intact and rib bones are firm to the backbone.
7. The vent is pink and protruding.
8. There is almost no odor, certainly no "fishy" one.

Fish that are not cleaned until the end of the day on the way in from the fishing grounds, at the dock, or worse, at home, cannot come up to these standards. To a greater or lesser degree, the eyes are dull, wrinkled and sunken; the skin colors are excessively faded; the gills are brown or gray with a cloudy mucous and have an offensive odor; the skin mucous is cloudy and/or ropy to the touch; belly walls may be ruptured (in some species the viscera may protrude or the rib bones may have broken from the backbone); the vent is brown and protruding; the odor is "fishy"—stale, sour or, in extreme cases, downright putrid.

Regardless of the fishing circumstances, the sportsman can present his family and himself with truly prime fare. If he's on a charter with a captain and a mate or with a guide, given the right approach (and the fact he's paying the bill), they should kill the fish immediately by stunning it or breaking the backbone—a simple technique with some species. This is usually done by putting a heavily gloved thumb in the mouth from the top of the head and snapping the head back. The gills are cut out or the whole head and gill area lopped off. The belly is slit from the vent forward to the gill cut and the viscera thumbed out.

When the belly of your catch (most species, that is) is slit—be sure it's done carefully—you may have caviar, which can be made from many fishes, on your hands. Should you have a female at the right season, you may have a bonus of excellent eating in the roe. Remove this carefully in one piece, wash off, and ice. While I have not had a chance to try every kind of roe, I've eaten most and have found only salmon not to be in the delicacy category—but that does make prime caviar! *WARNING:* Some blowfish and barracuda roes are considered poisonous.

The resulting cavity is thoroughly washed to remove any remaining viscera and blood. The fish should then be immediately iced to reduce its temperature as quickly as possible. Icing should be done with chips, rather than blocks, even though this sometimes means pounding, since chips should be put in the cavity and on top of the fish as well. For best results, the chips beneath the fish should be under a rack so the fish is not swimming dead in melted ice water. Small panfish, which are cooked and eaten "in the round" (uneviscerated), are the only exception to this procedure, but they too must be iced. Put them in layers with ice chips.

"Bleeding," a term frequently bandied about by sportsmen cooks, is taken care of by the beheading and eviscerating. After all, when the organs are removed (the lungs purify the blood and the stomach contains the bulk of the circulatory system) and the spinal blood is thumbed out, there's not much left.

Bleeding does have one advantage; it provides the whitest flesh possible. I do not agree that all tuna and salmon should be bled to remove even the backbone line. There is nothing wrong with it; it is edible, tasty and smooth-textured. However, should you decide to bleed a fish, immediately upon catching it, cut the throat and pull out the gill. Naturally, hold the head end down to drain. Eviscerate after draining, then rinse thoroughly. This is the bleeding method used with New England cod, haddock and such, particularly when they are intended for dry salting.

Sportfishing cruisers usually are equipped with wells to keep bait fish alive, and these do equally well keeping smaller species of catches alive until they can be handled at leisure. Just be sure there is a constant flow arrangement so the water does not become stale. Stale water will kill a fish by suffocation just as surely but not as efficiently as a knock on the head.

Large species are usually stunned on boating as a matter of safety. If they are intended for tournament or record entry where weighing and measuring are required, or for trophy mounting by a taxidermist who prefers to make his own incisions, knock the fish on the head, hoist him on the gin pole and leave him be; but don't plan on eating him. However, if you intend those mako steaks for the table (and they are every bit as good as, if not better than, swordfish) an agile mate can eviscerate him where he hangs. The whole point is to get that acid out of him quickly. A record setter or tournament winner can taste better than a promptly cared-for fish to only one person—the angler.

Small-boat or wading fishermen can delay caring for their catch for a bit, if they use a stringer properly and keep it in flowing water. While this doesn't help the fish, it will keep them alive longer than letting them flap in a pail of water or on the bottom of the boat. However, keep in mind that the stomach contains only a certain amount of food for the acids to work on. Freshwater-trout fishermen should be particularly careful in handling their catch. Trout, for some reason, seem to go bad faster than any other species.

If the fisherman is on his own, obviously something has to give, either the quality of the end product or a few extra casts. Since more people eat the fish than catch them, the pleasure and welfare of the majority should not suffer for the pleasure of the minority.

Because ice is not practical to lug along while wading a stream, put some wet moss or grasses in your creel, then the cleaned fish, then more wet stuff. If you wade deep and your creel or pocket gets into the creek, so much the better. Just keep your cleaned catch cool with moisture. If you don't wade deep, stop every now and then and dunk your catch; it will taste all the better for such treatment. Since trout is one of the species that will quickly loosen rib bones from the backbone, prompt care will make eating much more pleasant, particularly for that family member who just doesn't like bones!

In warmer weather, should the fisherman be completely unable to ice his catch, or to hold it in running water, he can still manage to get it home in good shape if he takes the time and trouble to do a temporary corning job. After cleaning and washing the belly cavity of the fish, it is thoroughly rubbed with common table salt mixed with pepper in the ratio of 1 tablespoon of pepper to 1 cup of salt. The proper amount of pepper can be added to a partially used market salt container and carried in the tackle box for such emergencies. The mix is also sprinkled on the skin side of the fish. Lay the fish in a container which can be covered with several layers of wet burlap propped well enough above the fish to allow for air circulation. They will keep well for at least 48 hours. If the fish are rolled in the salt and left packed with as much salt as will cling to them, they will keep for as long as 10 days. After thorough washing, these can be used in any manner desired.

When it comes to harvesting shellfish, the live well or box is an essential, second only to being sure that the waters are unpolluted. For that important information, check with the local Board of Health. Even if it's the youngsters who wade the mud flats for clams, give them some means of keeping their crop alive in flowing water; their sand pails won't do it. A wire-mesh floating box similar to, but smaller than, those used by boat liveries to maintain live bait is excellent, easy to make and handle, and serves a double purpose with all bivalves—clams, oysters, scallops and mussels.

These, if left in such a floating trap in tidal flow water, will flush themselves of undesirable sand and gravel, making the cleaning process in the kitchen much easier, and the eating more pleasant. All shellfish should be alive when used; bivalves should tighten and close when handled, crabs and lobsters should scrabble and fight to get away. If they don't actively object to the treatment they're getting, discard them; they are not fit to eat.

The floating live well can also come in handy as a source of soft-shelled crabs. When you go crabbing, check your catch over carefully. If you know the signs, you can pick the crabs that will shortly shed their outgrown houses to result in soft shells. A crab that is soon to molt will have a space between the upper and lower shells at the back between the swimming legs covered by a thin, semitransparent membrane. Frequently, if it's just about to pop out, you can see the line of the soft new white shell underneath. Save these crabs in a live well in free-flowing tidal water and, when they've shed and are white, you've got soft-shelled crabs that are entirely edible, white shell, innards and all. But do remember to feed them while they are in the well! Fishheads and scraps from your fishing trips will do fine.

There are a few exceptions to the rule of having shellfish argue with you on going into the pot—saltwater crawfish (spiny or rock lobster) and two subspecies of crabs (stone and king), but this applies only when these crustaceans are taken by divers or trap lifters who have ice at hand. When a crawfish is taken, an antenna is broken off at the head and the soft tip is broken off. The body is discarded after breaking it off by snapping backwards just behind the carapace (body shell). The narrow end of the antenna is then inserted into the anal opening at the base of the tail shields, pushed in about one fifth of the length of the tail, twisted in a half circle and pulled out. This removes the dorsal orin (alimentary tract) and cleans it for icing.

A trap lifter, wearing heavy-duty workshoes and gloves, can handle stone crabs as the professionals do, thereby assuring a supply for coming years. They take only the crusher claw (the larger of the two forward ones) and return the live and kicking crab to his waters to grow a new claw for harvesting in the future. The technique calls for a heavily protected foot on top of the crab and a strong arm and hand to break off the crusher. However, since a strong man can have considerable trouble with a big stone keeping the crusher and second claw from joining, and that crusher really does live up to its name, don't go experimenting; learn the technique and practice it with someone who really knows! In the meantime, handle stone crabs as you do all other crabs such as blue claw and soft-shells—keep them alive, and handle them with respect!

The Alaska king crab, since he is equipped with nipper walking claws rather than crushers, does not present such a problem. Remove alternate claws down each side, being sure to leave one feeder claw at the head so he can sustain himself while he, too, grows replacements. Since the king crabs grow to a six-foot spread, there's plenty of good food in the nippers.

The true lobster, the cold-water one taken off the northeastern coast of the United States and Canada, is a far different matter from the southern crawfish. He comes equipped with two heavy forward claws, one invariably larger than the other. This is his crusher and fighting claw, but both claws contain the most succulent meat. The lobster normally is taken in a trap and has his claws "pegged" when removed from it. A heavy short piece of wood is inserted in the hinge of the claw so that he cannot open it; then the lobster is kept alive in flowing salt water. There are two reasons for the peg; one, of course, is to prevent the lobster from taking hold of you, but perhaps the most important one is to prevent the lobsters from fighting in their confined quarters, a practice that can result in badly damaged creatures. Usually, unfortunately, live lobster is dropped into boiling sea or salted water head first and cleaned afterwards. A better technique is described on page 250.

Shrimps, while now usually bought already processed from the market, were once a favorite prey of the proper Victorians. Catching them provided a pleasant day in the open as well as good food; and those original Victorians of England were experts in their preparation. Again, the crustaceans were kept alive, formerly in a creel or basket, but today a floating well serves very nicely.

Whatever you take from the water, panfish or monster, bivalve or crustacean (or even more exotic things that are covered in Chapter VIII), remember to care for it immediately; it will pay dividends at the table.

CHAPTER TWO

Get Ready
for
the Table

PREPARATION
AND
BASIC COOKING
METHODS

Once the cleaning and cooling has been attended to, all that remains to be done is to prepare the catch for cooking. Methods here vary according to the species and how they are to be cooked. The major point is to take care of all the chores before you get home; taking scales off the kitchen ceiling is no fun. Some fish need no scaling; those that do may be either scaled or skinned. Obviously, if you are going to skin the fish, you don't have to scale it.

If scaling is necessary, first clip off the fins, as close to the skin as possible without cutting it. Use a commercial scaler as per instructions, or the blade of a heavy knife held at a 45-degree angle against the fish. Whichever you use, pull it from the tail to the head, against the scales.

Large firm-fleshed fish, for the most part, make excellent steaks. These are cut with a sharp knife through the fish at right angles to the backbone. They are best cut 1 to 1¼ inches thick, even for people who prefer thick sirloins. If a fish steak is cut much thicker than this, the outside tends to overcook. While the steak can be skinned, it is preferable to leave the skin on to hold the meat together while cooking; it peels off very easily after cooking.

Split fish can be broiled, baked in a liquid, poached, steamed, or fried. Splitting is much easier to do than filleting; however the bones are still present to worry the diner.

Actually, there are two methods of splitting fish, one through the abdominal cavity after the fish has been eviscerated; the other removes the backbone from the top, along with the viscera, making a belly cut unnecessary. The first method is the one most frequently used, while the second is usually recommended for salmon to be prepared in the Scandinavian manner.

When the backbone is removed, ribs can be cut free and pulled out with tweezers, unless the species is a particularly bony one such as bonefish or shad.

There is another boning method that results in an unbroken envelope of fish, entirely without bones, that can be stuffed and baked. This was evolved by my late husband, Dick, after we invited a friend for a baked striped bass dinner—and he informed us that he'd eat steak. It seems he lost more than his appetite if he ran into a bone.

This method works well with any of the fresh- or saltwater bass families, or any fish with a similar bone structure. After the fish has been eviscerated:

1. Make a cut on each side of the ventral (lower back) fin and pull it out back to front. With clippers or scissors, cut off the dorsal (front top) fin level with the back. Do not cut the skin. Slit the skin between the vent and the tail.
2. Keeping the knife at a 45-degree angle, start separating the meat from the backbone at the ventral opening. Flench the meat from the bone to the top of the back, not cutting the skin.

3. With scissors or clippers, cut the ribs free from the backbone and lay the whole section back flat.
4. Turn the fish around and repeat with the other side.
5. Remove the backbone.
6. Flench the rib bones free with the knife. Remove the remaining bony meat. With the fingers, check the remaining flesh to be sure all the bones are removed.
7. Lay stuffing all along one side of the fish, mounding in the rib area to re-form. Skewer or sew up, and you have a boneless fish for baking that can be cut like a meat loaf, and everyone gets plenty of stuffing.

Shad boning is an art in itself, and a difficult one. Foremost practitioners of it are the Helmrich Brothers of Williamsport, Pennsylvania, who supply beautifully boned shad to finer restaurants and clubs all over the world. It's a very tricky bit and not recommended for amateurs. While the Helmrichs can bone a shad in a very short time, keep in mind they are the third generation in their family to do it and they've had lots of practice.

Filleting, resulting in a boneless piece of meat with no waste and one optional piece of skin, is undoubtedly the most popular method of cutting, and one of the more difficult. This is a technique recommended primarily for firm-fleshed meat that will hold together in cooking, regardless of the method. Filleting is the first step in producing fish sticks and fish squares from thick fish and the first choice in handling flat fish such as flounder and sole. Here is the method, using such a flat fish:

1. Place the fish top (dark) side up; cut to the depth of the bones (but not into them) at an angle from the top of the head down to the end of the chin.
2. With a sharp knife held at an angle, gently work the flesh free from the bones, working toward the tail.
3. Turn the fish over and make a reverse angle cut on the underside.
4. Remove the bottom fillet in the same manner, cutting from the head toward the tail.

These fillets can be skinned, if desired, by gently working the knife blade between the skin and the solid piece of meat.

A tough-hided, spiny fish such as a catfish presents a skinning problem. Wearing heavy gloves and being careful not to stab yourself on one of their sharp spines (some of which secrete a fluid which will give you an extremely sore hand and possibly a fever), cut a ring around the head back of the skull. Using broad-billed pliers, grab the skin behind the head and peel it back to the tail. If the fish has not been eviscerated, make a cut at the back of the head from the top deep enough to cut the backbone; pull the head straight out from the body and the entrails will come out with it.

(Incidentally, jewelry hobbyists and youngsters appreciate some catfish heads. Boil them in plenty of water long enough for the flesh to fall off—45 minutes to an hour—and pick out the catfish "pearls"—the earbones—and the cross-shaped bone in which they are set. Both are used by hobby jewelers.)

The same skinning technique is used for any tough-skinned fish. This method with northern saltwater blowfish, for example, results in a fine restaurant's "chicken of the sea," a chicken-leg-shaped piece of solid meat with a single bone.

While there are advocates of unskinned eels, if you do not care for them, the easiest way to handle the eels is to slit the skin in a ring behind the head, nail the head to a board, and peel off the skin with pliers as if peeling off a tight glove.

If your bivalves have not spent enough time trapped in a floating box to flush themselves, 15 minutes in an acidulated solution will do the job. Add about 2 tablespoons of vinegar to a quart of water and let them sit in that for about 15 minutes. The acid acts as an irritant, annoying the bivalve into spitting out sand and grit. Whichever system you use, scrub them well under running water before dropping them into a cooking pot or opening them to eat raw. The bottom mud (and, on mussels, the beard which should be pulled off) adds nothing to the flavor or appearance. Never use, raw or cooked, any bivalve with a cracked or broken shell, nor a cooked one that refuses to open.

All raw bivalves can be opened the same way, harder shells naturally putting up more of a fight. While there are gadgets on the market that supposedly make the job easier for the novice, all you really need is a short, heavy knife available in most fishing stations. If commercial shuckers can handle literally barrels of clams and oysters a day, with just a bit of practice you can easily manage a dozen or so.

With the shallow bottom shell held in the palm of your hand, insert the knife between the lips of the shell at the point of the shell near the hinge. Force the knife in, cutting the flesh free from the top of the shell. The knife has to be angled slightly upwards to scrape along the upper shell. Remove the top shell and run the knife under the flesh in the bottom shell, freeing it completely.

(My father discovered a trick to make clams and oysters relax a bit; he puts them into the freezer for about 20 minutes before opening them.)

For service on the half shell, spill as little of the juice as possible, chill, and serve within an hour of opening. If they are not to be served raw, open them over a bowl and save the liquid for cooking; it helps the flavor of the finished dish.

Until the labeling laws were tightened, markets carried three different kinds of scallops. One simply was not a scallop; it was a scallop-shaped piece of meat cut out of skate wings. They were, of course, edible, but tended to be tougher than the real article. There are also deep-sea scallops, a true bivalve commercially taken.

The prize scallop, of course, is the tiny so-called Bay scallop, the original coming from Great South Bay off Long Island, New York and shipped to all parts of the country. These are protected by law but, if you are interested in trying a real delicacy and can do it legally, hunt for scallops, not just clams, in estuary waters. If they are carefully taken (the bottom not roiled up) they don't need any flushing, and they open easily. While it is true that just the muscle of the sea scallop is used, the entire estuarine scallop is not only edible but delicious.

(The use of just the muscle of even the sea scallop strikes me as a waste; in Europe they are not so profligate and use the whole of the meat. What got us into the practice remains a mystery to me.)

The best of fish fare is moist, tender and flavorful, and practically any cooking method chosen will produce the desired result if care is taken and you keep an eye on the cooking. Whatever the species of fish, whichever method is followed, fish is ready for the table when it "flakes" easily. To test for this just-right moment, gently insert a table fork, not a large kitchen one, and lightly twist. The flesh will break into obvious flakes.

If your recipe calls for keeping the fish warm while a sauce is prepared, remove it to a warmed platter in a warming oven (lowest possible temperature) just short enough of the flaking point to have the fish finish cooking (which it will do even in a very low oven) while the sauce is completed. This is a tricky bit of timing, admittedly, but practice will make perfection. If fish is overcooked it gets mushy and loses flavor and overcooked shellfish toughens.

Two cooking methods, simmering and steaming, usually require that the fish be wrapped in several layers of cheesecloth to hold it together, particularly soft-fleshed fish such as scrod and cod. While a New England menu may say "boiled cod," actually simmering or poaching is closer to the truth; the liquid is brought quickly to a boil and skimmed, the fish is added and the cooking reduced to a mere simmer. An active boil might well tear the fish to pieces, even if wrapped.

Steaming is done, again wrapped (and using parchment paper will keep down kitchen odors), on a greased rack above a boiling liquid.

Both these methods are used with either whole fish or large pieces, and always with a seasoned liquid (Chapter X).

Frying is undoubtedly one of the more popular ways of preparing fish and shellfish, whether a gentle sauté, a quick deep-fry or anywhere in between. Always be sure to use fresh fat or oil for frying, regardless of the depth of the fat. Fish quickly absorb alien flavors, a fact that makes the use of batters in deep-frying popular (Chapter X). When deep-frying, it is always advisable to use a deep-fry thermometer to read the temperature accurately. The fried-bread-cube method allows too much margin for error, and with improper temperature the end result can be tough, or soggy, depending on which side you err.

Pan-frying means to cook the food to a golden brown on one side in a small amount of fat (the fish is usually coated with seasoned dry ingredients) then turn and brown the other side. In sautéing, again only a small amount of fat is used, but the food without a coating is kept moving, either by frequent turning or agitating the pan, so that it does not develop a crisp crust.

Oven-frying is a relatively recently developed technique which saves spatter on the stove, frees a top burner for something else and, to my mind, is the easiest method. In this case the fish (steaks or sticks are best but any evenly sized pieces will do) is given a coarse coating such as half and half cornmeal and flour, or seasoned crumbs. Melt butter in a shallow baking pan while preheating a very hot oven. Put the coated fish in the pan in the oven and cook for the required time, turning once.

Broiling is an excellent method of preparation for the majority of firm-fleshed fish. However, fish with a low fat content should be generously treated with butter, bacon or oil to prevent drying, and the broiling rack should always be greased to prevent sticking. Fillets, split fish and steaks are the usual cuts for this type of cooking.

There is one other cooking technique unfortunately little practiced in this country but popular in much of the rest of the world (Latin America, Asia and Scandinavia) and that is cold cooking. This is a standard procedure for main courses as well as for appetizers in many lands which depend heavily on the waters for sustenance. Don't let the term upset you; it does not necessarily mean raw. In most cases it means a marinade which cooks the fish through chemical reactions.

Clams and oysters seem to be as far as we Americans are willing to go in the eating-raw department, and some people have an aversion to even that. This, to me, is somewhat deplorable. Scallops, which people never think of eating raw, are delicious. Whenever I sit and shuck them, I usually wind up eating a good portion of them raw, and without benefit of a fancy sauce. Even some fish are good completely raw, sliced very thin at an angle. The Orientals are particularly fond of preparing fish in this way, and they are truly experts in serving tasty and nutritious meals from the sea.

Approximate Cooking Times

STEAM fish for 10 to 40 minutes, depending on thickness of the piece.

POACH or SIMMER fish for 7 to 10 minutes per pound.

SAUTÉ fish golden in a medium-hot skillet for approximately 5 minutes for a fillet.

DEEP-FRY bite-sized pieces for 3 to 6 minutes in 390° fat.

DEEP-FRY croquettes of cooked chopped seafood for 2 to 4 minutes at 375° to 380°.

DEEP-FRY croquettes of raw chopped seafood for 5 to 6 minutes at 370°.

DEEP-FRY fritters of chopped cooked seafood for 2 to 5 minutes at 365° to 370°.

DEEP-FRY batter-dipped small panfish and raw whole shellfish for 2 to 6 minutes at 390°.

To judge baking time, estimate the weight of the cleaned, unstuffed fish. Cook in a preheated very hot (550°) oven for 15 minutes, then reduce the heat to hot (450° to 500°). Allow approximately 10 minutes per pound for up to 4 pounds, then 5 minutes more for each additional pound. For constant temperature baking, allow 10 minutes per pound in a preheated hot (450°) oven. Baked split fish or fillets can be cooked quickly (10 to 12 minutes total) in a preheated very hot (500°) oven or more slowly (25 to 30 minutes) in a preheated hot (450°) oven.

I have adopted a format for the recipes that should make things a bit less pressing in the kitchen. Wherever practical I have indicated with / the point at which preparation can be delayed. All the preparations before / can be done in the earlier part of the day; all after / should be done just prior to cooking and serving. Needless to say, unless specified otherwise, all the ingredients tended to before / should be refrigerated in the interim. At the finish of all preparations prior to /, in most cases the dishes can be frozen for future use, making it practical to double up on many of the recipes. Be sure to defrost any prepared dish slowly in the refrigerator.

Weights and Measures

The usual table of equivalents is due for a change in the foreseeable future when the United States converts to the metric system. Here are our current measurements (which are used throughout this book) and their metric equivalents:

1 quart = 2 pints, liquid or dry measure = 4 cups, liquid or dry measure = 8 gills, liquid measure = 32 ounces, liquid or dry

1 litre, the metric measure closest to our quart = 1.0567 liquid quart

1 ounce = 28.35 grams

1 pound = 453.6 grams

1 kilogram (1000 grams) = slightly over 2 pounds (2.205 pounds, to be precise).

While there is nothing more delicious than fresh fish eaten within hours of being caught, when a run is on it's the rare fisherman who's willing to release every fish that he and his family can't use immediately. Good days on open boat docks show burlap sacks and plastic bags filled with dozens of fish going home to small families. Well, neighbors like fresh fish, too—if they are cleaned. However, why give away all those good meals unless you have a fair trade agreement with the sportsman next door? With a little forethought and preparation you can preserve your excess catch for excellent out-of-season meals.

American Indians were preserving fish to provide food for lean periods long before the first white man saw these shores. They did it over a smoky fire, much as today's sportsman can. Sailing ships always carried barrels of salted fish, even though they frequently navigated waters that would give them fresh catches. Even today the Eskimo throws his catch onto the ice, lets it get rock hard, and stacks it like cordwood to feed both his family and his dogs. Since the years have proved the practicality of preserving fish by a variety of methods, why not put some fish aside for the future? Modern equipment and products make it easier than ever.

Freezing

The advent of the home freezer has saved much time and effort in the kitchen (and money in the pocket) for sportsmen all over the country. It not only preserves fresh raw fish and precooked fish, it prolongs the life of foods preserved by the old-time methods.

Materials used for freezing are of prime importance, no matter what you are preserving. If the wrappings allow air to get to the food, freezer burn will make it unpleasant and even unpalatable. To insure airtightness, double wrapping is recommended for all foods not in a liquid-filled container. While heavy-duty aluminum foil is undoubtedly best for an outer wrap (carefully sealed with freezer tape), for underwrappings you can use a freezer paper, made especially for the purpose and usually as readily available as foil. Parchment paper, available through commercial suppliers if not at your local market, is a nonporous paper which can also serve satisfactorily. Whatever the wrapping materials, seal all folds with freezer tape after smoothing the wrapping as close to the fish as possible.

There is another material, not as readily available, perhaps, but one which I find efficient and easy and quick to handle with the proper tools; and it separates from itself. This is *fuseable* cellophane. This is sealed not with freezer tape but with a warm iron. Some large hardware stores stock a narrow, handled iron that maintains the proper temperature for sealing this material. I had trouble finding one locally, so the manager of the local meat market was kind enough to give me the name and address of the maker of the iron he used to prepackage meats behind the counter. A letter brought a brochure describing several models at various prices. Since the only cellophane that is up to the job is fuseable, it would be wise to be assured of a supply before going on an iron hunt. A regular dry (nonsteam) clothes iron can also be used, but it must be very carefully cleaned after using and I found it awkward to handle.

When fish and shellfish are to be frozen raw, do all the steps preliminary to cooking before wrapping, with the exception of stuffing a baking fish. Always have foods thoroughly cleaned and trimmed before packaging: if they are not clean you will have more work to do when they defrost; if they're not trimmed, you're wasting freezer space. I find it most practical to package fairly large amounts together (to the capacity of the freezer shelves), which is why I prefer to use fuseable cellophane for an underwrap.

I package individual portions—one serving-sized fillet, half a swordfish steak (if that will make a portion) or as many as three small fillets together. These servings I heat-seal, spread on a freezing shelf or freezing tin (if I don't have a shelf free, I find that a large cookie sheet laid on top of thoroughly frozen foods does a good quick freeze); when they are frozen, I overwrap all of them together with taped foil and label. In this way I can take out only what is needed. Since the cellophane does not stick to itself the entire package does not have to be thawed. This system also prevents small packages from getting lost in the shuffle. It's a lot easier to find one large package of fillets than the necessary six or eight for a dinner when they are tucked into odd corners.

Flat cut pieces, such as fish steaks, can be packaged together with *two* sheets of parchment or freezer paper between, then wrapped and overwrapped. If two sheets of paper are used, steaks can be taken off the pile as they are needed. This system is not practical, however, unless both sides of the pieces are cut flat and they can be stacked in a pyramid or column. If two pieces of fish are put side by side to square off a package, be sure a double layer of paper divides them. If one piece of fish overhangs another, separating them can be a chore and the package will need partial defrosting. Packaging this way (with layers of paper rather than using the cellophane) slows the freezing process since the bulk of the package reduces the efficiency of the freezing shelf, although it can be used without damage to the final product.

Except when you are using fuseable cellophane, the wrapping technique is the same for both the under- and overwrappings; use the standard drugstore fold. The fish is laid lengthwise on a piece of wrapping material longer than the fish and about one quarter wider than the girth of the fish. The two long sides are brought together and folded over, then folded over once or twice more to bring it snug to the body, then folded in at an angle on both sides of each end to make a point. This point is again smoothed and flattened and folded in once to the fish, then folded in again and over the top fold. Tape is run along the length of the long fold down over the points to the bottom of the package. In overwrapping, try to make the long fold across the width of the fish, although some large fish may be just too big for that. In that case, turn the underwrapped package over so that the long seam will be on the other side of the piece. This, along with smoothing all the air possible out of the wrappings, will help prevent air spoilage.

There is one possible advantage to using oven-tempered foil for an under-wrap; individual packages can go still frozen in their underfoil into the oven. A 10- or 12-ounce cleaned frozen fish or fillet can be put into a pre-heated 450° oven for about 30 minutes; after that time open the foil and turn it back. Dot with butter and add your choice of seasonings. Bake for about 10 minutes more, until done. Larger fish, steaks or fillets (weighing about 2 pounds) will take about 55 minutes; a 3-pound fish about 1 hour and a quarter—both timings include opening the package for the last 10 to 15 minutes. Keep in mind, however, that the fish (if it's whole) cannot be stuffed if handled this way. To package for freezing for this cooking method, wash the fish well and pack it while still very wet; it needs the moisture in cooking.

Glazing is a freezing technique that works well with eviscerated whole fish, small panfish and roe. This is a system of building up a skin of ice about ¼ inch thick all over the fish, which keeps the air off as long as the ice is intact. If you use this method, you should check the glaze frequently and renew it as needed. No overwrapping is necessary if the glazing is done and maintained properly.

To glaze, dip the fish into ice cold water and wrap in parchment or freezer paper, then freeze, redip into ice water and refreeze, repeating until the necessary "skin" is built up. (Frankly, this method is a lot of work and very time-consuming, and also very cold on the hands.)

A third freezing method, employing an ice block, is the most effective for bivalves, and oddly enough, freshwater trout. Trout preserved in this way can be kept for months and will taste every bit as good as fresh caught; perhaps even better, since they can be enjoyed out of season. Waxed milk cartons are excellent for this purpose (cut off the tops) or use a bread tin. The fish, whole but eviscerated, are put in the container head to tail to take best advantage of the space. Partially fill the container with water. Freeze to the point where the fish are not floating free, then fill the container to the top with water and freeze so that no part of the fish is exposed to the air. At this point a milk carton can be overwrapped and labeled (and don't forget to note how many fish it contains!). If you are using a metal container, dip it briefly into hot water to loosen the ice block, slip out the ice and quickly wrap and label it. While an overwrapping is not necessary insofar as the quality of the fish is concerned, it does give you a way to label and is less likely to stick to a freezer shelf.

Whatever packaging method you use for whole fish, they will keep best if they are dipped first into a solution which will act as an antioxidant and flavor preservative. After rinsing (rinse saltwater fish in a solution of 1 tablespoon salt to 1 quart water) dip whole fish for 30 seconds into an ascorbic-acid (available at the drugstore) solution in the proportion of 1 part powder to 100 parts water (or follow the recommendations of the manufacturer). Low-fat fish dipped for 30 seconds into 1 quart water with ½ cup salt will keep for about 3 months, but the ascorbic-acid dip is recommended for longer storage.

As noted, bivalves are best frozen by the block method in small containers such as standard freezer boxes. Open the bivalves, saving the natural juices, and put into a container with the strained natural juices. Again only partially fill the container with liquid, partially freeze and then top with either the rest of the natural juice or water and finish freezing.

Frozen raw shrimp will keep up to 10 months if they are washed and beheaded but not shelled before freezing. Cooked shrimp, which will keep up to 3 months, are also best if left in their shells. Whichever system you use, fresh or cooked, flash freeze the shrimp first unwrapped and loose on a shelf or tin, then put them in a moisture- and vaporproof bag, excluding as much air as possible. (There is now available a home model food "preserver" suction pump that draws air from food bags.) By freezing shrimp loose you may take out only what you need, but each time the bag should be carefully resealed. Crawfish can, of course, be handled the same way.

For home freezing, crustaceans should be cooked first. While it is true that lobsters can be frozen live (and frequently are for restaurants), this requires a commercial unit that maintains a lower temperature and has a larger capacity than the usual home freezer. Crabs and lobsters should be boiled for 15 to 20 minutes (depending on size) until they are done in seasoned liquid (Chapters VII and X). After cooling, carefully pick the meat out of the shell and pack tightly into containers or bags to exclude as much air as possible. Since there is no liquid in the container, it is best to overwrap, if you use a box. Handled this way, the meat will last for several months. Cooked lobsters and soft-shelled crabs can be frozen in their shells if wrapped in foil, but they will keep this way for only a few weeks.

Many casserole dishes can, of course, be frozen before cooking. Recently, however, a new product on the market made bulk cooking and freezing of many dishes more practical by shortening the freezer to table time. The "Scotchpak" freezing kit allows you to store in your freezer individual cooked portions of any favorite dishes that have a sauce or liquid content. Drop the hermetically sealed pouches into boiling water, boil for a few brief minutes based on the volume of the pouch (they come in a variety of sizes), and you can serve a piping hot dinner in less time than that required for a TV dinner. Naturally several pouches can be heated together and they can all be different. These pouches are also good for freezing raw shellfish in their juices.

TV dinners are easily made up in your own kitchen, and usually please the ultimate diner more than the commercial ones since their combinations can be made to order. When making these up remember that if there is no sauce you should put butter on the vegetables and on any baked or poached fish. After the plate is arranged (divided foil dishes can be saved up or bought new in hardware stores), cover with a sheet of foil slightly larger than the dish and pinch it down well around the edges, then overwrap, tape and label. Cooking these dinners usually takes 45 to 50 minutes in a 350° oven. If you have used a fried food, fold back the foil top from only these foods for the last 10 minutes to crisp them. If you'd rather not take the space necessary for a whole dinner, you can flash freeze and pack bite-sized pieces of fried fish just as you do shrimp.

Whatever system you use in packing cooked fish or shellfish for freezing, it is best to undercook them somewhat the first time around so that the final cooking will bring the dish to perfection; cook them about three-quarters done.

Home freezer temperatures are apt to be rather varied, hence a list of storage times for various seafoods can be misleading. These are based on the food being held at 0° F. On that basis, lean fish that have been properly handled, dipped, and wrapped can be kept for about 8 months. Fish with a high fat content also properly treated will keep for about 6 months. Firm-fleshed fish are the most satisfactory to freeze. Naturally your freezer owner's handbook should be consulted as well.

Unless the ice-block method of freezing has been used, before cooking it is best to leave the fish wrapped and defrost it in the refrigerator, allowing approximately 6 hours per pound to defrost. An ice block can be set on a rack in the sink to drain as it melts, but as soon as the bulk of the ice is gone be sure to refrigerate the fish. Remove the small block of ice from the stomach cavity as soon as it will slip out. If you should suddenly find that you have defrosted more than you need and if the seafood is still ice-flaked, it can be rewrapped and refrozen. This is not really recommended, but if the flesh still has some ice slivers in it, it can be treated this way without danger.

Smoking

Smoking is not only one of the oldest methods of preservation, it is undoubtedly the method with the greatest variety of techniques. It can be as complicated as a permanent structure in the backyard or as simple as a shoebox-sized unit over your campfire, canned heat or stove, or even just your own gas or electric oven. Regardless of the means by which the smoking is accomplished it produces gourmet food from a nibble to a banquet, to be eaten either hot or cold. Smoking will add flavor to the bland, highlight and accent the flavorful. Whatever your catch, try smoking some of it, either at home or in a commercial smokehouse.

Many fishing and farming areas have smokehouses that will take care of your catch for you even if you have to do a convincing selling job. The commercial smoker who turned out marvelous smoked shrimp and sailfish in the Florida Keys assured us that redfish just weren't worth the effort of smoking. After convincing him that he wouldn't have to eat it and that he'd be paid for his efforts, we came out with one of the best canapés yet. Unfortunately, letting a commercial smokehouse handle your catch robs you of experimenting with the most fascinating aspect of the whole method; the great flexibility that can result in many different tastes from just one species of fish.

Smoking combines many factors. First, of course, is the flesh to be smoked. The smallest fish, such as herring and butterfish, are best "gibbed." (See p. 16.) Any pan-sized fish can be smoked whole after gutting. Shrimp, clams and oysters are, of course, prime candidates for smoking whole. Larger fish are best filleted (leave the skin on unless, like northern pike and barracuda, they have a highly aromatic hide), or else cut into steaks. The temperature of the smoke dictates whether the fish will be cold or hot smoked. Cold smoking (smoke temperature under 90°) results in a product that will keep longer and is frequently used in dishes that require further cooking. Hot smoking (temperature over 110°) produces a dish right then, hot, or else it should be eaten within the next few days, or frozen.

There are some points at which the person doing the smoking must make a decision that will affect the final flavor. First, after the choice of the fish (and it can even be fish out of the freezer since it doesn't have to be fresh caught) and the smoking temperature (usually dictated by the smoker equipment itself) comes the decision whether or not to salt the fish.

While all directions for smoking seem to require that the fish be first either brine-cured or dry-salt-cured before the heat treatment, I personally have found that, if you are going to use the smoked fish quickly or freeze it for storage, you do not have to "cure" the fish first *unless* you want to do so for flavoring. Salt, whether in solution or dry, does definitely tighten the flesh by drawing out its natural moisture. This can be an advantage in that it firms up the flesh so that it will hang better on a hook or rod. However, when this tightening takes place it almost inevitably means that the flesh is also toughening, at least relatively. It is wise to keep in mind that the smoke itself increases the strength of the tissues as it draws out additional moisture. A "kippered" fish, for instance, is always dry-salt-cured, then hot-smoked.

Salting can be done in a variety of ways. The two traditional ways are a brine solution and dry salting. Before brining, the cleaned fish are first soaked for 30 minutes in 1 gallon of water in which 1 cup of salt has been dissolved. This soaking draws further blood from the fish and helps leach it out. The brine solution, should you decide to use it, also offers a flavoring opportunity. The standard brine soaking solution in which the fish is immersed for from 2 to 4 hours, depending on its thickness and fat content, can be as simple as a saltwater solution strong enough to float a raw potato or it can be flavored. Should you want flavoring try adding, to each quart of water, ½ cup salt, ¾ cup sugar (white or brown), 2 tablespoons black pepper (crushed or ground) and, if you wish, 3 or 4 bay leaves.

After brining the fish should be washed in fresh water and hung in a cool, shaded breezy place for a few hours until a thin, shiny skin develops. It is then ready for hot smoking, which ideally should be done in two stages. The first half of the time (usually about 4 hours) it should smoke at a temperature of about 110°. At the end of this time the smoke should be intensified and the temperature brought up to about 160° for an additional 3 to 4 hours, at which point the fish should be completely cooked and flavored with smoke.

Dry salting, as a preliminary step to smoking, is far simpler and quicker than when dry salting is used as a preservative by itself. For smoking, the freshly washed fish is sprinkled generously with salt on the flesh side to the depth of about $\frac{1}{16}$ inch. Let it absorb the salt completely (this takes about an hour) before hot smoking for about 8 hours in a smoke temperature of about 160°.

Cold smoking produces a better preserved result but also takes considerably longer to accomplish. For cold smoking with dry salting, first soak the fish for 30 minutes in 1 gallon of water with 1 cup salt. Then wash the fish with fresh water and drain off surplus moisture. The fish, either split or whole, is then dredged with fine salt. Pack the fish with as much salt as will cling to them in layers (with more salt scattered on each layer) in a non-metallic container and allow to stand for 6 hours if split and flattened out, for 12 if whole. Rinse in fresh water and allow to dry in a cool, shady, breezy place until the shiny skin develops. Smoking will be accomplished in anywhere from 1 to 5 days in a smoke temperature of not over 90°. Not too much smoke must be produced for the first part of the smoking time.

Another way in which smoked fish can be flavored is through the source of the smoke. Smoking is done over hardwood—chips or sawdust. Apple, pear and peach wood all add their flavors to the smoke. In California manzanita roots are a popular fuel for smoke, as are palmetto roots in Florida. The choice of the wood will change the final flavor. Sometimes, if fruitwood is not available, try adding some fresh fruit peels (apple, pear) to the wood; that, too, will add an interesting touch.

One of the simplest ways of making smoked fish is by using your oven. Naturally this will result in hot smoking. (A shoebox-sized unit made in Sweden also does hot smoking.) To use your oven, salt the pan-sized fish with table or seasoned salt, brush or sprinkle generously with Liquid Smoke, and allow to rest covered in the refrigerator overnight. Thread S hooks through the shoulders or heads of the fish and hang them from an oven rack. (It will save a messy cleanup job if a lower rack is covered with foil to catch the drippings.) Smoke the fish in a preheated 400° oven for 10 to 15 minutes, then reduce the temperature to 225° until they are firm and dry. This can take 1 to 3 hours, depending on size.

In any smoking the seafood should be as "open" as possible. If the fish has only been gutted, make sure that the belly cavity is wide open; prop it open if necessary. When it comes to fillets, or small things such as shrimp and oysters (which you can hardly hang!) use a rack made of hardware cloth— and be sure that it's *hardware*, not the plastic product they are now selling for screening.

The Norwegian process that produces some of the finest smoked salmon available anywhere makes a liar out of anyone who is rash enough to set down rules for smoking. For those lovely pink slices, they start with a 16- to 20-pound salmon fresh from an ice-cold stream. The fish is not scraped nor washed, but the head and tail are cut off and the backbone and entrails removed by cutting lengthwise along the back. The belly is wiped clean with absorbent paper, allowing some of the blood to be absorbed into the flesh. A thick layer of 4 pounds salt mixed with 5 ounces sugar is spread on a wide board on which the fish is laid skin side down. Another thick layer of the same salt-sugar is spread on top. All this is topped with another board and left overnight. The next day a weight is placed on the top board to compress the flesh. The fish remains this way for 3 days, then the salt is wiped away and the fish is washed with ½ tablespoon saltpeter (from the drugstore) dissolved in brandy. It is then smoked for about 8 hours. The fish is not considered ready to eat until 6 days later when it is sliced; while waiting, it is kept covered in a cool place.

A variation of this method can be used with fillets. Place them skin side down on a board heavily spread with salt. Sprinkle the flesh well with salt, then with a layer of sugar moistened with brandy. After 3 hours, spread on more salt. After standing for 2 to 2½ days, the fillets are smoked—naturally, for less time than a whole fish.

In several Norwegian dishes calling for smoked salmon, where a lighter flavor is desired, the fish is handled in the following manner. A 3- to 3½-pound middle section of salmon is washed, filleted and washed again. After wiping the fillet with a damp cloth, place it skin down on a heavily salted board, sprinkle the flesh with superfine granulated sugar and cover with buttered muslin. After letting it stand in a cool place for 24 hours carefully scrape off all the salt. The fish is then lightly smoked.

Norwegians smoke cod to use in their equivalent of our New England boiled dinner. A 6- to 9-pound cod is eviscerated and wiped dry. Sugar is sprinkled in the belly cavity and salt is put in a thin layer on the skin side. After the cod sits in a cool place for 3 days, the salt is scraped off, and the fish is wiped and hung to dry for awhile. It is then lightly smoked for about 3 hours. For the Norwegian boiled dinner, the cod is skinned and cooked whole in boiling water for a few minutes.

With any smoked fish, slice it diagonally and on an angle to avoid toughness as well as to provide larger slices.

When it comes to the actual smoking unit, it can be as simple as a reconstructed barrel, a converted old refrigerator, or a permanent outbuilding, depending on your ambition and talents with a hammer and nails. If you do build your own, or have it built, the position of the fire pit determines whether you are going to wind up with hot or cold smoking. Sporting magazines frequently run "how to" articles on building your own smokehouse, or plans can be obtained from the U.S. Fish and Wildlife Service, Washington, D.C. 20240.

Construction of your wood-burning smokehouse limits you to one smoking process, and presupposes the attention of a fire watcher for whatever time is needed—which can be a week or more, as noted. Under these conditions, it is not surprising that many people throw up their hands before they even start.

Electricity has come to the rescue. There are manufactured smokehouses available that use electric hot plates to smolder hardwood sawdust. These units are, of course, portable. Most practical in this line, however, is the unit for which plans are available from the U.S. Department of Agriculture and Oregon State University where it was designed. The plans call for two heating elements with a 3-position heat control so that either cold or hot smoke can be produced. While the plans call for 5 trays, the unit can easily be converted to use for hung fish.

The shoebox-sized unit mentioned earlier is undoubtedly the smallest practical one available and is a most flexible one to use. Imported from Sweden, it can be used over canned heat, a campfire or your own stove. The fish is set on a rack over hardwood sawdust (a small pouch of it comes with the unit, and you can order larger quantities), and the rack is just large enough to hold two 10-inch trout. This little gadget, incidentally, has shown me that possibly only the rule of needing heat is inviolable when it comes to smoking techniques. I usually smoke trout without any previous brine soaking, and, when doing them in pairs, vary the salt I use. One I will dust liberally with regular salt inside and out, and on the other I'm generous with seasoned salt; then I smoke both for 20 to 30 minutes. The difference in the results is amazing. One thing I've found is that with this technique the fish comes out moister than after brining since there is no salt concentration to solidify the tissues. While technically this is smoking, it is not smoking as a preservative process, but a cooking one. Trout cooked this way make an exotic main course served hot, or an unusual hors d'oeuvre served hot or cold. Small bits of fish or shrimp are best prepared this way with no preliminary soaking.

In any smoking, always plan a piece for nibbling to check on flavor and texture. Fish can dry out quickly and, in the process, lose a great deal of its natural flavor. When you are working with a naturally flavorful fish or shellfish, the intention should be to accent its natural flavor and blend in the smoke flavor. This whole method of preservation (or cooking) is so much a matter of personal taste, it is quite conceivable that your own smoking times may be either more or less than the so-called standard times.

When the fish have been thoroughly cooled after smoking, they should be double wrapped and frozen as with fresh fish or they can be kept for a considerably shorter time by other methods. They can be lightly brushed with a vegetable oil or dipped into melted paraffin. Both form a protective coating, but, of course, when the paraffin hardens it becomes brittle and requires careful handling. Wrap each fish in wax paper and store in a dry, cool place; warmth and moisture hasten spoilage.

Smoked shellfish are best stored in a liquid for future use. Commercial packers usually use a light, unflavored oil and a canning process. Since the majority of home smokers, if they intend to save their smoked products for future use, will put the results in the freezer, it is wise to remember that oil does not freeze well. It is best, if you intend to freeze bivalves, to save their natural juices when you are shucking them and use these juices for the freezing. They can be used as is (adding water if needed to fill the container), or seasoned.

Air Drying

Air drying of low-fat-content fish is little practiced in the United States except in the northeastern coastal regions, which is logical in view of the fact that the method, called "rackling," was introduced by the Scandinavians whose home climates were similar to the area's. The fish are beheaded just forward of the shoulder and split and cleaned by removing the backbone. The sides are cut through in long 1-inch-wide strips from the collarbone to the tail. After thorough cleaning and soaking in a standard brine solution for 1 hour, they are suspended in a shady, breezy place to dry, a process that takes from 1 to 2 weeks, depending on the weather. The end product is usually used without any further preparation as a fish "jerky," but can be soaked and simmered to use like salted fish.

Along the Gulf of Mexico shrimp are dried for use in Creole and Mexican dishes, and to be sent North as a party delicacy. After a thorough washing, unshelled shrimp are boiled until cooked in a salt solution in the proportion of ½ cup salt to 1 quart water. They are then spread in a thin layer to dry in the sun—not in the shade, as in rackling. For the first day stir them every half hour. Since they must be taken in at night, or at the first sign of rain, and moved to well-ventilated cover, a clean window screen supported off the ground makes a handy rack. If the weather is good, they will be dry and hard at the end of 3 days, at which time they are shelled. If there's a larger quantity to be shelled than you can manage one by one, the shrimp can be put in a sack and pounded to crack off the shells. The contents of the sack can then be screened as you would sand through screen with ¼-inch mesh. (The shell crumbs will fall through the mesh if they are well pounded.) The loss of weight in drying is considerable: after shelling, the shrimp will weigh about one eighth of the original weight. The dried meats can be ground and mixed with sauces for canapé spreads (see Chapters VII and X), nibbled as they are, or, as with dehydrated food, soaked and cooked.

Salting

Salting has been a standard means of preserving fish for centuries. While the lean fishes are most easily cured by this method, when fat fish are successfully preserved in this way they are of the highest quality. Since this system requires less time and skill than air drying, and is not so dependent on weather conditions (at least with brine salting), it is much more widely practiced in homes around the country. Whichever salting process you use, either brine salting or dry salting, be sure to use the purest salt available and the finest grain you can find. Salt which is virtually chemically pure (with less than 1% impurities) results in a milder, more pleasant flavor which does not need prolonged freshening. The finer salt naturally forms a brine more quickly and penetrates the flesh more rapidly than a coarser grind. Standard curing salt is available from salt companies, butcher supply firms and often from rural feed stores.

Brine salting is a system of alternating layers of cleaned fish with salt, under a weight, so that a natural brine is formed from the moisture of the fish dissolving the salt. Because the amount of salt required is dependent upon its purity and the size of the grain, the temperature (warm weather requires more salt), the size of the fish and its fat content (larger and fatter need more) and length of curing, once again no hard and fast rules can be set down. As a guideline, however, to prevent "burn" from an excess of salt or spoilage through fermentation as a result of using too little, the salt total should be between one quarter and one third of the weight of the fish.

The fish, with the exception of herring, are cut so as to lie flat in one piece; usually the backbone split is used. For ease of handling the shoulder or collar plate is left on; this is particularly important if you intend to smoke the fish afterwards. To facilitate the penetration of the brine, the flesh is scored at 1- to 2-inch intervals along the length but not through the skin so that the piece will lie flat. Large fish can be filleted; thick-skinned, spiny or large-scaled fish should be skinned.

Wash the fish thoroughly in fresh water, then soak for 30 to 60 minutes in a brine of ½ cup salt to 1 gallon water to draw any blood and cut any remaining skin slime. After draining for 5 to 10 minutes, dredge them with as much salt as they will hold and rub extra salt into the scorings. Then pack them skin side down into a container such as a stoneware crock, starting with a light layer of salt, so as to form an even layer. Depending on the sizes and shapes involved, this may mean forming a pinwheel or placing the fish head to tail; do not let the fish in each layer overlap any more than is unavoidable. Add a thin layer of salt and another layer of fish at right angles to the preceding layer. Stagger the layers and arrangement as much as is necessary to form even layers so that pressure, when applied, will be as equal as possible on all the pieces of fish. Place the top layer of fish skin side up. Put a loose wooden cover on the top layer and a weight on top of that to compress the fish and force out the brine-making moisture. Small fish will generally be completely brined in about 48 hours, while larger, fatter fish may take as much as 10 days. When brining is completed, scrub the fish in a fresh full-brine solution with a stiff brush, then repack in a crock with a light scattering of salt between the layers which are well pressed down. Then fill the crock with a fresh full-brine solution and store in a cool, dark place. Properly preserved and stored this way, fish will keep for about 9 months if attention is paid to the brine solution every few months. At the first sign of fermentation (which occurs most rapidly in warm areas) drain off the old brine, scrub and repack and rebrine as before.

Herring are handled a bit differently. They should be plump, prime specimens and brined immediately on catching; don't hold them on ice. They can be brine-salted whole or gibbed. Since they should be free of feed (which is hard to guarantee.in a whole fish), it is best to gib them, as follows: Hold the herring with the back to the palm, with the head between the thumb and forefinger, leaving the throat clear. Stick a short-bladed knife up under the gill cover with the edge of the blade toward the stomach and give a sharp twist upward and outward. With practice, throat, pectoral fins, gills and main gut will come out with this one operation. Then thoroughly scrub the herring in a brine solution to remove scales and leach out the blood; then drain.

As with other varieties, dredge them well with salt and put a layer of salt in a crock. Place them on their backs and pack closely together so as to make an even layer. Sprinkle each layer with salt, with each subsequent layer arranged at right angles to the preceding layer. Pack the top layer backs up and salt a bit more than the rest. Fill the crock with a fresh full-brine solution, close tightly, and store in the traditional cool dark place. The brine solution should be replaced every 2 months.

Dry salting, while a curing method best adapted to warmer climates, is popular in the New England area. This is the traditional way of curing cod, that area's virtual trademark. Dry-salted fish (cod, cusk, haddock, mackerel) can be bought in many parts of the country in wooden boxes or tubs.

Fish to be dry salted should be bled immediately when they are caught. Cut the throat and remove the gills. Ice them, then when ready to salt, clean and cut them (either through the backbone line or the belly) so that they lie flat. Be sure not to remove the collar plates, since these hold the fish together for further treatment. Clean the fish very well, inside and out, removing all signs of black skin, blood, etc. Wash the fish thoroughly in 1 gallon water with 1 cup salt. Scrub fish with a stiff brush to be sure it's clean, and then drain well to remove as much moisture as possible.

As with brine salting, dredge the fish well with salt. Lay it out on a layer of salt in a container where the moisture that forms will drain away; here you don't want any brine. If you have to stack them in layers, salt the layers. As with brine salting, the fish are laid skin side down, with the top layer skin side up. The usual proportion of salt is 1 pound to 4 pounds of fish.

After 48 hours to a week (it depends on the temperature and the humidity —a shorter time is needed if it's warm and dry), remove fish from the salt and scrub well again in a brine solution so that no salt remains on the surface. Drain them well and start the drying process.

This drying process is done in the shade (sunlight will result in a "rusted" product) and, naturally, in an area with free-flowing air circulation. A hardware-cloth screen raised on legs a few feet off the ground does an excellent job. Prop cheesecloth over the fish, so flies will not "blow" and spoil the fish. A breezy location results in the best product; the rapid evaporation of moisture produces a clear color in the flesh. Again, the fish are placed skin side down, but they should be turned several times the first day.

The screens (or at least the fish) must be brought indoors at night; the moisture in night air results in mold. If the weather turns bad and you can't put them out the next day, salt them again lightly. Brush any loose salt off when you can again put them out in the air. As usual, there are no set timetables for the drying period; the best way to tell if they are sufficiently dried is to pinch the thick section of the flesh. If your fingers don't leave an impression, they are ready for packing.

Dry-salted fish are wrapped in wax paper and traditionally packed in the thin, wooden boxes or tubs you find in the market. However, at home these are not too easy to come by, particularly with lids that are tight. Here you can overwrap and freeze. Even in the wooden containers, they should be kept in the usual cool, dry place.

Dry salting can be done with virtually any fish, although the fatter ones are trickier to do properly and do not keep as well. For the majority of recipes (and tastes) dry-salted fish should be freshened (soaked in fresh water) for anywhere from ½ hour to 12 hours. Some fish really drink up the salt; as an example, dry salted mackerel may need 12 hours for freshening; dry salt cod needs about 1 hour.

Caviar, of course, is salted roe. Some methods, used with mullet, shad and striped bass roes, result in a sausagelike product; others result in the more familiar (and expensive) form. The methods are covered in Chapter VIII.

Pickling

Pickling is not often practiced with seafood at home, yet the possibilities are far wider than those indicated by the small assortment found on market shelves. Pickled herring, of course, is easily found, and pickled shellfish is sometimes available, generally imported, in gourmet shops. Yet practically any edible product from either fresh or salt water can be pickled.

Pickling, as a preservative, is always done after a preliminary brining, as for smoking. The actual pickling liquid is, of course, vinegar based and this should be distilled vinegar; cider and flavored vinegars have a very variable acetic-acid content and the residues may give the final result an off taste. As with any form of pickling, the liquid, seasoned with spices, is boiled and poured hot over the drained and rinsed fish or shellfish pieces packed in sterilized jars, the lids are put on the jars and then tightened down. Be sure to test the seal after the jars have cooled.

Canning

Canning presents problems. Actually canning of fishery products should *not* be attempted at the nonprofessional level. Some years ago the Fish and Wildlife Service of the Department of the Interior ran a series of tests on home-canned fish that showed most unhappy results. Their conclusions were that 1) fishery products *must* be canned under pressure. This means with a pressure canner, not the hot-water bath most frequently used for home canning. 2) Methods of canning are not flexible. 3) Not all edible fishery products can be canned successfully. 4) The only acceptable point of variance in canning would be in the seasonings used.

In view of this it is perhaps safest if I simply recommend that all those interested in canning fish get a copy of the U.S. Department of the Interior Conservation Bulletin number 28 from the Government Printing Office, Washington, D.C. 20401. At the price (15 cents) it's well worth it for what you learn about what *not* to do.

CHAPTER FOUR

Recipes
for
Firm-Fleshed
Fish

Moist Fish

Moist, firm-fleshed fish are undoubtedly the most popular on the table; they are most flexible in the kitchen, and lend themselves to a wide range of recipes. The fishes that fit this group range all the way from small-boy sunfish and crappies from fresh water (and dad's sporting freshwater bass) to the coastal permit and pompano and the ocean's colorful and exciting dolphin.

APPETIZERS

GREEK COLD FISH

2½ lbs. fillet of flounder
   flour
⅓ cup olive oil

3 shallots, minced
½ cup white-wine vinegar
½ tsp. rosemary

Dredge fillets with flour. Fry in oil until golden. Remove fish and pour excess oil from pan. Add remaining ingredients to pan and simmer, stirring, until drippings are incorporated. Arrange fillets in bottom of shallow glass dish and pour vinegar mixture over. Cover and refrigerate at least overnight.
SERVES about 8.

CEVICHE À LA BAJA CALIFORNIA

¾ lb. skinned and filleted dolphin
½ cup Mexican or Key lime juice
   (or lemon juice), plus 1 lime
¼ tsp. salt, approximately

2 tsps. soya sauce
2 tsps. sugar
1 tbsp. minced onion

Cut fish into ½-inch cubes and place in a small deep bowl. Mix lime juice, salt, soya sauce and sugar and pour over fish. Cover and chill for at least

6 hours. Mix fish with onion and add more salt if needed. Squeeze on juice of fresh lime.

SERVES 6.

SOUTH AMERICAN CEVICHE

---

1 (1½-lb.) red snapper, skinned and boned
1 cup fresh Mexican or Key lime juice
½ cup olive oil
¼ cup minced onion
2 tbsps. minced, peeled canned green chile peppers

1 garlic clove, minced
1½ tbsps. salt
1 tsp. freshly ground pepper
dash of Tabasco

chopped fresh coriander (cilantro)

Cut fish into thin strips. Cover strips with lime juice; refrigerate for 4 hours. Drain. Blend remaining ingredients and toss with fish strips. Chill. Garnish with coriander and serve.

SERVES 4 to 6.

JAPANESE SASHIMI

1½ lbs. filleted, skinned porgies

Pour boiling water over fish, then drain off. Pour ice water over fish, drain, and pat dry. Slice very thin on the diagonal and serve with freshly grated horseradish and soya sauce blended with vinegar and lemon to taste.

SERVES 10 to 12.

SOUTH AMERICAN ESCABECHE

2 lbs. skinned grunt fillets, in 2-inch
    cubes
6 tbsps. Mexican or Key lime juice
    (or lemon juice)
    flour
    butter
    ripe olives, quartered limes or
      lemons

1 garlic clove, crushed
⅓ cup orange juice
2 tbsps. olive oil
½ cup minced green onions
    dash of Tabasco or cayenne
    salt

Dip fish into 3 tbsps. lime juice and dust with flour. Sauté quickly in melted butter until golden brown. Arrange in a shallow bowl. Make sauce of garlic, remaining lime juice, orange juice, olive oil and onions, Tabasco and salt to taste. Pour over fish, cover, and refrigerate for 24 to 48 hours. Garnish with olives, lemons, or limes. Fresh coriander, ground cumin seed or toasted coriander seeds can be added to sauce.

SERVES 6 to 8.

REVERSE ESCABECHE

2 lbs. pompano fillets
¾ cup olive oil
1 cup sliced onion rings
1 cup sliced carrots
1 cup sliced celery
4 garlic cloves, minced
½ cup white-wine vinegar

1 cup water
1 tsp. thyme
2 whole cloves
1 bay leaf, crushed
¼ tsp. crushed peppercorns
1 tbsp. salt
½ cup flour

Combine half of the oil with onions, carrots, celery and garlic. Cook, stirring, over low heat for 10 minutes. Stir in the vinegar, water, thyme, cloves, bay leaf, peppercorns and salt and bring to a boil. Reduce heat, cover, and simmer for 20 minutes. Cut fish into 2-inch cubes; dust with flour. Brown quickly in remaining oil until golden. Arrange in large shallow dish. Pour on hot marinade, spread vegetables on top. Cool to room temperature, cover tightly and refrigerate for 24 to 48 hours.

SERVES 6 to 8.

SOUPS

COLOMBIAN OKRA AND FISH SOUP

6 servings pompano fillets
2 garlic cloves, chopped
2 fresh hot peppers, seeded and chopped
⅛ tsp. ground cumin seed
⅛ tsp. ground allspice
2 medium onions, minced
1 large tomato, peeled, seeded and chopped
2 qts. fish stock
juice of 1 lemon

2 cups okra, quartered
1 lb. small yams, peeled and cut into 1-inch pieces
2 ripe plantains, peeled and diced
2 tbsps. butter
2 tbsps. tomato paste
1 tbsp. Worcestershire sauce
salt and pepper

Add garlic, hot peppers, cumin seed, allspice, onions and tomato to the stock and bring the mixture to a boil. Reduce heat and simmer for 15 minutes. Add lemon juice to a pan of salted water, bring to a boil, and add the quartered okra. Bring again to a boil and then drain, add the okra to the stock with the yams and plantains. Cook over low heat for 1 hour. Sauté the fillets in the butter until golden and cut into 1-inch pieces. Add to the soup with tomato paste, Worcestershire sauce and salt and pepper to taste. Simmer for 30 minutes longer.

SERVES 6.

FRENCH FISH SOUP WITH COGNAC

1½ lbs. flounder fillets cut into chunks
3 tbsps. olive oil
1 tbsp. minced garlic
1 cup minced onion
2 tsps. crumbled whole saffron
½ tsp. chopped fresh or dried thyme
3 drops Tabasco
½ tsp. salt

⅛ tsp. freshly ground pepper
1 cup dry white wine
4 cups water
⅓ cup tomato purée
1 tsp. crushed fennel seeds
3 tbsps. Cognac
2 cups heavy cream

Heat the oil in a kettle, add garlic, onion, saffron and thyme. Cook, stirring, until onion is wilted. Add fish, and season with Tabasco, salt and freshly ground pepper. Cook briefly, stirring to break up fish. Add wine, water, tomato purée and fennel seeds. Bring to boil and simmer for 15 minutes, stirring occasionally. Add Cognac, stir in cream, and bring to a boil. Simmer for 10 minutes.

SERVES 8.

JAPANESE FISH CHOWDER

1½ lbs. porgies, boned and cut into small chunks (save trimmings)
5 cups dashi or tangle soup
6 mushrooms, sliced
1 lb. tofu (bean curd), diced

¼ cup lemon juice
¼ cup white vinegar
⅓ to ½ cup soya sauce
1 Japanese leek, thinly sliced

Bring *dashi* to a boil, add fish trimmings, and boil for 10 minutes. Strain out fish trimmings. Add mushrooms, *tofu* and fish. Bring to a boil, reduce heat, add lemon juice and simmer until done. Serve with vinegar, soya sauce and leek.

SERVES 6.

ENTRÉES

ALGERIAN BAKED FISH

6 (12- to 16-oz.) mutton snappers, cleaned, with heads on
1 tsp. minced garlic
¼ cup fresh lime juice
½ cup water
¾ cup sliced onions
12 pitted green olives, sliced

½ tsp. salt
½ tsp. pepper
½ cup olive oil
2 bay leaves, crushed
1 tbsp. each of capers and caper liquid

Rinse fish and cut 2 gashes on each side. Place in a lightly oiled baking dish.

Blend remaining ingredients and smooth mixture over fish. Bake for 10 minutes at 550°, reduce heat to 425° and bake for 7 to 10 minutes longer.

SERVES 6.

BAHAMA FILLETS

---

2 lbs. Atlantic yellowtail snapper fillets
1 small onion, chopped
salt
1 tsp. prepared mustard
dash of Tabasco
1 tsp. Worcestershire sauce

2 tsps. lemon juice
few drops of white vinegar
¼ lb. butter
1 tomato, diced
3 parsley sprigs, minced
pinch of curry powder
pinch of paprika

Arrange the onion on the bottom of a baking dish just large enough to contain the fillets. Salt fillets lightly and lay them on the onion. Mix mustard, Tabasco, ½ tsp. Worcestershire, lemon juice and vinegar and spread on fillets. Cover fillets just to the top with hot water. Bake in a 350° oven for about 15 minutes.

Make a sauce. Melt the butter and heat until it starts to brown. Add tomato, parsley, curry powder, paprika and remaining Worcestershire. Stir for a few moments. Pour over cooked fish.

SERVES 4.

CARIBBEAN BAKED FISH

5- to 6-lb. baking gray snapper
½ cup Mexican or Key lime juice
½ tsp. salt
¼ tsp. fresh ground pepper
½ cup olive oil
1 large onion, thinly sliced
½ tsp. dried thyme
½ tsp. orégano

1 bay leaf, crumbled
1 medium onion, minced
2 garlic cloves, minced
1 fresh hot pepper, seeded and minced
1 tbsp. chopped parsley
½ cup ground toasted almonds
1½ cups fish stock

Mix lime juice with salt and pepper and pour over fish, inside and out. Set aside to marinate while dressing is made. Pour 6 tbsps. olive oil into a baking dish. Arrange sliced onion in the dish; sprinkle with thyme, orégano, bay leaf and salt and pepper. Sauté minced onion and garlic in remaining olive oil until tender but not browned. Add hot pepper, parsley, almonds and ½ cup fish stock; mix well. Drain fish and pour marinade over onions in the baking dish with remaining 1 cup fish stock. Place fish in dish; spread almond dressing on top and sides of fish. Bake uncovered at 400° for 40 to 45 minutes.

SERVES 6.

CHINESE SWEET AND PUNGENT FISH

1 (3-lb.) snapper, cleaned and left whole
1 cucumber, peeled, seeded and cut into matchsticks
1 carrot, peeled, and cut into matchsticks
1 sweet pickle, cut into matchsticks
1 tsp. chopped fresh gingerroot
½ cup minced onion

2 tbsps. salt
2 tbsps. sugar
½ cup vinegar
½ cup water
4 tbsps. oil
1 tbsp. cornstarch
2 tbsps. soya sauce
2 garlic cloves, minced

Combine cucumber, carrot, pickle, gingerroot, onion, 1 tsp. salt, sugar, vinegar and ½ cup water. Marinate the fish in this for 45 minutes. Drain fish, but reserve the marinade. Place fish on a rack over 2 qts. water flavored with remainder of salt and 2 tbsps. of the oil. Steam fish for about 20 minutes, or until tender. Strain the vegetables from the marinade and reserve both. Mix cornstarch and soya into liquid. Heat remaining oil and brown the garlic. Add the marinade liquid and cook, stirring, until thickened. Correct seasonings. Return vegetables to sauce and heat, but do not cook. Drain fish and pour the sauce over it.

SERVES 4.

HAWAIIAN BAKED FISH

1 (3- to 5-lb.) Lane snapper, cleaned
1 tsp. salt
1 cup small bread cubes
¼ cup liquid skim milk
1 tbsp. bacon drippings
1 tbsp. minced onion

1 tsp. minced parsley
½ tsp. salt
pinch of pepper
3 slices of bacon
ti leaves, oiled cheesecloth or aluminum foil

Rub the inside of the fish with 1 tsp. salt. In a bowl blend bread, milk, drippings, onion, parsley, salt and pepper. Stuff the fish lightly with this mixture; sew or skewer the opening. Arrange bacon slices on top of fish. Wrap fish in leaves, cheesecloth or foil. Bake in 325° oven for 20 minutes per pound.

Serves 6 to 8.

KEYS FISH STUFFED

1 lb. red snapper fillets
1 (3-lb.) red snapper, prepared for baking
1 egg white
1 tsp. salt
⅛ tsp. white pepper
few drops of Key lime juice

3 pickled okras, thinly sliced
1 tsp. minced fresh dill
Key lime slices
sprigs of fresh dill

Pound the fillets or put through a fine grinder. Gradually add the unbeaten egg white, pounding vigorously. Season with salt, pepper and Key lime juice; stir in the okra and minced dill. Use to stuff the fish; skewer fish closed. Bake in lightly greased baking dish at 375° for about 30 minutes, or until done. Serve garnished with Key lime slices and sprigs of dill.

Serves 6.

MEXICAN FISH IN ADOBO SAUCE

8 pargo (snapper) fillets
  salt
  cooking oil
4 red chiles (anchos), roasted and de-
    veined
2 onions, chopped

3 garlic cloves, minced
4 cuminseeds
1 tsp. orégano
2 cups peeled and seeded tomatoes
  juice of 2 oranges
  pepper

Rub fish with salt; fry lightly in oil. Grind chiles with onions, garlic, cumin-seeds, orégano and tomatoes. Fry this sauce in the fish frying oil. When thick, remove from heat and add orange juice. Lay fish slices in a buttered baking dish, alternating with sauce./Cover and bake at 350° for 30 minutes. Season with salt and pepper to taste.
    SERVES 8.

PAKISTANI FILLETS

4 (1½-lb. total) Lane snapper fillets
1 tbsp. flaked or grated coconut
1 garlic clove
2 canned California green chiles,
    rinsed and seeded
½ tsp. sugar
1 tsp. salt

1 tbsp. coconut milk or cow's milk
2 eggs
¼ cup cow's milk
½ medium-size cucumber, peeled,
    seeded and minced
1 tbsp. butter
  paprika

Arrange fillets in a single layer in greased baking dish. Whirl smooth in a blender, or mash in a mortar with a pestle, the coconut, garlic, chiles, sugar, salt and coconut milk. Spread evenly over fish. Add eggs and cow's milk to cucumber; beat until well blended and pour over fish. Dot top with butter and bake at 325° for 20 to 25 minutes. Garnish with paprika.
    SERVES 4.

PUERTO RICAN FRIED SPOTS

4 lbs. Lane snapper, cut into 1-inch
    slices
2 tsps. and 2 tbsps. salt
1 cup olive oil
2½ lbs. onions, sliced
24 ripe olives
1 (4-oz.) can of pimientos, drained

2 tbsps. vinegar
2 bay leaves
1 large garlic clove
1½ cups water
2 tbsps. capers
2 (8-oz.) cans tomato sauce

Make a sauce of ½ cup of the oil, 2 tsps. of the salt and remaining ingredients except fish and garlic. Simmer for 1 hour. Brown the garlic clove in ½ cup oil; remove garlic. Salt the fish slices with 2 tbsps. salt and fry in garlic-flavored oil over medium heat for about 7 minutes on each side. Cover fish with sauce.
    SERVES 12.

SPANISH FISH PIE

6 snapper fillets
3 tbsps. olive oil
½ cup ground almonds
4 onions, chopped
2 garlic cloves, minced

1 bay leaf, crumbled
    salt and pepper
6 medium-size tomatoes, peeled,
    seeded and chopped
3 cups seasoned mashed potatoes

Heat the oil and sauté the almonds for 5 minutes, stirring frequently; remove the almonds. Sauté the onions and garlic for 10 minutes, stirring frequently. Add more oil, if needed. Add bay leaf, seasonings to taste and tomatoes; cook over very low heat for 10 minutes, stirring occasionally. Grind 1 fillet; cut remaining fillets into thirds. Reserve one third of tomato mix as sauce. Force balance of tomato mixture through a sieve. Add ground fillet and sautéed almonds. Cook over low heat for 10 minutes, stirring frequently. Butter a 9-inch casserole and line bottom and sides with mashed potatoes, saving some for the top. Arrange layers of fish and tomato mixture, and top with potato. Bake at 425° for 30 minutes. Heat reserved tomato sauce and serve on the side.
    SERVES 4 to 6.

SPANISH BAKED FISH

1 (4- to 6-lb.) snapper, cleaned but whole
1 cup water
2 tsps. salt
olive oil
4 strips of bacon

2 cups canned tomatoes
½ cup young peas
4 tsps. minced onion
1 tsp. minced green pepper
1 small garlic clove

Soak the fish for 5 minutes in 1 cup water in which the salt has been dissolved. Drain. Slit the skin of the fish in several places on each side to keep it flat. Brush with olive oil. Put 2 strips of bacon on a greased pan. Put in fish and cover with 2 remaining strips. Mix remaining ingredients and pour over. Bake at 550° for 10 minutes; reduce to 350° and bake for about 30 minutes longer, or until done, basting from time to time.

Serves 4 to 6.

VERACRUZ HUACHINANGO

8 individual red snapper fillets or steaks
½ cup olive oil
1 tsp. minced onion
1 garlic clove, minced
2 cups tomato sauce
2 peppercorns, ground
2 whole cloves

⅛ tsp. ground cinnamon
1 to 2 tbsps. chile powder
½ tsp. sugar
18 green olives, sliced
3 potatoes, boiled and diced
4 slices of white bread, sautéed and cut into strips

Heat half of the oil and in it sauté the onion and garlic until transparent. Add tomato sauce and spices and cook gently for about 30 minutes to blend well. Add sugar (and water, if the sauce is too thick) and olives. Heat the rest of the oil in a separate pan and sauté the fish. When the fish is done add to the sauce with the potatoes. Garnish with sautéed bread strips.

Serves 8.

VENETIAN FLATFISH

2 whole flounder (1 per serving), cleaned and skinned
3 tbsps. butter
2 tbsps. chopped mint
1 tbsp. minced parsley
1 small garlic clove, mashed
salt and pepper
1 large onion, thinly sliced
½ cup white wine
½ cup water

Cut a large X in each side of the flounders. Make a paste of 2 tbsps. butter, mint, parsley, garlic and salt and pepper to taste. Press into slashes on sides of fish. Cook onion in 1 tbsp. butter until soft and yellow; add wine and cook for 10 minutes. Add water, and salt and pepper to taste; simmer. Meanwhile broil fish, turning once until fish flakes. Pour sauce over fish and serve.
SERVES 2.

FRENCH ROE OMELET

2 small flounder roes
½ cup ground raw flounder
2 tbsps. salt
2 tbsps. salted butter
1 tbsp. chopped shallot
salt and pepper
2 tbsps. sweet butter
1 tsp. lemon juice
dash of cayenne
dash of grated nutmeg
2 tbsps. sour cream
6-egg omelet mixture
2 to 3 tbsps. oil from canned anchovies
8 flat anchovy fillets
½ cup capers

Blanch roe in simmering water with 2 tbsps. salt for 5 minutes. Drain, cool, and skin. Mash with a fork. Melt 1 tbsp. salt butter in a pan. Add shallot, ground raw fish, and salt and pepper to taste. Cook for 3 or 4 minutes, stirring. Add the mashed roe and the remaining salt butter and cook for 2 or 3 minutes, stirring. Add the sweet butter, lemon juice, cayenne and nutmeg. Mix in sour cream and heat. Cook the omelet. Before folding it, spoon the roe and fish mixture over it. Fold over and brush top with anchovy oil. Top with anchovy fillets and scatter capers around.
SERVES 4.

ISRAELI POACHED FISH

2 (1-lb.) flounder fillets
2 cups water
2 tbsps. lemon juice
½ tsp. salt
¼ tsp. pepper
2 small onions, chopped

1½ tbsps. butter
½ cup dry white wine
1¼ cups sliced mushrooms
1 cup dairy sour cream
1 tbsp. flour

Bring water and 1 tbsp. juice to a boil. Add seasoning and fish immediately; reduce heat to a simmer. Cook for 15 minutes. Make the sauce.

Sauté onions in butter until clear. Add wine, mushrooms and remaining lemon juice. Cook until mushrooms are soft. Scald sour cream and stir into the onion mixture. Add flour to thicken slightly. Simmer for 5 minutes. Pour over fish.

SERVES 2.

IRISH FILLETS

12 flounder fillets
1 cup fish stock or bottled clam juice
¾ cup white wine
2 shallots, minced

1 cup heavy cream
5 tbsps. butter
2 egg yolks
salt and pepper

Roll up the fillets and tie or pin; place in saucepan and cover with stock, wine and shallots. Simmer fish until it flakes. Transfer fillets to a warmed platter, cover, and keep warm. Cook remaining poaching liquid over high heat until reduced by one third. Add heavy cream and cook until reduced by one fourth. Remove pan from heat and whisk in butter, bit by bit. Beat in egg yolks and heat sauce very slowly; do not let it boil. Season with salt and pepper to taste and pour over fillets.

SERVES 6.

ISRAELI FILLETS WITH ALMONDS AND GRAPES

6 flounder fillets
flour seasoned with salt and pepper
5 tbsps. butter
2 tbsps. oil
½ cup green seedless grapes or raisins (plumped in hot water and drained)

½ cup blanched and slivered almonds
3 tbsps. consommé
juice of ½ lemon
dash of Worcestershire sauce

Dust fillets with seasoned flour. Sauté in 2 tbsps. butter and the oil for 3 or 4 minutes each side. Remove fish and keep warm. In same skillet melt 2 tbsps. butter and stir in grapes; cook for 2 or 3 minutes and spoon over fish. In same skillet melt 1 tbsp. butter and sauté almonds until lightly browned. Stir in consommé, lemon juice and Worcestershire; heat and pour over fish.

SERVES 6.

IRISH FILLETS IN CIDER SAUCE

1½ lbs. plaice fillets
pinch of paprika
½ cup cider
4 tbsps. butter
3 tbsps. flour
salt and pepper

½ cup light cream
1 tbsp. chopped parsley
6 medium-size mushrooms, blanched and sliced
1 tbsp. chopped parsley

Put fillets in a shallow baking pan; sprinkle with paprika. Pour on the cider. Bake at 375° until fish barely flakes, basting occasionally. Remove fillets to a hot casserole and keep hot. Melt butter in a saucepan, stir in the flour, and gradually add the fish cooking liquid. Stir until smooth and thickened. Bring to a boil. Reduce heat and season to taste. Slowly add cream and cook, stirring, over very low heat until hot, but do not let boil. Add mushrooms and pour over fish. Put under broiler until sauce is bubbly and lightly browned in spots. Sprinkle with parsley.

SERVES 4.

FRENCH TURBAN

8 skinless sole fillets
1 tbsp. butter
  salt and white pepper

1 recipe fish or shellfish mousse

Butter a 7- to 8-cup mold. Season the sole lightly with salt and pepper. Lightly score the fillets on the side from which the skin was removed and lay that side up as you line the mold, covering the bottom and up the sides and leaving the ends over the edge. Pack the mousse mixture in the mold and fold the fillet ends over the top. Bake at 375° for about 1 hour, as with mousse. Serve with warm sauce of your choice.

SERVES 6 to 8.

FRENCH FILLETS MEUNIÈRE

6 sole fillets, washed and patted dry
  flour
  salt and pepper

½ cup butter
  juice of 1 lemon
2 tbsps. chopped parsley

Dip fillets into flour seasoned with salt and pepper. Sauté in half of the butter until golden. Remove and season. Melt remaining butter in a separate skillet and let it turn brown. Add lemon juice and parsley and pour over the fillets.

SERVES 6.

CHINESE STEAMED STEAKS

3 to 4 lbs. lingcod in 2-inch steaks
6 to 8 dried Chinese mushrooms
½ tsp. salt

2 slices of fresh gingerroot, cut into slivers about ¼-inch thick
1 tbsp. soya sauce

Cover mushrooms with hot water and let stand for about 1 hour. Wash mushrooms well, then pinch off and discard stems. Squeeze mushrooms dry. Arrange fish steaks in a pan; sprinkle with salt; decorate with gingerroot and mushrooms. Cover dish with double thickness of wax paper. Put on a rack above 1 or 2 inches of boiling water. Cover pan snugly and simmer rapidly for about 14 minutes, or until fish flakes. Pour soya sauce over just before serving.
SERVES 6.

SEA SQUAB PROVENÇALE

2 lbs. northern puffer, rinsed and dried
flour seasoned with salt and pepper

½ cup olive oil
2 garlic cloves, chopped
2 tbsps. chopped parsley

Roll fish in seasoned flour. Heat oil and sauté garlic. Add fish and sauté over moderate heat for 8 to 10 minutes, or until lightly browned. Remove to heated platter. Add parsley to the oil and pour over fish.
SERVES 4.

SPANISH WINE-BAKED FISH

2 (1 ½-lb.) pompano
12 strips of lean bacon
4 or 5 strips of salt pork
   salt and pepper
2 tbsps. chopped fresh mushrooms

1 tsp. minced parsley
1 tbsp. beurre manié
½ cup fish stock
½ cup white wine or lemon juice
2 tbsps. tomato purée

Place 6 bacon strips in a buttered shallow baking dish. Add fish and place strips of salt pork on top. Season with salt and pepper. Sprinkle with mushrooms and cover with remaining bacon strips. Sprinkle on parsley and dot with *beurre manié*. Mix stock and wine or lemon juice with tomato purée and spoon on. Cover with buttered brown paper and bake, basting once, at 400° for 20 minutes. Remove paper and bake for 5 minutes longer.

SERVES 4.

MALAYSIAN FISH IN COCONUT CURRY

4 permit fillets, cut into halves
   salt
⅓ cup oil
2 cups thinly sliced red onions
2 tsps. ground ginger
¼ cup ground cashews
½ tsp. dried ground chile pepper

¼ tsp. ground saffron
2 cups coconut cream
3 tbsps. lime or lemon juice
1 tsp. sugar
1 tbsp. cornstarch

Wash and dry fillets and salt lightly. Brown in 3 tbsps. of the oil. Remove from heat. Heat remainder of oil and sauté onion slices until soft but not browned. Remove half of onions. Add to the pan the ginger, cashews, chile pepper, saffron and coconut cream. Bring to a boil and add lime juice. Mix sugar and cornstarch together and add to sauce. Return fish to sauce and cook over low heat for 10 minutes. Serve with reserved onions.

SERVES 6 to 8.

COLOMBIAN BAKED FISH

1 (4-lb.) whole pompano, cleaned
garlic salt
pepper
4 cups small bread cubes of fresh
bread with no crusts, dried overnight
1 cup minced peeled and seeded cucumber
3 tbsps. chopped onion
¼ cup toasted almonds

2 tbsps. chopped capers
1 tsp. dried sage
dash of ground cloves
6 tbsps. butter
¼ cup white wine
salt
2 strips bacon
ground blanched almonds
melted butter and white wine, half
and half

Rub fish inside and out with garlic salt and pepper. Make stuffing of all remaining ingredients except bacon, ground almonds, melted butter and wine. Season with salt and pepper. Stuff fish and close opening. Score both sides of fish lengthwise and bury a strip of bacon in each slash. Make a heavy paste of ground almonds, melted butter and wine. Spread a ⅛-inch-thick layer of the paste over the top and sides of fish. Bake in a well-buttered pan at 350° until browned, without turning. Baste with butter if the paste dries too much. SERVES 6.

BURMESE CURRIED FISH BALLS

2 lbs. rabbitfish fillets
½ cup sesame or peanut oil
3 onions, minced
2 fresh chile peppers, peeled, seeded
and minced, or ½ tsp. dried ground
chile pepper

4 garlic cloves, minced
1 tsp. grated lemon rind
1 tsp. turmeric
2 tsps. salt
¼ cup flour
3 tomatoes, chopped

Grind the fillets or chop very fine. Heat ¼ cup oil. Add onions, chile peppers, garlic, lemon rind, turmeric and salt. Sauté for 10 minutes, stirring frequently. Remove one third of mixture and add fish to it. Chop or grind together until smooth, or blend in small batches. Form into walnut-sized balls and roll lightly in flour. Add remaining oil to pan and heat. Add the balls and brown on all sides, stirring frequently./ Add tomatoes and cook over low heat for 25 minutes. SERVES 6.

LATIN AMERICAN CORIANDER FILLETS

3 lbs. dolphin fillets
2 cups court bouillon
2 tbsps. unsalted butter
1 medium-size onion, minced
½ cup chopped blanched almonds
3 canned green Serrano chiles or fresh hot green peppers, seeded and chopped

2 cups coarsely chopped fresh green coriander, stems and leaves
salt and fresh-ground pepper

Poach fish in court bouillon until it flakes easily. Remove and keep warm. Reserve poaching liquid. Melt butter in a small pan and sauté onion until tender but not browned. Combine with almonds, chiles, coriander and 1½ cups poaching liquid and whirl in blender until smooth. Season. Add more stock if needed for consistency: sauce should be like heavy cream. Heat without letting it boil. Pour over warm fillets.
SERVE 6.

BAJA CALIFORNIA BREADED FISH

3 lbs. dolphin fillet

Marinade:
½ cup lemon juice
¼ cup salad oil
1 or 2 small garlic cloves, mashed
1 tsp. salt

2 eggs beaten with 2 tbsps. milk

2 tbsps. dry white wine
¼ cup minced onion
1½ tsps. dried orégano
¼ tsp. pepper

fine dry bread crumbs
butter and cooking oil

Blend marinade, add fillets, and let stand for 20 minutes. Drain fish and dip into egg coating made of milk beaten into eggs. Coat with crumbs. Put on wax paper, not touching, and let stand for 5 minutes. Brown on all sides in a small amount of half-and-half cooking oil and butter.
SERVES 6.

ITALIAN FILLETS WITH PARMESAN

4 individual portion-sized dolphin
    fillets
salt and pepper

butter
4 thin slices of Parmesan cheese
¼ cup fish stock

Place fillets in a buttered skillet; sprinkle with salt and pepper and dot with extra butter. Brown gently on both sides. Top each fillet with slice of cheese and sprinkle on the stock. Cover and simmer slowly for about 5 minutes, until the cheese melts. (Can be done either in the oven or on top of the stove.)
    SERVES 4.

HAWAIIAN SAUTÉED FISH

6 individual slices of dolphin, ¼ inch
    thick
⅓ cup chopped scallions with tops
2 tbsps. white sesame seeds, toasted
    and ground

1 tbsp. sesame oil
dash of pepper
3 tbsps. soya sauce
1½ tbsps. butter or sesame oil

Mix scallions, sesame seeds, 1 tbsp. oil, pepper and soya sauce. Dip fish into this mixture. Sauté in butter or oil until lightly browned.
    SERVES 6.

HAWAIIAN BROILED FILLETS

4 mahimahi (dolphin) fillets, cut
    into serving pieces
salt and pepper
3 tbsps. salad oil

1 tbsp. soya sauce
2 tbsps. lemon juice
1 tbsp. minced parsley

Season fillets with salt and pepper. Broil 3 inches from the source of heat for about 7 minutes, basting frequently with mixture of oil and soya sauce. Turn and broil for 4 more minutes, basting occasionally. Arrange on a warm platter.

Heat remaining basting sauce with fish drippings, lemon juice and parsley, and pour over fish.

SERVES 4.

NORWEGIAN MOUSSE

1½ lbs. northern kingfish fillets
2 egg whites
2 cups heavy cream
¾ tsp. salt

¼ tsp. fresh ground pepper
¼ tsp. grated nutmeg
dash of cayenne

Grind fillets 4 times, or blend in small batches at high speed, until very finely shredded, then pound with wooden spoon or mallet. Put in a bowl over cracked ice. Gradually beat in egg whites with a whisk or wooden spoon. Stir in the cream a little at a time, making sure it is thoroughly absorbed. Season and let stand over ice for 1 hour. Stir mousse and pour into a buttered mold. Cover with wax paper or buttered brown paper. Place mold in a pan with 1 inch of hot water. Bake at 350° for about 25 minutes, or until firm. Unmold and serve hot with a hot seafood-seasoned sauce.

SERVES 4.

IRANIAN DATE-NUT STUFFED FISH

1 (4-lb.) kingfish, split and boned
    for baking
½ cup cooked rice
½ cup ground almonds
½ lb. chopped, pitted dates
1 tsp. sugar
½ tsp. ground ginger

¼ lb. butter, melted
2 tsps. salt
½ tsp. black pepper
¾ cup chopped onions
½ cup water
½ tsp. ground cinnamon

Wash fish and let stand in salted water for about 5 minutes. Drain and pat dry. Mix together rice, almonds, dates, sugar, half of the ginger and 2 tbsps. butter. Stuff fish with the mixture and close the opening. Pour half of remaining butter into a baking dish and arrange the fish in it. Sprinkle with salt, pepper, remaining ginger and remaining butter. Add onions and water. Bake at 350°, basting frequently, for 1 hour. Sprinkle with cinnamon; raise heat to 450° and move fish to top rack of oven until browned.

SERVES 4.

THAI STEAMED FISH PUDDING

1½ lbs. flying fish fillets, ground very fine
2 tbsps. shrimp or anchovy paste
1½ cups coconut milk
4 tbsps. minced scallions
2 tbsps. grated cabbage

1 tbsp. minced garlic
1 tsp. grated lemon rind
½ tsp. dried ground chile pepper
salt and pepper
1 egg
½ cup heavy cream

Blend ground fish with shrimp paste, coconut milk and remaining ingredients except egg and cream; season with salt and pepper to taste. Beat for a few minutes then beat in the egg. Divide among 6 individual baking dishes. Spoon cream on top and cover with foil. Set in a pan of hot water. Bake at 325° for 1 hour, or until set.

SERVES 6.

ITALIAN-STYLE FLIERS

---

6 (1-lb.) flying fish

¼ tsp. pepper

Marinade:
1 cup olive oil
1 tbsp. chopped fennel
1 small garlic clove, mashed
leafy tops of 3 celery ribs, chopped
1 tbsp. lemon juice
1 large bay leaf
3 parsley sprigs
½ tsp. salt

Stuffing:
½ lb. pork fat, minced
2 fennel sprigs, chopped
1 onion slice, minced
3 or 4 parsley sprigs, chopped
1 tbsp. minced chives
2 small shallots, minced

1 cup tomato sauce

Make the marinade. Let the fish marinate in it for 1 hour. Meanwhile make the stuffing. Moisten stuffing with enough marinade to give spreading consistency. Divide stuffing into 6 portions. Oil 6 sheets of brown paper each large enough to wrap 1 fish. Lay a portion of stuffing on paper. Lay fish on top of stuffing and wrap the fish securely. Put in shallow baking pan with half of the unstrained marinade. Bake at 350° for 20 minutes, basting frequently and turning once. Remove the papers, set fish aside, and scrape the stuffing back into the pan. Add the tomato sauce and bring to a boil. Pour stuffing and sauce into a hot shallow serving dish and lay fish on top.

SERVES 6.

BAKED FLIERS

flying fish fillets

Put fillets in a buttered shallow baking dish. Season with salt and pepper. Dot with butter and top with sliced raw mushrooms. Add sour cream almost to cover. Bake at 300° for 30 to 35 minutes.

BAJA CALIFORNIA BROILED FLIERS

6 (1-lb.) flying fish	paprika
¼ lb. butter	1 to 2 tbsps. tarragon vinegar
salt and pepper	1 tsp. minced gherkin pickle

Slash the backs of the fish to prevent curling. Melt butter and season with salt, pepper and paprika. Roll fish in melted butter and broil under medium heat for 10 minutes on each side. Sprinkle with vinegar, pickle and remaining browned butter just before serving.

SERVES 6.

JAPANESE BARBECUED FILLETS

2- to 3-lb. piece of sablefish, filleted
¼ cup soya sauce
2 tbsps. lemon juice

½ cup dry sherry
½ tsp. grated fresh gingerroot, or ¼ tsp. ground

Place fish skin side down in greased baking dish. Mix remaining ingredients and simmer for 2 or 3 minutes, or until slightly thickened. Brush onto fish flesh and let stand for 30 minutes. Cover dish and bake at 350° for about 15 minutes, basting several times.
SERVES 4 to 6.

SPANISH ORANGE FILLETS

6 (6-oz.) freshwater bass fillets
milk
flour
4 tbsps. butter
salt and white pepper
1 tbsp. minced onion

⅔ cup orange juice
¼ cup dry white wine
1 tsp. grated orange rind
segments of 2 large oranges, peeled

Dip fillets into milk, then dust with flour; sauté in 3 tbsps. butter until well browned on both sides and flesh flakes easily. Sprinkle with salt and pepper to taste and keep warm. Cook minced onion in butter remaining in the pan until soft. Stir in orange juice, wine and grated rind. Season with salt and pepper and simmer for 5 minutes. Strain sauce into another pan and blend in remaining 1 tbsp. butter. Add orange segments and heat through. Arrange segments around fillets and pour sauce over.
SERVES 6.

POLISH FILLETS IN SOUR CREAM

2 lbs. freshwater bass fillets
salt and pepper
flour
3 tbsps. butter

4 tbsps. grated Parmesan cheese
1 cup dairy sour cream
3 tbsps. buttered crumbs

Season fish, dust with flour, and brown lightly in butter. Arrange in a shallow dish. Sprinkle thickly with cheese. Mix sour cream with ½ tsp. flour and spread over fish. Sprinkle with buttered crumbs. Bake at 450° for about 20 minutes.

SERVES 4.

KASHMIR FILLETS

6 freshwater bass fillets
2 garlic cloves, minced
½ tsp. ground chile pepper
⅛ tsp. ground cuminseed
¾ tsp. salt

¼ tsp. pepper
4 tbsps. butter
½ cup sour milk or buttermilk
2 tsps. lemon juice

Mix garlic, chile, cuminseed, salt and pepper; rub into fillets. Melt butter and brown fillets well on both sides. Add sour milk and lemon juice, and cook over low heat until liquid is absorbed.

SERVES 6.

BRETON MINTED FILLETS

1 lb. freshwater bass fillets
½ cup heavy cream

Court Bouillon:
1 cup water

1 carrot, chopped
½ tsp. salt
1 onion, chopped
3 sprigs of fresh mint

Make court bouillon and simmer for 30 minutes; strain and let cool. Add the fillets and bring gently to a boil. Reduce heat and simmer until the fillets are done. Drain and reserve ½ cup stock. Keep fish warm while blending and heating (without boiling) the reserved stock and the cream. Pour over fish before serving.

SERVES 2 or 3.

CANADIAN ROAST FISH

1 (4-lb.) smallmouth bass   ½ tsp. pepper
   lemon juice   ⅓ cup melted butter
2 tsps. salt

Wash fish in cold water to which lemon juice has been added. Wipe fish dry. Rub with mixed salt and pepper. Slash sides slightly to prevent curling. Place in a roaster and pour on the melted butter. Roast at 350° for 30 minutes, basting frequently. Serve with mustard sauce.
SERVES 4.

BOLIVIAN BAKED FILLETS

6 portion-sized barracuda fillets   2 tbsps. heavy cream
½ lb. butter   ½ tsp. grated nutmeg
2 onions, chopped   ½ cup sherry
3 cups bread crumbs   1 tbsp. salt
4 egg yolks, beaten   1 tsp. pepper

Melt half of the butter and sauté the onions for 10 minutes, stirring frequently. Add bread crumbs and cook over low heat, stirring for 2 minutes. Remove from heat and stir in the yolks. Add cream, nutmeg, and half of the sherry, salt and pepper. Divide into 6 parts. Roll a fillet around each part and fasten with food picks or poultry pins. Melt remaining butter, add fillets, and sprinkle with rest of sherry and salt and pepper. Bake at 400° for 30 minutes, basting frequently.
SERVES 6.

TURKISH FILLETS

2 lbs. porgy fillets
salt and fresh-ground black pepper
1 bunch of green onions with tops, chopped
2 green peppers, seeded and thinly sliced

3 tbsps. olive oil
½ cup water
2 tomatoes, thinly sliced
1 lemon, thinly sliced
½ cup chopped parsley

Wash and dry fillets, fold in half, and place in a buttered casserole. Sprinkle with salt and pepper to taste. Mix onions, peppers, oil and water, and cook, covered, over medium heat for 10 minutes. Spread over fillets. Place tomato and lemon slices on top. Bake at 350° for about 25 minutes. Garnish with parsley.

SERVES 4.

JAPANESE SIMMERED FILLETS

2 lbs. porgy fillets
½ cup water
5 tbsps. soya sauce

2 tbsps. mirin or sherry
¾ cup snow peas or ¾ cup 1¼-inch pieces of cauliflower or celery

Bring water to a boil; add soya and mirin. Add fish and weight it so that it doesn't move. Simmer until fish flakes. Remove fish and keep warm. Boil vegetables in fish water until tender. Serve vegetables with fish.

SERVES 4.

FOIL-BAKED FISH

2 lbs. boned fish, cut into serving pieces

Arrange on foil. Top with 1 sliced medium-size onion. Make sauce of juice of 1 lime or lemon, 2 tbsps. butter, large dash of Worcestershire sauce, dash of soya sauce, salt and pepper to taste and 3 tbsps. mayonnaise. Add sauce to fish and dot with extra butter. Double-fold the foil and bake on coals (or in 350° oven) for 20 to 25 minutes.

SERVES 4.

SANDDABS

Clean and dry sanddabs. Dip into milk seasoned with salt and pepper, then into fine dry crumbs. Arrange on a greased baking sheet and dot with butter or sprinkle with salad oil. Bake at 450° for 8 to 10 minutes; or sauté in butter until browned and tender.

WEST COAST SIZZLING FISH

Sanddabs, cleaned but whole, or other individual-size flat fish

Preheat metal steak plates in 500° oven. Sprinkle fish lightly with salt and pepper, dredge with flour and shake off excess. Put 2 tbsps. butter in each hot steak plate and swirl to coat. Turn fish in butter to coat both sides. Arrange fish on plates and return to 500° oven. Cook until done without turning: 4 to 6 minutes for small fish, 8 to 10 for larger.

ITALIAN PANFISH IN WHITE WINE

2 lbs. cleaned crappies	1 tbsp. minced parsley
2 tbsps. butter	1 bay leaf, crumbled
1 onion, chopped	1 cup white wine
1 carrot, chopped	2 tbsps. raisins, plumped
1 garlic clove, minced	salt and pepper

Melt butter; fry onion, carrot, garlic, parsley and bay leaf. Add the fish and the wine, and enough water to cover fish. Poach gently for about 25 minutes, covered. Remove fish and reduce sauce over high heat by half. Add raisins and salt and pepper to taste.

SERVES 4.

BURMESE CROQUETTES IN COCONUT CREAM

2 lbs. sunfish fillets
2 onions, sliced
½ tsp. dried ground chile pepper
3 garlic cloves, minced
1 tbsp. minced fresh gingerroot, or
   ½ tbsp. ground

2 tbsps. lemon juice
1 tbsp. cornstarch
2 tsps. salt
1 cup oil
1 cup coconut cream

Grind the fillets fine with one of the onions, the chile, garlic and ginger. Blend in lemon juice, cornstarch and salt. Shape into small croquettes and chill, covered, for about 1 hour. Heat oil and sauté remaining onion until browned. Remove onion from oil and brown croquettes. Remove croquettes and pour off all but 1 tbsp. oil. Blend in coconut cream, bring to a boil, and return croquettes. Cook over low heat for 10 minutes. Garnish with browned onion rings.

SERVES 6.

ITALIAN FILLETS WITH MARSALA

4 grunt fillets
flour seasoned with salt and pepper
4 tbsps. butter

¼ cup marsala
¼ cup fish stock

Dust fillets with seasoned flour and sauté in bubbling butter. Add marsala and stock and cook, uncovered, until the fillets are tender and the sauce somewhat reduced.

SERVES 4.

GRITS AND GRUNTS

Split grunts and sprinkle flesh with salt. Let stand for 1 hour. Boil gently for 1 hour. Serve with grits and Old Sour or Key lime juice.

CANADIAN PANFISH

Poach fish in simmering water until barely done. Remove and skin. Broil for 5 minutes. Blend 1 tbsp. lemon juice with 3 tbsps. sweet butter per fish and pour over.

SOUR CREAM FISH

4 croakers, cleaned
  salt and pepper
1 cup sour cream

2 tbsps. butter
2 tbsps. water
1 tbsp. minced parsley

Put fish in a very well-greased dish; barely cover bottom with water. Season with salt and pepper and bake at 400° for 15 to 20 minutes, basting 2 or 3 times. Scald the cream in a double boiler with butter and water. Add parsley and pour over fish. Return to oven for 5 minutes. Dust with paprika.
    SERVES 4.

BOURRIDE PROVENÇAL

1½ lbs. assorted firm fish, cut into chunks
6 small firm fish fillets
2 onions, chopped
2 tomatoes, peeled, seeded and chopped
  bouquet garni of thyme, bay leaf, fennel and parsley

2 garlic cloves, chopped
1 qt. water
  salt
  pinch of saffron
2 egg yolks
6 slices of garlic toast, sautéed
1 cup aïoli sauce

Bring vegetables and herbs to a boil in the water, salted to taste. Add the chunks of fish and simmer for 15 minutes. Add saffron. Remove fish and keep hot. Cook the broth down for a few minutes. Strain and rub the vegetables through a sieve. Measure and reheat 1¾ cups broth. Poach fillets in this until tender, remove and keep hot. Beat egg yolks; add 2 to 3 tbsps. broth to yolks, then gradually add this to rest of broth, stirring. Cook gently over hot water until slightly thickened; do not let boil. Arrange a piece of garlic toast in a deep dish with a fillet on top. Cover with *aïoli* sauce. Surround toast with pieces of fish and pour broth over all.

SERVES 6.

COOKED AND LEFTOVER FISH

JAPANESE FISH SOUP

8 oz. broiled fish, broken into small pieces

5 oz. mild miso (if granular, grind fine)

8 oz. tofu (bean curd), diced

5 cups dashi

2 leeks, sliced

Mix all but leeks and bring to a boil. Add leeks, let them become warm, and serve.

SERVES 6 to 8.

ENGLISH-STYLE KIPPERED FISH

1 lb. salted and smoked sablefish, cut into serving pieces

1½ lbs. small (less than 1½ inches in diameter) new potatoes

2 cups water

2 garlic cloves, mashed

1 tsp. salt

¼ tsp. pepper

2 tbsps. melted butter

1½ tbsps. lemon juice

Scrub potatoes. Place them in a small pan and add the garlic, salt and pepper; cover and simmer for 10 minutes. Set fish pieces on top of potatoes and continue cooking, covered, for 8 to 10 minutes, or until potatoes are tender. Drain fish and potatoes and drizzle on melted butter mixed with lemon juice. Add more salt and pepper to taste.

SERVES 4.

FISH TURNOVERS

---

1 cup flaked cooked fish
1 cup flour
¼ tsp. salt
4 tbsps. butter
  pepper
  ground thyme
  dillweed
  chopped parsley

1½ cups cooked rice
1 (4-oz.) can mushroom pieces,
  drained
2 hard-cooked eggs, sliced
1 egg, beaten
  melted butter
  lemon juice

Make a pastry of flour, salt, butter and enough cold water to moisten (about 2 tbsps.). Chill for at least 2 hours. Roll into a large oval ⅜ inch thick on a floured board. Put onto oiled and floured cookie sheet. Season fish with salt, pepper and herbs to taste. On half of the oval alternate layers of rice, mushrooms, egg slices dotted with butter, and fish, ending with rice. Fold dough over, crimp edges, and brush with beaten egg. Make 2 or 3 vertical slashes for vents in top. Bake at 450° for about 15 minutes. Serve with melted butter seasoned with lemon juice to taste. Individual turnovers can, of course, be formed.

SERVES 4.

HUNGARIAN PIQUANT CROQUETTES

---

3 cups flaked cooked and boned fish
3 tbsps. butter
3 tbsps. flour
½ cup chicken stock
¼ cup dry white wine
2 tbsps. sweet pickle relish
2 tbsps. anchovy butter

2 tsps. capers
1 tsp. grated onion
  few drops of Tabasco
  salt
  fine bread crumbs
  fat for deep-frying

Melt butter; blend in flour. Add stock and wine and cook over low heat, stirring, until thick and smooth. Blend in fish, pickle relish, anchovy butter, capers, grated onion, Tabasco and salt to taste. Heat thoroughly. Chill overnight.

Form mixture into small balls and roll in crumbs. Fry in deep hot fat heated to 365° until brown and crisp. Drain, and serve hot with caper cream sauce. SERVES 6.

INDOCHINESE FISH WITH ANISE SAUCE

2 lbs. fried fillets, cut into bite-sized pieces
¼ cup oil
¾ cup minced scallions
3 garlic cloves, minced
½ tsp. ground chile peppers
2 tsps. sugar

1 tsp. ground aniseed
2 tbsps. vinegar
1½ cups water
2 tsps. anchovy paste

Heat the oil and sauté the scallions in it for 5 minutes. Stir in all but fish and anchovy paste; simmer for 20 minutes. Blend in anchovy paste, add fish pieces, and cook for 5 minutes longer. SERVES 6 to 8.

ISRAELI BAKED FISH

1 lb. poached fish fillets, broken into small pieces
3 tbsps. butter
3 tbsps. flour

¾ cup white-wine court bouillon
¼ cup light cream
1 cup grated Cheddar cheese

Melt butter, blend in flour, and gradually add court bouillon and cream. Thicken, stirring. Add half of the cheese and stir until melted. Add fish. Spoon into individual baking dishes (6 for appetizer, 3 for main course) and top with remaining cheese. Bake at 350° until bubbly, about 10 minutes. SERVES 6 for appetizer, 3 for main course.

Oily Fish

Firm-fleshed fish that have a relatively high fat content (all of which smoke well) are primarily saltwater fish, ranging from the swift wahoo and rainbow runner to the heavy tuna that makes an angler really bend his back. Eels, both fresh- and saltwater, come into this group and the large anadromous and landlocked family of salmon.

Salmon are in a bad way, as all anglers are aware. In 1972 many of the Canadian salmon waters were closed because of the pressure on the fish population created by commercial fishery activities. Limits, where still permitted, are greatly reduced.

The Coho salmon, which has caused a tremendous fishing furor in the Great Lakes, has also managed to absorb much too much DDT. However, these salmon can be trimmed of those portions where most of the DDT is concentrated; unhappily these are the fatty portions which contribute much to the salmon's flavor. If you take Coho, it is best to cut the fish into steaks, then, after skinning, cut off the strips of darker meat on each side of the flesh, the flesh surrounding the backbone and the area immediately around the belly section. True, you are discarding a fair amount of meat, but it's undoubtedly a good idea to do it, at least until scientists announce that DDT levels have decreased to a safe point . . . if they ever do.

Bonito, which many anglers look upon solely as a bait for billfish, is a game fish—the Oceanic bonito, that is—and is also edible. Obviously, it has possibilities. The California bonito is canned, and only the state's "Tuna" law keeps it from being called that on market shelves.

APPETIZERS

ECUADORIAN CEVICHE

1 (1½-lb.) king mackerel, skinned and
    boned
fresh lemon or lime juice
1 cup orange juice
1 cup salad oil

1 onion, thinly sliced
1 fresh hot red or green pepper,
    seeded and minced
1 garlic clove, minced
salt and pepper

Cut fish into bite-size pieces, and cover with lemon or lime juice. Let fish stand chilled for 4 hours, or until fish is opaque. Drain and toss gently in mixture of remaining ingredients.

SERVES 4 to 6.

HAWAIIAN MARINATED APPETIZER

1½ lbs. fresh king mackerel fillets, sliced into long narrow strips
juice of 3 limes
½ cup chopped scallions
4 tomatoes, peeled and diced
salt and pepper
Tabasco

Put fish in a glass or earthenware bowl; add lime juice. Cover and chill for several hours. Drain and rinse in very cold water. Mix mackerel with scallions and tomatoes. Season with salt, pepper and Tabasco to taste; it should be spicy. Chill.

SERVES 6.

FRENCH GREEN EELS

3 lbs. eels, cut into 1-inch pieces
1 cup olive oil
1 qt. fish stock
½ cup chopped mixed herbs (chervil, mint, chives, puréed spinach)
juice of 3 lemons
2 cups white wine
salt and pepper

Heat the oil and sauté the eel pieces for 5 minutes, turning them in the oil. Add stock; bring to a boil, and cook for 5 minutes. Add herbs, lemon juice, wine, and salt and pepper to taste. Bring to a boil. Remove from heat and let stand until cool.

SERVES 6 to 8.

ITALIAN MARINATED EELS

Cut eels into chunks and fry in olive oil until three-fourths cooked. Measure enough red wine to cover eels in a deep dish. Add a dash of salt and a dash of sugar. Boil wine for 10 minutes. Add the frying oil and a few bay leaves. Pour over the fish, cool, cover, and refrigerate overnight.

ITALIAN SKEWERED EELS

Scrub small finger-thick eels well and cut with scissors into 4-inch sections. Thread onto skewers alternating with bay leaves; salt heavily. Broil 6 inches above a charcoal fire for 20 to 25 minutes; or eels can be cooked in the oven.

POLISH ROULADE OF EEL

1 medium-size eel (about ½ lb.)	2 or 3 pickled gherkins
salt	pepper
4 to 6 medium-size mushrooms, sliced	1 raw egg
	4 cups strong vegetable broth
1 tbsp. butter	2 tbsps. vinegar
5 hard-cooked eggs	1 lemon

Split the eel and remove backbone. Salt inside and out. Sauté mushrooms in butter. Chop 3 hard-cooked eggs, the gherkins and mushrooms. Season to taste and bind with raw egg. Stuff into eel. Wrap stuffed eel in cheesecloth and roll tightly together. Put in as small a pan as possible. Add broth and vinegar and simmer, covered, for 30 minutes. Let cool in broth; remove cheesecloth and chill. Garnish with remaining eggs and the lemon, sliced or cut into wedges. Slice eel and serve with seasoned mayonnaise.

SERVES 2 to 4.

MEXICAN AGUJA

Wash small needlefish, up to 4 inches long, in salted water but do not eviscerate or behead. Fry very quickly in deep, hot fat. Serve hot.

SOUTH AFRICAN PICKLED APPETIZER

12 thin slices of salmon, cut into halves	3 tbsps. curry powder
4 tsps. salt	½ tsp. dried ground chile pepper
1 tsp. pepper	1 cup seedless raisins
¼ cup oil	2 tbsps. sugar
6 large onions, sliced into thin rings	1 tsp. turmeric
	3 cups vinegar

Wash and dry the fish. Mix 1 tsp. salt with 1 tsp. pepper and sprinkle over fish. Heat oil and brown the fish on both sides. Remove and cool. Add 4 onions to the oil and brown. Mix 2 tbsps. curry powder with chile pepper, raisins, sugar, turmeric and 3 tbsps. vinegar. Arrange alternating layers of fish, fried onions and spices in a bowl. Combine remaining onions, vinegar, salt and curry powder and boil for 15 minutes. Pour over the fish and let stand for 1 hour. Cover and refrigerate for at least 2 days. Will keep for 2 weeks.
SERVES 6 or more.

TAHITIAN RAW FISH IN LIME JUICE

1 lb. bonito, skinned and boned	salt and pepper
1 large onion	coconut cream
1 cup lime juice	

Slice the fish ¼ inch thick and put a layer on the bottom of a deep bowl. Cut half of the onion into thin slices and mince the rest. Sprinkle a thin layer of minced onion over fish and sprinkle on lime juice and seasoning. Continue building layers until done, reserving a bit of lime juice. Cover and refrigerate for about 3 hours. Drain, rinse with fresh water, and drain again thoroughly.

Serve with reserved lime juice sprinkled on and accompany with a dip of coconut cream and sliced half of the onion in rings.

SERVES 4.

Gravlax, or gravad lax as some spell it, presumably comes from the old Scandinavian technique of preserving salmon before the days of refrigeration. The story goes that it was treated, wrapped and buried underground until ready. Or was it only buried in the sense that it was put out of sight for the required length of time? Regardless of the history, today's is just as good.

SWEDISH GRAVLAX VARIATIONS
Swedish "Buried" Salmon

2-lb. skinned center-section fillet
4 tbsps. sugar
2 tbsps. salt
12 whole peppercorns, coarsely
    ground

1 tbsp. minced fresh dill, or
1 tsp. dried dillweed

Mix together sugar, salt, pepper and dill and pat lightly into all sides of the fish. Place salmon in a flat-bottomed, close-fitting dish. Sprinkle with any remaining mix. Cover and chill for at least 24 hours or up to 4 days (it gets too salty if left longer). Weight to make slicing easier. Spoon juices over fish occasionally. Slice thinly across the grain. Serve with toast or dark rye bread and mustard sauce.

SERVES 8 to 12.

PICKLED SALMON

2-lb. center-section fillet with skin
1 tsp. dried dillweed
1 tsp. dill seeds
3 tbsps. salt

4 tsps. sugar
¼ tsp. fresh-ground pepper
¼ tsp. ground allspice
¼ cup red- or white-wine vinegar

Mix dillweed and seeds (or use 1 tbsp. minced fresh dill) and sprinkle half on the bottom of a flat dish the salmon closely fits. Put salmon skin side down in dish and sprinkle with remaining dill. Mix salt, sugar, pepper and allspice and distribute evenly over salmon, patting lightly into flesh. Pour vinegar over. Cover dish with plastic film and set a heavy (1 pound or more) weight on it. Refrigerate for at least 2 days, spooning juices over fish occasionally. After 1 day, remove weight. Will keep for about 1 week before getting too salty.

SERVES 8 to 12.

MARINATED SALMON

2-lb. skinned center-section fillet
6 tbsps. minced fresh dill, or 3 tbsps. dried dillweed

2 tbsps. salt
1½ tbsps. sugar
½ tsp. fresh-ground pepper

Sprinkle half of the dill on the bottom of a flat, close-fitting dish. Mix together salt, sugar and pepper and pat firmly onto fish on all sides. Put fish in dish and sprinkle with remaining salt mix and dill. Cover with clear plastic film, add weight, and refrigerate for at least 24 hours or up to 4 days; spoon juices over occasionally. Serve thinly sliced with lemon juice squeezed on to taste, or thick sour cream, or dot with mustard.

SERVES 8 to 12.

SWEDISH SALMON

2 lbs. salmon in 2 fillets with skin
2 to 3 cups fresh dill
20 white peppercorns

7 tbsps. salt
6 tbsps. sugar

Wash fillets only if necessary, and then quickly, and dry well. Put a layer of fresh dill in a bowl. Crush peppercorns and mix with salt and sugar. Rub flesh with some of this and sprinkle some on top of dill. Put 1 fillet, skin down, on top of dill. Put a layer of dill on top and sprinkle on some of the salt mix. Put the other fillet on top, skin up, thick side over thin. Add another layer of dill and rest of salt mixture. Cover and weight. Cool for 6 to 24 hours, turning several times without disturbing layers. Scrape off seasonings. Slice fish slantwise toward the skin. Garnish with sprigs of dill.

SERVES 8 to 12.

SWEDISH SALMON SOUR

Fish cut into 3-inch chunks.

Cook until done in 1 qt. water with 1 cup cider vinegar, 1 tsp. salt and ¼ tsp. pepper, 1 tbsp. sugar and 2 bay leaves. Chill in its own liquid. Serve for cold supper, or cut smaller for appetizers.

SOUPS

ALASKAN FISH CHOWDER

1½ lbs. salmon
2 qts. water
1 sprig of fresh thyme, or pinch of dried
1 sprig of fresh tarragon, or pinch of dried
2 slices of bacon
2 onions, minced

2 parsley sprigs, minced
3 carrots, minced
3 or 4 medium-size potatoes, minced
1 celery rib, minced
1 beef bouillon cube
salt and pepper
1 (1-lb.) can solid-pack tomatoes

Simmer salmon in water with thyme and tarragon until it flakes easily, about 15 minutes. Remove salmon, and skin and bone it and break into chunks. Strain cooking liquid and reserve. Cook bacon, onions and parsley together for about 5 minutes, until limp. Add to liquid. Bring liquid to a boil; add carrots, potatoes, celery, bouillon cube and salt and pepper to taste. Cook until vegetables are done, about 15 minutes. Add tomatoes and salmon; simmer for about 10 minutes.

SERVES 8.

RUSSIAN FISH SOUP

1 lb. fresh salmon, skinned, boned
    and cubed
2 leeks
4 cups water
1 medium-size onion, quartered
1 parsley sprig, minced
1 carrot, cut into thin strips
1 celery rib, thinly sliced
2 tbsps. butter
2 tbsps. tomato purée

1 bay leaf
4 or 5 peppercorns
½ tsp. dried thyme
1 garlic clove
1 tbsp. capers
2 tbsps. pimiento-stuffed olives,
    sliced
salt and pepper
dairy sour cream

Slice green tops of leeks and put in a saucepan with the water, the onion and parsley. Bring to boil and simmer for 15 minutes. Strain, reserving liquid; discard vegetables. Slice white part of leeks and sauté with carrot and celery in butter until softened. Add reserved liquid and tomato purée. Tie bay leaf, peppercorns, thyme and garlic in a cheesecloth bag and add. Bring to a boil and simmer for 15 minutes. Remove bag and add capers, olives and fish. Simmer very gently until fish is done. Season with salt and pepper to taste. Serve with topping of sour cream. (This can also be made with leftover poached or steamed fish.)
    SERVES 6.

CLEAR SALMON SOUP

head, fins, tail and bones from a
    filleted salmon
8 cups water, approximately
1 medium-size onion, chopped
1 garlic clove, crushed
½ tsp. coriander seeds

1 tbsp. salt
1 tbsp. butter
1 tbsp. olive oil
1 tsp. dillweed
⅛ tsp. cayenne
chopped fresh parsley for garnish

Simmer all but parsley, uncovered, for about 1½ hours. Adjust salt and cayenne to taste. Strain, add parsley before serving.
    SERVES 6.

RUSSIAN SOUP WITH WINE

1½ lbs. salmon steaks (6, about 1-
    inch thick)
2½ cups fish stock
  2 tbsps. minced fresh dill

salt and cayenne pepper
3½ cups champagne or sauterne
lemon slices for garnish

Arrange steaks in a skillet; add boiling stock. Boil over high heat for 5 minutes. Reduce heat and simmer for 15 minutes more. Remove fish from stock and remove skin and bones. Put fish in a heated tureen. Sprinkle with dill. Season stock with salt and cayenne to taste and pour into tureen over fish. Bring wine just to a boil and add to tureen. Garnish with lemon slices.
    SERVES 6.

CATALINA CHOWDER

½ lb. Pacific yellowtail, in bite-size
    pieces
3½ cups fish stock
 8 oz. wide egg noodles
 1 cup chopped watercress

1 tbsp. chopped parsley
1 tbsp. chopped scallions
1½ cups milk
  salt and pepper

Bring stock to a boil; add noodles and cook, uncovered, stirring occasionally, for 5 minutes. Add watercress, parsley, scallions and fish and cook over low heat for 15 minutes. Remove from heat, add milk, and season to taste. Chill and serve cold. (To make it richer, use half and half instead of milk.)
    SERVES 4.

HAWAIIAN CHOWDER

1½ lbs. fresh tuna, skinned, boned
    and cubed
¼ lb. salt pork, diced
1 cup minced onion
2 cups diced potatoes

3 cups boiling water
2 cups light cream
½ tsp. salt
⅛ tsp. white pepper
⅛ tsp. ground ginger

Render the salt pork and discard the pieces. Add onion and fish to the fat and cook over low heat for 5 minutes. Add potatoes and water. Cover and cook over low heat for 30 minutes. Stir in cream and seasonings. Heat without boiling and correct seasonings.

SERVES 6.

MARTINIQUE FISH SOUP WITH CAPERS

2 lbs. fish, at least half tuna	1 cup minced celery
3 lbs. fish bones and trimmings	2 garlic cloves, minced
2½ cups water	¼ cup flour
3 parsley sprigs	½ tsp. salt
1 small celery rib with leaves	dash pepper
3 tbsps. butter	½ tsp. cayenne pepper
1 cup minced onion	½ tsp. dried thyme
¾ cup minced green pepper	⅓ cup drained capers

Combine bones, water, parsley and celery ribs, and simmer for 15 minutes. Drain and reserve stock. Heat butter and cook onion, green pepper, minced celery and garlic, stirring until wilted. Sprinkle with flour. Add fish and fish stock, stirring. Add salt, pepper, cayenne and thyme. Simmer until fish flakes easily. Beat soup briskly to break up fish. Add capers. Bring to boil and simmer for 5 minutes. (Can also be made with leftover steamed fish; in that case, add fish with the capers.)

SERVES 6.

ENTRÉES

ALASKA BAKED FILLETS WITH DRESSING

6 individual salmon fillets	4 tsps. minced onion
6 tbsps. butter	salt and pepper
¾ cup minced celery	¼ cup ketchup
4 cups fresh bread crumbs	butter

Melt butter and sauté celery for 10 minutes, or until tender. Combine with crumbs, onion, 1 tsp. salt and ½ tsp. pepper. Moisten with enough ketchup to hold together. Sprinkle fillets with salt and pepper on both sides. Arrange half the fillets (the larger ones) on greased foil in a baking dish. Top with dressing. Top dressing with smaller fillets. Dot with butter. Cover dish and bake at 350° for 25 to 30 minutes. Cut each in half to serve.

SERVES 6.

CANADIAN BREADED SALMON

1 (1-inch-thick) center-cut salmon slice

Wipe slice dry and sprinkle lightly with salt. Dip into well-beaten egg, then into very fine bread crumbs seasoned with pepper and chopped parsley. Sauté in vegetable oil over high heat, turning only once, until golden brown. Drain on paper towels and serve with lemon wedges and tartar sauce.

SERVES 1 or more.

FINNISH-RUSSIAN TURNOVERS

2½ lbs. skinned salmon fillets, cut from tail section
2 tbsps. butter
1 tbsp. lemon juice
1 tsp. salt
2 tbsps. minced parsley
3 tbsps. minced fresh dill
salt and pepper
pastry for 2-crust pie
1½ cups cooked buckwheat groats, bulgur, or cracked wheat
¼ cup butter, melted and cooled
3 hard-cooked eggs, sliced
1 egg, beaten

Sauté salmon in 2 tbsps. butter for 2½ minutes on each side. Sprinkle with lemon juice and salt. Trim fillets along edges to make a smooth line. Chop trimmings, plus enough extra to make 1 cup. Mix chopped salmon with parsley, dill, and salt and pepper to taste. Roll out half of the dough in a circle ¼ inch thick. Place on lightly greased cookie sheet. Spread chopped salmon mixture over pastry to ½ inch of the edge. Top with cooked wheat; drizzle on the melted butter. Make a layer of egg slices and finally arrange the whole fillets on top. Roll remaining dough and drape over mounded filling. Moisten the edges of the bottom crust and press or pinch edges of top to bottom to seal. Brush with beaten egg, and make some decorative small slashes in top as vents. Bake at 375° for 35 minutes or until browned. If frozen, bake without thawing 1 hour with a sheet of foil loosely over the top for the first 30 minutes.

SERVES 6.

FRENCH TORTE

¾ lb. skinned salmon fillets
pastry for 2-crust 9-inch pie (flaky pastry preferably)
8 mushroom caps
¾ cup soft butter
½ cup light cream
½ cup dry white wine
dash of grated nutmeg

salt and pepper
2 large egg whites, beaten stiff
2 tsps. minced fresh tarragon
2 tsps. minced fresh parsley
1 tsp. chopped chives
¼ cup melted butter
juice of ½ lemon

Roll out half of pastry into a thin round and line a 9-inch pie pan. Roll out the rest into a thin round also. Chill. In a blender whirl ½ lb. salmon and mushroom caps. Stir in soft butter, cream and wine. Season with nutmeg and salt and pepper to taste. Fold in egg whites. Spoon half of the mixture into the pastry-lined pie pan. Cover filling with remaining ¼ lb. salmon cut into thin slices. Sprinkle lightly with salt and pepper. Spoon on remaining purée and cover with the second round of pastry. Seal edges. Cut a 1-inch circle from center top of pastry. Combine remaining ingredients and set aside. Bake torte at 400° for 30 to 40 minutes, or until pastry is golden. Just before serving pour herb and melted butter and lemon juice mixture into hole.

SERVES 6.

JAPANESE SALMON

Soak fish in soya sauce for 2 hours. Broil. Serve with parched sesame seeds or poppy seeds.

POLISH BAKED STEAK WITH MADEIRA

½-lb. salmon steak or chunk
   salt and pepper
   few strips of salt pork
1 truffle

juice of ½ lemon
½ cup Madeira
½ tbsp. flour
1 tbsp. butter

Season fish with salt and pepper; lard with salt pork and thin strips of truffle. Arrange in a buttered shallow dish and cover with greased brown paper. Bake at 350°, basting from time to time. When half done, sprinkle with lemon juice and add wine. Bake until slightly browned. Blend flour and butter and mix in, stirring, to thicken the sauce.

SERVES 1.

SCANDINAVIAN DILLED FISH BAKE

1 (4-lb.) thick salmon fillet
   salt and pepper
1 cup dairy sour cream

1 egg yolk
½ tbsp. minced fresh dill

Put salmon, skin side down, in a greased shallow baking dish. Sprinkle lightly with salt and pepper. Bake uncovered at 400° for about 15 minutes, or until fish will flake. Mix sour cream, egg yolk and dill. Spread mix over salmon and return to oven for about 5 minutes.

SERVES 8 to 12.

SCOTTISH BAKED STUFFED FISH

4- to 5-lb. whole salmon, cleaned
½ cup minced onion
¼ cup butter
2 tbsps. oil
2 cups dry bread crumbs

1 cup ground cooked ham
⅓ cup minced parsley
1 tsp. dried tarragon
   salt and pepper
4 slices of salt pork

Sauté onion in butter and oil until tender but not brown. Mix well all but fish and salt pork to make a stuffing. Season with salt and pepper to taste. Stuff fish, close opening, and put fish in a lightly oiled baking pan. Top with salt pork. Bake at 350° for 40 to 50 minutes, or until done. Remove pork. Serve salmon plain or with hollandaise sauce (p. 355).

SERVES 6 to 8.

SCOTTISH GRILLED STEAKS

6 salmon steaks

Rub steaks with chopped fresh dill, brush with oil, and sprinkle with lemon juice. Put on an oiled broiling pan and broil about 2 inches from the source of heat for 5 or 6 minutes. Turn, and brush tops with oil. Broil for 4 or 5 minutes more, or until done. Season with salt and pepper.

SERVES 6.

SCOTTISH FISH WITH ANCHOVY SAUCE

3- to 4-lb. center slice of fresh salmon	1 garlic clove
3 cups fish stock	1 bay leaf
a curl of lemon peel, diced	6 peppercorns
¼ cup melted butter	½ tsp. ground allspice
1 cup red wine	½ tsp. salt
4 mushrooms, trimmed and sliced	½ cup brown sauce or gravy
1 small onion, chopped	2 tbsps. butter
several parsley sprigs	2 tbsps. anchovy paste

Simmer fish in stock with lemon peel for about 30 minutes, or until done. Drain, reserving stock, and pour the melted butter over the fish on a heated platter; keep warm. Reduce the salmon stock to 2 cups. Add wine, mushrooms, onion, parsley, garlic, bay leaf, spices and salt. Simmer for 30 minutes. Strain and stir in brown sauce or gravy. Heat. Just before serving stir in butter and anchovy paste.

SERVES 8.

SWEDISH FISH PUDDING

½ lb. fresh salmon, cut into thin
   slices
butter
fine bread crumbs
1½ lbs. potatoes, peeled and thinly
   sliced

2 onions, thinly sliced
pepper
minced fresh dill
3 eggs, well beaten
2 cups milk

Butter a baking dish well and sprinkle with bread crumbs. Build alternating layers of potato, onion and salmon slices. Sprinkle each layer with a little pepper and dill. Continue until all ingredients are used, ending with a layer of potatoes. Combine eggs and milk well and pour over layers Bake at 350° for 30 to 40 minutes, or until potatoes are done. Serve with melted butter.
   SERVES 6.

JAPANESE FRIED FISH

1 (6 lb.) tuna chunk
1 cucumber
salt and pepper
4 tbsps. cornstarch

2 tbsps. sesame oil
2 tbsps. white vingear
1 tbsp. ground ginger
3 tbsps. soya sauce

Cut fish lengthwise into 6 pieces. Cut cucumber lengthwise into halves, then into 1-inch pieces. Sprinkle fish with salt and pepper. Make a paste of cornstarch and a little water and spread on fish. Fry fish in sesame oil. Salt cucumber slices. Make a sauce by blending vinegar, ginger and soya sauce. Mix fish and cucumber and serve sauce on the side.
   SERVES 6.

ALASKA BAKED FISH

1 (4-lb.) tuna chunk, with skin
2 cups bread crumbs
2 tbsps. chopped onion
1 tbsp. chopped parsley
1 tsp. dried sage

4 tbsps. melted butter
1 cup fish stock
  salt and pepper
6 strips of bacon

Wash and dry fish; split open. Mix all but bacon to make stuffing. Season to taste. Put stuffing on top of one half of fish, fold other side over, and skewer together. Put in a buttered dish. Lay bacon across top and bake at 350° for 1 to 1½ hours.
  SERVES 8 to 10.

ITALIAN BROILED FISH

Cut thin slices from the stomach area of tuna, brush with oil, and broil.

ITALIAN STEWED FISH

Cut thin slices of tuna from the stomach area, brush with olive oil and fry. Drain. Stew in garlic-flavored tomato sauce for 30 minutes.

JAPANESE BOILED FISH WITH VEGETABLES

1 (6 lb.) tuna chunk
5 tbsps. water
6 tbsps. soya sauce
½ tsp. white vinegar
1 tsp. grated fresh gingerroot

1 tsp. sugar
1 cup coarsely chopped small turnips
  or halved Brussels sprouts or
  chopped celery or chopped cauliflower

Scale and clean fish. Boil water and 5 tbsps. soya sauce. Add fish, cover, and boil for 5 minutes. Remove from heat. Add vinegar, gingerroot, sugar, 1 tbsp. soya sauce and vegetable of your choice. Boil until vegetable is barely tender.
SERVES 6.

ITALIAN FISH GNOCCHI

2 lbs. fresh tuna, skinned and boned
1 cup coarse French bread crumbs
¾ cup hot milk
1 tsp. salt
    dash of pepper
¼ tsp. grated nutmeg
1 egg, slightly beaten
3 egg yolks
½ cup plus 2 tbsps. butter, melted
¼ cup flour

Combine the crumbs and milk and mix well. Mash fish thoroughly. Add crumbs, salt, pepper, nutmeg, whole egg and yolks and ½ cup melted butter. Mix until well blended. Shape mixture into rolls 3 inches long and 1 inch thick. Lightly coat with flour. Put remaining 2 tbsps. melted butter in a saucepan. Add tuna rolls and boiling water to cover. Simmer, uncovered, for 10 minutes. Serve with your choice of sauce.
SERVES 4 to 6.

FRENCH STEAKS

2 lbs. tuna steaks
1 cup and 1 tbsp. white-wine vinegar
3 tbsps. olive oil
2 small onions, chopped
2 tomatoes, peeled and quartered
    salt and pepper

Put fish in a shallow dish with 1 cup vinegar. Cover tightly and marinate for 24 hours, turning occasionally. Heat oil and sauté the drained tuna for about 2 minutes per side, or until lightly browned. Remove fish to a casserole. In the fish skillet, sauté onions for about 3 minutes. Add tomatoes and cook for 3 minutes more. Season to taste. Pour tomato mixture over fish and cover casserole. Cook over low heat for about 15 minutes. Just before serving stir in remaining tbsp. vinegar.
SERVES 6.

HAWAIIAN FISH WITH VEGETABLES

2 lbs. skinned and boned tuna, cut into ½-inch squares
½ cup plus 2 tbsps. soya sauce
piece of green gingerroot, crushed
2 tbsps. cornstarch
3 tbsps. salad oil

5 medium-size onions, sliced
¼ lb. snow peas
⅓ cup sugar
2 tbsps. sake
¼ tsp. MSG

Marinate tuna squares 15 minutes in ½ cup soya with gingerroot for 15 minutes. Drain. Dredge with cornstarch, and sauté in oil until golden. Remove fish from pan and sauté onions until tender but not browned. Stir in snow peas, sugar, sake and 2 tbsps. soya and MSG. Add fish squares and cook for 5 minutes, stirring frequently.

Serves 6.

· JAPANESE BROILED FISH

6 servings of bonito
½ tbsp. salt

¼ cup soya sauce
¼ cup mirin

Slightly salt fish. Skewer each serving with 2 skewers to keep fish from spinning. Broil until lightly brown. Dip into mixture of soya and *mirin;* broil briefly again. Dip again and broil again, or baste. Remove skewers and serve.

Serves 6.

COLD CHINESE SWEET AND SOUR FISH

1 (2-lb.) piece of bonito
3 cups boiling water
3 large onions, sliced
¾ cup raisins
1 tsp. salt

juice of 1½ lemons
¼ cup vinegar
1½ tbsps. sugar
1 egg yolk, beaten

Put bonito in a shallow pan; pour on the water. Add onions and raisins and sprinkle with salt. Simmer for 20 minutes. Turn the fish and add lemon juice, vinegar and sugar. Cook for 20 minutes longer, basting several times. Remove fish to a glass dish. Strain juice and reheat it. When boiling, slowly pour over the beaten yolk, then pour mixture over fish and chill.

SERVES 6 to 8.

NORWEGIAN FRIED EELS

3 lbs. eels, skinned and boned

3 tbsps. brandy

¾ cup lemon juice

1 recipe Basic Frying Batter

Cut eels into 3-inch pieces. Mix brandy and lemon juice and marinate eels in it for 1 hour. Drain, dry well, and coat with frying batter. Fry in deep fat heated to 375° until crisp. Drain. Serve with a sauce of your choice.

SERVES 6 to 8.

ITALIAN STEWED EELS

2 lbs. eels

2 large onions, chopped

1 carrot, chopped

1 small celery rib, chopped

handful of chopped parsley

2 cups water or fish stock

1 tbsp. wine vinegar

grated rind of ½ lemon

Boil vegetables in water or stock. When almost soft, strain and reserve liquid and vegetables separately. Cut eels into 3-inch pieces. Put alternate layers of eel and vegetables in a casserole; pour on reserved liquid. Cover and bake slowly, barely simmering, for 3 hours. Add vinegar and lemon rind. Boil for a few minutes longer.

SERVES 4 to 6.

ITALIAN STEWED EELS IN WHITE WINE

1¼ lbs. eels, cut into 1-inch pieces
3 tbsps. oil
2 tbsps. butter
1 garlic clove, minced
  grated rind of ¼ lemon

1 tsp. tomato paste
½ cup white wine
2 or 3 sage leaves, crushed
  salt and pepper

Melt oil and butter and brown the eels a bit. Add garlic, lemon rind, tomato paste softened with a bit of water, wine, sage and salt and pepper to taste. Simmer for 30 minutes.

SERVES 4.

ITALIAN SKEWERED EELS WITH HERBS

Cut eels into 3- or 4-inch chunks. Thread on skewers alternating with bay, sage and rosemary leaves (moistening them makes them easier to thread). Brush with oil and cook over hot coals, or in a broiler, basting with drippings. Alternately, they can be marinated in oil seasoned with lemon juice, salt and pepper for 1 hour; during broiling baste with the marinade.

FRENCH EEL MATELOTE

2 lbs. skinned eels, cut into 1-inch
    pieces
4 shallots, chopped
2 tbsps. butter
2 tbsps. flour

salt and pepper
4 cups red wine
6 small white onions
1 parsley sprig

Sauté the shallots in half of the butter until tender but not browned. Blend in flour and salt and pepper to taste. Add wine and bring to a boil. Reduce heat and simmer over very low heat, covered, for 1 hour. Sauté onions in remaining butter until tender. Add onions and eels to wine mixture with parsley and cook for 15 minutes, until eels are tender.

SERVES 6.

ENGLISH BAKED EELS

Cut eels into 3-inch pieces, then rub with suet. Put in a buttered baking dish and dot with butter. Cover and bake at 350° until tender, 30 to 45 minutes. Serve with sweet-sour sauce.

ENGLISH EEL STIFLE

6 small eels, skinned and cut into 4-inch pieces
butter
6 large potatoes, peeled and sliced

4 large onions, sliced
flour
pepper
1-inch cube of salt pork, minced

Butter a large baking dish and arrange alternating layers of eel, potato and onion, sprinkling each with flour and pepper. Sprinkle top with salt pork and dot well with butter. Add enough hot water to barely cover. Cover dish and bake at 375° for 30 to 40 minutes, until everything is tender.
SERVES 6.

FRENCH SAUTÉED EELS

2 large eels or several small ones, skinned
flour
6 tbsps. olive oil

salt and pepper
3 garlic cloves, chopped
¼ cup chopped parsley

Cut eels into 3-inch pieces. Dredge pieces with flour and sauté quickly in hot oil until tender, about 7 or 8 minutes. Season to taste and add garlic and parsley. Toss all together for a minute or two. Arrange on a platter and pour on pan juices.
SERVES 6 to 8.

JAPANESE STEAKS

4 individual Pacific Yellowtail steaks   1 tbsp. fresh lime or lemon juice
2 tsps. salt

Sprinkle half of the salt on the steaks and let stand for 30 minutes. Sprinkle on remaining salt. Broil 6 inches from the source of heat for about 4 minutes per side, or until done. Sprinkle with lemon juice and serve.

SERVES 4.

CHINESE SIMMERED FISH

4 whole butterfish, cleaned but with   1 tbsp. sherry or mirin
   skins on   1 tbsp. soya sauce
3 tbsps. cooking oil   ¼ tsp. sugar
2 thin slices of fresh gingerroot   4 scallions, sliced into rings

Thoroughly dry fish. Heat oil, add ginger, and cook for 1 minute. Add fish and fry for 1 minute each side. Add sherry, soya sauce and sugar. Sprinkle scallions on fish. Cover and simmer gently for 5 minutes.

SERVES 4.

ORIENTAL STEAKS

2 lbs. king mackerel steaks   ½ tsp. pepper
¼ cup orange juice   ¼ cup soya sauce
2 tbsps. ketchup   2 tbsps. melted butter
2 tbsps. chopped parsley   1 tbsp. lemon juice
1 garlic clove, minced   ½ tsp. dried orégano

Put steaks in a single layer in a shallow baking dish. Combine remaining ingredients. Pour over fish and let stand for 30 minutes, turning once. Remove fish, reserving sauce for basting. Put fish on a greased broiler rack and broil about 4 inches from source of heat for about 8 minutes, basting. Turn, baste, and broil until done.

SERVES 6.

HAWAIIAN BROILED FILLETS

3 lbs. king mackerel fillets
1 cup soya sauce
¼ cup sugar

2 garlic cloves, crushed
piece of green gingerroot, crushed
1 scallion, minced

Make a marinade with all ingredients except mackerel, and soak fish for 1 hour. Drain. Broil until firm and done.

SERVES 6.

BAHAMIAN NEEDLES

1 (24- to 36-inch) needlefish, cleaned
  and cut into 3-inch pieces
flour

salt and pepper
butter

Roll pieces of fish in seasoned flour and fry quickly until crisp in shallow melted butter.

SERVES 1.

COOKED AND LEFTOVER FISH

ENGLISH APPETIZER EGGS

1 cup flaked cooked salmon
6 hard-cooked eggs
¼ cup mayonnaise
1 pimiento, chopped

1 tsp. minced onion
1 tbsp. lemon juice
1 tsp. salt
¼ tsp. cayenne pepper

Cut the eggs into halves and carefully scoop out the yolks. Blend yolks well with remaining ingredients and stuff the whites. Chill.

SERVES 6 or 12.

COLD SCANDINAVIAN BISQUE

1 cup cold flaked cooked salmon
½ garlic clove
1 small onion, sliced
½ green pepper, chopped
1 tbsp. butter
1½ cups milk

¼ cup chopped dill
2 tbsps. dry sherry
¼ tsp. Tabasco
¼ tsp. pepper
½ cup heavy cream

Sauté garlic, onion and green pepper in the butter. In a blender, purée the sautéed vegetables and all the rest except the cream. Cover and blend on high speed for 15 seconds, or until smooth. Leave motor running and pour in the cream. Chill.

SERVES 4.

FINNISH FISH PIE

2 lbs. poached salmon, skinned and flaked
pastry for 2-crust pie
1 tsp. minced fresh dill

3 egg yolks
salt and pepper
2 tbsps. chopped parsley
⅔ cup sour cream

Roll out half of pastry and fit into a 9-inch pie pan. Mix remaining ingredients and season to taste. Fill the pastry-lined pan. Cover with remaining pastry. Cut vent./ Bake at 400° for 30 to 35 minutes, until pastry is browned and filling is bubbly. Serve hot or cold.

SERVES 8.

CANADIAN COLD FISH MOUSSE

2 to 2½ cups poached salmon
1 cup mayonnaise
½ cup heavy cream
1 envelope unflavored gelatin
½ cup poaching liquid
¾ tsp. salt
¼ tsp. fresh ground pepper

3 tbsps. chopped parsley
2 tbsps. minced scallions
1 tbsp. chopped chives
1 tbsp. chopped fresh tarragon
2 tbsps. lemon juice
2 tsps. prepared Dijon mustard

Whirl one quarter of the fish with one quarter of both mayonnaise and cream in a blender until smooth. Continue until all is blended. Soak gelatin in the poaching liquid. Add salt, pepper, parsley, scallions, chives, tarragon, lemon juice and mustard to the fish. Stir to mix well. Dissolve gelatin over low heat and stir into salmon mixture. Pour into a lightly greased 6-cup mold, or individual molds, and chill for at least 3 hours. Unmold on greens.

SERVES 6.

SCOTTISH FISH PIE

1½ cups cooked salmon
    pastry for 1-crust 9-inch pie
1 medium-size onion, thinly sliced
1 tbsp. butter
1½ cups light cream

5 eggs
2 tbsps. grated Swiss or Gruyère cheese
salt and pepper

Roll out pastry and line a 9-inch pie pan; chill. Break up salmon with a fork. Sauté onion in butter until golden. Stir in salmon and cook for 1 or 2 minutes. Beat light cream, eggs and cheese together with salt and pepper to taste. Add salmon mixture and pour into pastry-lined pan. Bake at 350° for 30 to 35 minutes, or until custard is done and pastry golden. Serve hot or cold.

SERVES 6.

SWEDISH COLD PLATE

1 lb. cold cooked salmon, sliced
½ lb. mushrooms, sliced
½ lb. asparagus, cooked and chilled
⅓ cup olive or salad oil

2½ tbsps. white-wine vinegar
¼ tsp. salt
¼ tsp. dry mustard

Make an attractive arrangement of fish, mushrooms and asparagus. Mix oil, vinegar, salt and mustard. Spoon over dish and chill for at least 1 hour. Serve with a dressing based on sour cream.

SERVES 6.

SCOTTISH FISH WITH CUCUMBER

4 cups cold cooked salmon, lightly flaked
1 small cucumber, peeled, seeded and chopped
½ cup minced parsley

2 scallions, minced
1 tbsp. chopped chives
3 tbsps. salad oil
juice of ½ lemon
black pepper

Combine salmon, cucumber, parsley, scallions and chives. Make dressing of oil and lemon juice and pour over salmon. Add pepper to taste. Toss lightly. Serve on greens accompanied with a sauce based on sour cream.

SERVES 4.

ENGLISH FISH SALAD

2-lb. piece of poached salmon, cut into 6 slices
lettuce
1 cup flavored homemade mayonnaise

3 hard-cooked egg yolks, sieved
capers

Put a salmon slice on a bed of lettuce. Top with mayonnaise, decorate with egg yolks and capers.

SERVES 6.

INDIAN KEDGEREE

2 cups flaked cooked or canned
  salmon
1 cup raw rice
2 qts. water
1 tbsp. salt
2 garlic cloves
2 tbsps. butter

2 tbsps. flour
1 cup clam broth or fish stock
3 tbsps. cream
1 tbsp. (or more to taste) curry
  powder
1 tbsp. anchovy paste
½ cup heavy cream

Boil rice in water with salt and garlic. Remove garlic; drain rice. Measure out 2 cups and add to salmon. Melt butter, gradually add flour, and then add broth or stock; cook, stirring, until thickened. Remove from heat, add cream, and let cool. Add curry powder and anchovy paste and blend. Whip cream and fold into sauce. Add rice-salmon mixture, stirring gently. Oil a 6-cup mold (or 6 individual molds). Fill molds, cover, and chill for 6 to 12 hours. SERVES 6.

SPANISH FISH SALAD

1 scant lb. cooked tuna, cut into
  bite-size cubes
1 (16-oz.) can chick-peas, drained
1 (16-oz.) can artichoke hearts,
  drained

1 cup sliced celery
½ cup pimiento-stuffed olives
⅔ cup garlic-flavored dressing

Combine first 5 ingredients. Add dressing and toss gently but well. Chill. SERVES 4 to 6.

INDIAN CURRIED FISH SALAD

2 cups flaked cooked salmon, chilled
¼ cup mayonnaise
2 tbsps. lemon juice
½ tsp. curry powder
¼ tsp. salt
  dash of pepper

2 tsps. chopped chutney
1 medium-size cucumber, sliced and
  peeled
1 green onion, chopped
2 hard-cooked eggs, sliced

Combine mayonnaise with lemon juice, curry powder, salt, pepper and chutney. Combine fish, cucumber, green onion and egg slices. Divide dressing among the salads.

SERVES 4.

MEDITERRANEAN TUNA SALAD

1 cup flaked cooked tuna
1 (6-oz.) jar marinated artichoke hearts
⅓ cup olive oil
3 tbsps. white-wine vinegar
½ tsp. crumbled dried tarragon
¼ tsp. salt

1 garlic clove, minced
1 (2-oz.) can anchovy fillets with capers, chopped
4 thin slices of red onion, in rings
½ lb. raw mushrooms, sliced
1½ cups cherry tomatoes, cut into halves

Drain marinade from artichokes into a bowl. Make a dressing with olive oil, marinade, vinegar, seasonings and chopped anchovies. In a bowl arrange alternating layers of tuna, artichoke hearts, onion rings, mushrooms and tomatoes. Pour on dressing and chill as long as overnight.

SERVES 4 to 6.

SMOKED AND SALTED FISH

GERMAN EEL SOUP

¾ cup chopped smoked eel
¼ cup dried apricots
¼ cup pitted prunes
2 cups boiling water
2 tbsps. butter
¾ cup chopped onion
¼ cup thinly sliced leek
2 cups white wine

1 (13½-oz.) can chicken consommé
1 tsp. salt
½ tsp. ground thyme
½ tsp. ground savory
1 tbsp. flour
2 tbsps. wine vinegar
¼ cup raspberry jam
¼ cup dairy sour cream

Soak dried fruits in boiling water for 10 minutes. Drain, chop fine, and set aside. Melt butter and sauté onion until tender but not browned. Add leek, white wine, consommé, salt, thyme, savory and chopped fruits. Cover and simmer for 10 minutes. Remove from heat. Blend flour with vinegar. Whisk this mix, together with jam and sour cream, into soup. Heat just to boiling, stirring constantly. Add smoked eel and cook for 1 minute to heat. Garnish with parsley.

SERVES 6.

FRENCH SMOKED SALMON SOUFFLÉ

6 oz. smoked salmon, slivered
2 tsps. lemon juice

⅓ cup chive-cheese spread

Blend with standard 4-egg soufflé mix/and bake at 350° for 40 minutes, or until puffed and golden brown. Soufflé may be refrigerated before baking for up to 4 hours; in that case, bake for about 55 minutes.

SERVES 8 to 10.

RUSSIAN COULIBIAC

1 recipe brioche dough, mixed the day before
¼ lb. smoked salmon, chopped
3 tbsps. melted butter
¼ cup dairy sour cream

1 raw egg
1 cup cold cooked rice
2 hard-cooked eggs, chopped
1 tsp. snipped fresh dill

Butter a brioche mold or loaf tin 9 x 5 x 3. Make a filling by combining salmon, rice, melted butter, sour cream and dill; mix well. Line the buttered mold with two thirds of the rolled-out brioche dough. Fill center with filling. Top with remaining rolled-out dough. Dampen edges of dough and press together to make a firm seal. Decorate with dough trimmings. Cover with a towel and let rise in a warm place (85°) free from drafts for about 1 hour,

until dough rises somewhat above pan edges. Combine the raw egg with 2 tbsps. water and brush top of brioche. Bake at 350° for 30 minutes, or until golden brown. Cover top lightly with foil and bake for 50 minutes longer. Let stand in the mold on a wire rack for 30 minutes. Turn out and serve warm.
SERVES 8.

IRISH LOAF PUDDING

1½ cups flaked cooked smoked
    salmon
2 cups milk, scalded
1 cup half-cooked rice, drained
2 tbsps. grated onion
2 tsps. salt

1 tsp. pepper
2 tbsps. lemon juice
3 tbsps. chopped parsley
3 eggs, beaten
½ cup melted butter

Combine milk, rice, onion, salt and pepper with lemon juice, salmon and parsley. Mix well; correct seasonings. Add beaten eggs and sugar, stirring in thoroughly. Pour into a buttered baking dish and bake at 350° about 45 minutes until firm and brown. Serve with melted butter.
SERVES 6.

SCANDINAVIAN SMOKED FISH WITH CUCUMBER

2 or 3 thin slices of smoked salmon
8 to 10 thin slices of cucumber
1 cup ice water
3 tbsps. white vinegar

1 tbsp. sugar
1 tsp. salt
½ tsp. pepper
1 tbsp. capers

Score cucumbers before slicing. Make a marinade with ice water, vinegar and seasonings and marinate cucumbers. (This makes enough marinade for 2 small cucumbers.) Drain cucumbers and mix with salmon and capers. Serve with sour cream and dill sauce.
SERVES 1.

FRENCH SMOKED FISH VINAIGRETTE

½ lb. smoked salmon
1 tsp. minced onion
1 tbsp. minced scallions

1 tbsp. capers
2 diced cooked potatoes
6 tbsps. vinaigrette sauce

Cut salmon into ⅛-inch-thick slices and cut slices into small squares. Carefully blend salmon, onion, scallions, capers and potatoes. Spoon vinaigrette carefully through the mix, and chill for at least 1 hour.
SERVES 4 to 6.

JAPANESE SUSHI

16 thin slices of smoked king mackerel
1 cup raw rice
1¼ cups water

2 tsps. soya sauce
2 tbsps. vinegar
1 tsp. sugar
½ tsp. salt

Wash rice; combine with water. Cover and cook over low heat for 20 minutes, or until tender and dry. With a fork stir in soya sauce, vinegar, sugar and salt. Pat flat on a board or plate and cool. Shape into 32 small balls or small patties. Cut mackerel slices into halves and wrap around rice balls.
SERVES 8 to 10.

HAWAIIAN SMOKED FISH SPREAD

1 lb. smoked tuna
¼ cup ice water
½ tsp. salt

12 scallions, minced
4 tomatoes, peeled, seeded and chopped

Soak the tuna in cold water for 3 hours, changing the water 3 times. Drain well; skin and bone fish, and shred the flesh finely. Add ice water and salt to scallions and mash to a paste. Combine tuna and tomatoes and crush in a mortar until very smooth (or use a blender). Add scallions and mix well. Chill.
SERVES 8 to 12.

NEW ENGLAND BROILED SALT FISH

2 lbs. salted king mackerel fillets

Soak fish in water overnight. Drain, wipe dry, and brush both sides with melted butter. Put skin side down on a greased broiler 3 inches below the source of heat and broil for 5 to 10 minutes, or until browned, basting once or twice. Turn and broil and baste. Serve with cream sauce.
SERVES 4 to 6.

Dry Fish

The relatively dry firm-fleshed fish adapt readily to all types of cooking, so long as they are given the needed moistening. This can be in the form of butter spread on a broadbill swordfish steak (or a mako shark's, which is virtually indistinguishable at the table) or a sauce or stock. These fish also lend themselves to baking with a moist stuffing and basting liquid.

While the broadbill and mako are familar on many restaurant menus (where they call mako "Block Island Swordfish"), not too many people are aware that the marlins make most satisfactory fare when treated properly. Since my walls are simply not adequate for the display of mounted billfish, I long ago decided that bill mounts were all I could happily live with. Not wanting to waste the remainder of the fish, I have talked fishing resort cooks on both the Atlantic and Pacific into serving it to me, and I've made converts of nonbelievers with sample bites. Obviously, billfish offer a great deal of edible meat, much more than can be eaten at a sitting, unless you entertain on a large scale. There is still no reason for waste, however; smoked billfish is excellent, plain or blended, as an hors d'oeuvre. Italians, who have always been excellent seafood cooks, frequently boil billfish and serve it cold with a sauce. Often, too, they interchange it with tuna in their sauced recipes.

APPETIZERS

CANADIAN PICKLED APPETIZER

---

1 (3-lb.) walleye, skinned and
    boned
3 cups olive oil
1 cup vinegar
10 peppercorns
3 bay leaves

2 large onions, sliced
    salt
    juice of 1 large lime
¼ cup flour
2 large garlic cloves, crushed

Cut fish into 1-inch pieces. Mix 2 cups olive oil, the vinegar, peppercorns, bay leaves, sliced onions and ½ tsp. salt. Simmer for 30 minutes; cool. Rinse fish and pat dry. Sprinkle on lime juice and season with salt. Flour both sides lightly. Heat remaining 1 cup oil and brown garlic; remove garlic. In the same oil brown the fish pieces over moderate heat. Reduce heat and cook the fish for 15 minutes. Fill a deep glass dish with layers of fish topped with cooled dressing.

SERVES 6 to 8.

PORTUGUESE PICKLED FISH

1½ lbs. swordfish, skinned
1½ cups white vinegar
½ cup water
2 garlic cloves, thinly sliced
5 or 6 dried small hot chile peppers

1 bay leaf, crumbled
½ tsp. salt
    olive oil or salad oil
1 large red onion, thinly sliced
3 to 4 tbsps. minced parsley

Cut fish into 1-inch cubes. Mix vinegar, water, garlic, chile peppers, bay leaf and salt and pour over fish in deep glass bowl. Cover and chill 1 to 4 hours. Drain and save marinade. Dry fish and arrange pieces slightly separated on broiling pan. Brush generously with oil and broil about 6 inches below source of heat for about 8 minutes, or until done. Do not turn. Combine onion and reserved marinade in a pan. Bring to a boil and simmer 3 or 4 minutes. Arrange fish cubes on plate, sprinkle with parsley and top with well-drained onions. Pour on heated marinade. Serve warm or at room temperature.

SERVES 10 to 12.

SOUPS

CENTRAL AMERICAN CHOWDER

2 lbs. filleted and skinned marlin, cubed
¼ lb. smoked bacon, cubed
2 medium-size onions, chopped
2 celery ribs, chopped
1 green pepper, chopped
2 medium-size potatoes, cubed
3½ cups canned tomatoes
1 tbsp. raw rice
Worcestershire sauce
Tabasco
salt and pepper
1 cup milk

Try out the bacon. Add onions and brown. Add fish, celery, green pepper, potatoes, tomatoes, rice and seasonings to taste. Simmer gently for 1½ to 2 hours. Remove from heat and stir in milk. (Very good reheated the second day.)
SERVES 8.

SOUTH AMERICAN CHOWDER

1 (4- to 5-lb.) grouper, skinned and boned
2 large onions, chopped
1 large green pepper, chopped
2 garlic cloves, minced
3 tbsps. olive oil
2½ cups canned tomatoes
½ of 6-oz. can tomato paste
4 cups boiling water
1 bay leaf
pinch of dried orégano
6 medium-size white potatoes, diced
salt and pepper
½ cup dry white wine

Cut fish into chunks. Brown onions, green pepper and garlic in oil. Add tomatoes and tomato paste and simmer for a few minutes to blend. Add boiling water, bay leaf and orégano. Add potatoes and salt and pepper to taste. Simmer; when potatoes are half done, add chunks of fish and white wine. Cook gently until fish tests done.
SERVES 8 to 12.

ENTRÉES

BAHAMA STUFFED FISH

1 medium-size hogfish, split to lie flat
1 medium-size onion, chopped
1 small green pepper, chopped
2 garlic cloves, mashed
1 tbsp. butter
1 tbsp. Worcestershire sauce
  salt and pepper
  paprika
6 slices of stale bread
1 egg

6 (½-inch) slices of raw potato

Sauce:
1 onion, minced
3 garlic cloves, mashed
½ green pepper
1 tbsp. olive oil
1 (6-oz.) can tomato paste
2 cups water
  salt and pepper

Sauté onion, green pepper and garlic of first group in butter. Add Worcestershire and seasonings to taste. Moisten bread, squeeze dry, and tear into pieces. Add bread and egg to mixture. Stir well and simmer over low heat for 5 minutes. Use to stuff fish. Close opening. Put potato slices in the bottom of a buttered baking dish. Add fish and bake at 350° for 45 minutes to 1 hour, until fish is done.

Make sauce by sautéing onion, garlic and green pepper in oil. Add tomato paste, water, and salt and pepper to taste and simmer for 20 minutes. OR: sauce can be made and poured over fish before baking; in that case, cover pan while baking.

SERVES 4.

CANADIAN BROILED FISH

6 individual freshwater perch
½ cup dried bread crumbs
¼ cup minced onion
4 tbsps. butter
1 tsp. chile powder

½ tsp. salt
⅛ tsp. dried marjoram
⅛ tsp. pepper
⅛ tsp. dried thyme

Split fish so they will lie flat; remove backbones. Wipe fish with a damp cloth and lay in a shallow dish. Blend remaining ingredients and spread mixture over fish. Broil slowly 6 inches from the source of heat for about 15 minutes, or until done.

SERVES 6.

RUMANIAN FISH AND VEGETABLE CASSEROLE

6 individual servings of freshwater perch
1 cup olive oil
2 cups diced potatoes
1½ cups shredded cabbage
1 green pepper, cut into julienne pieces
2 cups diced eggplant
1 cup chopped onions

2 garlic cloves, minced
2 tomatoes, chopped
½ lb. okra, sliced
⅛ tsp. dried thyme
1 bay leaf
4 tsps. salt
1 tsp. pepper
2 tbsps. butter

Heat oil to bubbling in a casserole. Carefully add potatoes, cabbage, green pepper, eggplant, onions, garlic, tomatoes, okra, thyme, bay leaf, 2 tsps. salt and ½ tsp. pepper. Mix lightly. Bake at 350° for 30 minutes. Season fish with rest of salt and pepper and arrange on vegetable bed. Dot with butter. Bake for 45 minutes more.

SERVES 6.

SPANISH BAKED FISH WITH TOMATO

3½-lb. piece of mako shark
12 tbsps. soft butter
1 tsp. salt
¼ tsp. pepper
 juice of 2 lemons
2 tbsps. dry white wine

Sauce:
1 medium-size onion, chopped

2 tbsps. butter
3 tomatoes, chopped
1 fish head
1 cup white wine
1 cup water
1 bay leaf
½ tsp. salt
 pinch of pepper
2 tbsps. flour

Coat fish well with butter blended with salt, pepper, lemon juice and wine. Bake at 350° for 40 minutes, or until done, basting twice with butter, lemon and wine. Meanwhile, make the sauce. Brown chopped onion in butter; add tomatoes and rest of ingredients except flour. Cover and simmer for 30 minutes. Stir in flour smoothly and simmer, uncovered, for 15 minutes longer. Force through a food mill. Serve sauce with the baked fish.

SERVES 4.

HAWAIIAN BARBECUED FISH

---

3 lbs. marlin steaks, 1 inch thick	¾ cup salad oil
¾ cup lemon juice	1 tbsp. grated lemon rind
2 tbsps. prepared horseradish	½ tsp. dried basil
½ tbsp. salt	½ tsp. dried orégano
¼ to ½ tsp. pepper	

Make a marinade of all ingredients except fish. Pour over fish and marinate, chilled, overnight. Drain, reserving marinade. Grill fish slowly, or broil 6 inches from the source of heat for 5 to 7 minutes on each side, basting frequently with the marinade.

SERVES 8.

BAHAMIAN BAKED STEAKS

---

4 (8-oz.) marlin steaks	2 large tomatoes, peeled and seeded
½ cup olive oil	pinch of saffron
1 large onion slice	2 tbsps. dark rum
1 large green pepper, seeded and sliced	salt and pepper
	½ cup bread crumbs
½ small hot red pepper, seeded and sliced	2 tbsps. chopped parsley
	melted butter

Wipe steaks with a damp cloth. Place in a buttered baking dish and bake at 350° for 8 to 10 minutes. Meanwhile, make a sauce of oil, onion, green and hot peppers; simmer for 5 minutes. Add tomatoes and saffron, and simmer for 5 minutes. Blend in rum and salt and pepper to taste. Pour sauce over fish; bake for 5 minutes more. Combine bread crumbs and parsley; add enough melted butter to moisten. Sprinkle over fish. Brown quickly under broiler.

SERVES 4.

SINALOA BROILED FISH

4 swordfish steaks, ¾ inch thick
2 tbsps. butter
2 tbsps. lemon juice

1 garlic clove, minced
1 tsp. dry mustard
6 flat anchovy fillets, chopped

Heat butter, lemon juice and garlic until butter is melted. Put steaks on a well-greased broiler rack and put in preheated broiler 3 inches from the source of heat. Baste with the lemon butter. Broil for 6 to 8 minutes, or until lightly browned. Turn, rub dry mustard into second side, sprinkle evenly with anchovies, and baste again with lemon butter. Broil until fish is browned and done, about 5 minutes longer.

SERVES 4.

MANZANILLO BAKED STEAKS

4 swordfish steaks, about ½ lb. each
½ tbsp. salt
⅛ tsp. pepper

6 tbsps. olive oil
½ cup sliced green onions

Sprinkle fish generously with salt and pepper. Brush with oil to coat heavily on both sides. Put fish in a single layer in a baking dish. Sprinkle on green onions. Bake, uncovered, at 350° for about 20 minutes.

SERVES 4.

TURKISH SKEWERED FISH

1½ lbs. swordfish, skined and boned
6 tbsps. olive oil
7 tbsps. lemon juice
1½ tsps. salt

2 tbsps. grated onion
¼ tsp. paprika
10 bay leaves
1 tbsp. chopped parsley

Cut fish into 1½-inch cubes. Combine in a bowl 2 tbsps. oil, 3 tbsps. lemon juice, 1 tsp. salt, the onion, paprika and bay leaves. Add fish and toss gently. Cover and refrigerate overnight. Drain fish and thread on 6 skewers. Broil for 6 minutes on each side. Make a dressing of remaining ingredients and serve fish hot with dressing at room temperature.

SERVES 6.

SPANISH SAFFRON FISH

1½ to 2 lbs. swordfish steaks, 1 inch
  thick
3 garlic cloves, minced
1 slice of white bread, torn apart
2 parsley sprigs, chopped

1 bay leaf, crumbled
  olive oil
1 tsp. ground saffron
1½ cups water

Sauté the garlic, bread, parsley and bay leaf in a little oil until lightly browned. Mash the mixture with the saffron in a mortar (or use a blender), slowly adding water to give the consistency of a thin sauce. Pour over fish. Bake at 350° until done, about 20 minutes.

SERVES 6.

CHINESE STEAMED FISH

1- to 1½-lb. sheepshead, cleaned but
  with head on
2 tbsps. dry sherry
2 tbsps. lemon juice
2 tbsps. soya sauce

2 tbsps. salad oil
1 tsp. salt
½ tsp. pepper
½ tsp. ground ginger
2 scallions, cut into ½-inch pieces

Lay fish on a double thickness of foil with the edges turned up all around. Put on rack that will be above 1½ inches of water in a Dutch oven. Bring water in Dutch oven to a boil; place rack with fish in position. Combine rest of ingredients and pour over fish. Cover pot tightly and steam the fish for about 15 minutes, or until done, basting occasionally with sauce.

SERVES 3 or 4.

SOUTH AMERICAN BAKED FILLETS IN WHITE WINE

1 (3-lb.) grouper, filleted
6 tbsps. butter
½ lb. mushrooms, sliced
1 bunch scallions, sliced
½ cup dry bread crumbs

pinch of dried thyme
1 bay leaf
salt and pepper
1 cup dry white wine

Put fillets in a buttered baking dish. Dot with 2 tbsps. butter. Lay mushrooms and onions on top; dot with 2 tbsps. butter. Sprinkle on crumbs and seasonings. Dot with 2 tbsps. butter. Pour wine into dish and cover lightly. Bake at 350° for about 20 minutes, basting occasionally.

SERVES 4.

BRAZILIAN FILLETS

2 lbs. grouper fillets, skinned
1 cup dairy sour cream
1 tsp. lemon juice
¼ cup grated cheese

1 tbsp. grated onion
½ tsp. salt
2 dashes of hot pepper sherry
paprika

Put fillets in a single layer in a well-greased baking dish. Combine all but paprika and spread mixture over fish. Sprinkle with paprika. Bake at 350° for 25 to 30 minutes.

SERVES 4.

SPANISH BROILED FISH WITH FENNEL

1 (5- to 6-lb.) striped bass
½ tbsp. fennel seeds*
½ cup olive oil

¾ tsp. salt
fresh black pepper
½ cup dry bread crumbs

Coarsely crush fennel seeds. Make a ¼-inch-deep score through the fleshiest part of the fish. Mix oil, salt, fennel and plenty of pepper together. Brush some onto fish. Broil 4 inches from the source of heat for about 25 minutes, or until just cooked, without turning. Brush twice with oil mix while cooking. Mix crumbs with remaining oil and sprinkle over fish. Broil for 5 minutes more to brown.

SERVES 6.

* The original recipe eliminates the fennel seeds and the fish is cooked over an open fire in which dried fennel twigs are in flame.

CANADIAN WINE-BAKED FISH

1 (3- to 4-lb.) striped bass
12 small white onions
2 tbsps. chopped parsley
2 tbsps. butter

2 cups dry white wine (about)
¾ tsp. salt
¼ tsp. pepper

Grease a baking dish and line with parchment paper. Add fish, onions, parsley and butter. Add wine (to cover) and salt and pepper. Bake at 375°, basting every 10 minutes. Allow 10 minutes per pound under 4 lbs., adding 5 minutes for each pound over 4.

SERVES 8.

DALMATIAN FISH STEW

2½ lbs. unskinned fillets of striped bass, cut into 12 pieces
lemon juice
2 onions, sliced
¾ cup olive oil
1 garlic clove, minced

1 cup dry red wine
⅓ cup white vinegar
scant ¼ cup water
4 tbsps. tomato paste
1 tsp. salt
½ tsp. pepper

Sprinkle fish with lemon juice. Sauté 1 sliced onion in oil until transparent. Add fish, flesh side down, then garlic and the other onion. Lightly brown fish, turn. Add wine, vinegar, water, tomato paste, salt and pepper. Simmer, uncovered, for 1 hour, occasionally spooning the sauce over and shaking pan to keep fish from sticking.

SERVES 6.

IRANIAN STUFFED FISH

1 (4-lb.) striped bass, split and boned
½ cup cooked rice
½ cup ground almonds
½ lb. pitted dates
1 tsp. sugar
½ tsp. ground ginger

¼ lb. butter, melted
2 tsps. salt
½ tsp. black pepper
¾ cup chopped onions
½ cup water
⅛ tsp. ground cinnamon

Wash fish and let stand in salted water for about 5 minutes. Drain and pat dry. Mix rice, almonds, dates, sugar, half of the ginger and 2 tbsps. butter. Stuff fish with this mixture; close opening. Pour half of the remaining butter into a baking dish. Arrange fish in the dish. Sprinkle with salt, pepper, remaining ginger and butter. Add onions and water. Bake at 350° for 1 hour, basting frequently. Sprinkle with cinnamon. Increase heat to 450° and raise fish to top rack of oven to brown.

SERVES 4.

ORIENTAL BAKED FISH

1 (3-lb.) striped bass
3 tbsps. butter
salt and fresh-ground pepper
2 medium-size green peppers, cubed
½ lb. mushrooms, sliced
2 tbsps. oil

1 cup orange juice
1 tbsp. soya sauce
2 slices of fresh gingerroot, minced
1 tbsp. cornstarch
¼ cup chicken broth or stock

Grease a sheet of heavy foil with 1 tbsp. butter. Put on fish, seasoned inside and out with salt and pepper, and dot with remaining butter. Close foil tightly and put in a baking pan. Bake at 350° for 30 minutes, or until fish flakes. Meanwhile, sauté peppers and mushrooms in oil until barely tender, 3 to 5 minutes. Add orange juice, soya sauce, ½ tsp. salt, ⅛ tsp. pepper and the ginger. Bring to a boil. Mix cornstarch and broth and add to sauce. Cook, stirring constantly, until thickened. Pour sauce over fish or serve separately.
SERVES 4.

ROMAN SIMMERED FISH

1 (3-lb.) sea bass, washed and patted
dry
2 tsps. salt
½ tsp. pepper
4 tbsps. butter
½ cup chopped onion
½ cup chopped flat anchovy fillets

1 garlic clove, minced
4 tbsps. chopped parsley
2 cups dry white wine
½ cup water
2 tbsps. olive oil
½ lb. fresh mushrooms, sliced
1½ tbsps. flour

Dust fish inside and out with salt and pepper. In a saucepan large enough to hold entire fish, melt butter. Stir in onion, anchovies, garlic and 2 tbsps. parsley. Cook, stirring, for 1 minute. Stir in wine and water. Bring to a boil and cook over moderate heat for 5 minutes. Add fish, cover pan loosely, and cook over low heat for 40 minutes. While fish is cooking, heat oil in sauce-pan and sauté mushrooms and rest of parsley for 5 minutes. Stir in flour. Transfer fish to a platter and stir cooking liquid into mushrooms. Heat, stirring, to boiling. Cook over medium heat for 5 minutes. Correct seasonings and pour over fish.
SERVES 4 to 6.

SPANISH BAKED FISH

1 (4-lb.) sea bass
1 large garlic clove, minced
1 green pepper, minced
1 onion, sliced and in rings
4 tbsps. olive oil

1 tbsp. white-wine vinegar
1 bay leaf
1 tsp. dried orégano
paprika
salt and pepper

Score the side of the fish; lay it in a baking dish. Sprinkle on the garlic and green pepper. Lay on onion rings. Mix oil and vinegar and pour on. Put bay leaf on the center and crush the orégano over all. Sprinkle with paprika, salt and pepper and bake at 350° until done, about 1 hour.
SERVES 6.

CHINESE DEEP-FRIED FISH

2 lbs. sea bass fillets, or 1 (4-lb.) fish*
¼ cup flour

1 egg, beaten
¼ cup cornstarch

Make a batter of flour, cornstarch and egg with bit of water. Coat fish and fry at 350° for about 10 minutes for whole fish, less for fillets. Serve with sweet and sour sauce.
SERVES 4.

* Chinese leave the head on whole fish for this preparation.

CHINESE FISH STRIPS

1½ lbs. sea bass fillets, cut into diagonal strips about ¼ inch thick
1 egg white
4 tsps. water
2 tsp. cornstarch
salt

3 tbsps. sesame oil
1 small garlic clove, thinly sliced
¼ lb. fresh snow peas
¼ lb. water chestnuts, sliced
2 tsps. and 1 tbsp. dry sherry
1 tsp. sugar

Combine egg white with 2 tsps. water, 1 tsp. cornstarch and a pinch of salt. Put fish in this mixture for 2 or 3 minutes. Cover bottom of skillet with 2 tbsps. oil and heat until just warm. Add the fish strips; cook for about 3 minutes and drain on paper towels. Heat 1 tbsp. oil with garlic. Stir in snow peas and water chestnuts and cook for 1 or 2 minutes. Combine 2 tsps. sherry with 2 tsps. water, 1 tsp. cornstarch, the sugar and a dash of salt; add to vegetables. Stir in fish strips carefully. Cook for about 3 minutes, or until sauce is thickened and fish is heated through. Sprinkle with 1 tbsp. sherry before serving.

SERVES 3 or 4.

CHINESE STEAMED FILLETS

1 lb. sea bass fillets	¼ cup chicken stock
1 tbsp. salad oil	¼ cup dry white wine
½ cup sliced green onions	4 tsps. soya sauce
1 cup sliced fresh mushrooms	1 tbsp. cornstarch
1 or 2 tbsps. minced fresh gingerroot	1 tbsp. water

Heat oil and cook fish for about 1 minute, turn carefully. Sprinkle with onions, mushrooms and gingerroot; add stock, wine and soya sauce. Cover and let steam in the liquid, not over it, for about 10 minutes, or until done. Remove fish. Mix cornstarch and water and add slowly to pan liquid. Cook, stirring, until slightly thickened. Pour over fish.

SERVES 2 or 3.

CHINESE STEAMED FISH WITH BAMBOO SHOOTS

1 (1¼-lb.) saltwater bass	3 slices of fresh gingerroot, shredded
3 or 4 dried Chinese mushrooms	3 slices of fat salt pork, or 2 bacon
1 tsp. salt	strips
2 scallions, cut into shreds	1 tbsp. sherry
1 (4-oz.) can bamboo shoots, shredded	

Wash and clean mushrooms; soak in hot water to cover for 20 minutes. Drain, reserving 1 tbsp. of the water. Shred mushrooms. Slash fish at 45° angle every inch on both sides. Rub inside and out with salt. Put on a dish, or on double layer of foil with edge turned up, on top of a rack over boiling water. Mix shredded vegetables and gingerroot and spread on fish. Lay salt pork or bacon on top. Mix sherry and mushroom liquid and drizzle on the fish. Cover pot and steam for about 10 minutes.

SERVES 4.

FIJI BAKED FISH WITH COCONUT CREAM

1 (3-lb.) sea bass
2 cups fresh or dried coconut

1½ cups heavy cream
2 tsps. salt

Combine coconut and cream and bring to a boil. Remove from heat and let cool for 30 minutes. Press through several layers of cheesecloth; discard pulp. Sprinkle fish with salt and lay in buttered baking dish. Pour on coconut cream. Bake at 350° for 50 minutes.

SERVES 6.

FINNISH BAKED FISH

1 (2-lb.) walleye
  salt and pepper
8 tbsps. butter
1 small onion, chopped
1 cup cooked rice
1½ cups chopped cooked spinach

1 egg, beaten
1 tsp. seasoned salt
¼ cup lemon juice
⅓ cup dried bread crumbs
¼ cup water

Season fish inside and out with salt and pepper. Melt 2 tbsps. butter and sauté onion until golden. Mix rice, spinach, onion, egg and seasoned salt. Use this to stuff walleye; close opening. Sprinkle fish on both sides with lemon juice, then coat with crumbs. Melt 3 tbsps. butter in a shallow baking dish. Add fish; dot with 3 tbsps. butter and add the water. Bake at 350° for about 1 hour, basting occasionally.

SERVES 6.

CANADIAN CAMP FISH

Butter a sheet of foil well; lay on walleye fillets. Cover with dots of butter, sliced onions, sliced fresh tomatoes (or canned, with some juice). Build 2 layers, alternating onions and tomatoes. Salt and pepper well. Make drugstore fold of foil loosely around fish and put on campfire rack. When the top of foil puffs, cook for 3 minutes more and pierce foil. Open and serve.

KEYS FILLET

Broil one side of a snook fillet; turn and spread with mayonnaise, and broil until done. Sprinkle with Key lime juice.

WEST INDIES BAKED BOX

cowfish, trunkfish, whole

Slit belly carefully. Reach in and remove entrails and fillet of solid meat and liver (yellow, fatty material). Discard entrails. Chop fillet and liver with onion, tomato and celery, and season with salt and pepper. Restuff into cavity, skewer opening, and bake at 350° for 25 to 30 minutes.

CANADIAN BAKED STEAKS

1 (3- to 4-lb.) muskie, cut into 1-inch steaks
salt and pepper
3 tbsps. soft butter
1 tbsp. flour
½ cup dairy sour cream
1 onion, minced
1 tbsp. butter
½ tsp. sugar
1 bay leaf
2 tbsps. grated Parmesan cheese
2 tbsps. buttered dry crumbs
1 tbsp. freshly grated horseradish

Put steaks in a buttered pan and rub with salt and pepper. Spread on soft butter and bake at 400° for 10 minutes. Stir flour into sour cream smoothly. Sauté onion in 1 tbsp. butter until golden; add to sour cream with sugar and bay leaf. Spoon onto fish. Bake for 10 minutes, basting occasionally. Sprinkle with cheese and buttered crumbs and bake until crumbs are browned. Remove fish to platter and stir horseradish into sauce in pan. Pour sauce over fish.

SERVES 6.

POLISH STEAMED FISH

1 (3- to 4-lb.) red drum
2 cups horseradish sauce

2 cups vegetable stock

Cut fish halfway through into serving pieces. Put on a rack over boiling stock in a heavy pan. Cover and steam for 10 minutes. Spread with horseradish sauce, cover again, and steam over very low heat until done. Serve with strained horseradish sauce and stock.

SERVES 6 to 8.

CANADIAN FOILED FISH

2-lb. chunk of muskie
  white-wine vinegar

1 tsp. salt

Soak a cheesecloth in white-wine vinegar. Wipe fish with soaked cloth. Sprinkle with salt. Wrap in foil and bake at 450° for about 45 minutes.

SERVES 4 to 6.

ITALIAN BAKED FILLETS WITH PROSCIUTTO

1 (3-lb.) red drum, filleted but not
 skinned
½ cup olive oil
½ cup lemon juice
¾ tsp. dried orégano

½ tsp. dried basil
½ tsp. minced garlic
1 cup sliced onions
½ cup chopped prosciutto ham
½ cup bread crumbs

Mix oil, lemon juice, ¼ tsp. orégano, the basil, garlic and onions in a medium-sized baking dish. Add fillets, flesh side down, and let them soak, unrefrigerated, for 1 hour. Discard onions, but reserve liquid marinade. Sandwich fillets, skin side out, with prosciutto. Bake at 325° for 30 minutes, basting 2 or 3 times with marinade. Spoon liquid out of pan and mix it with crumbs and remaining ¼ tsp. orégano. Spread over top of fillets. Brown under broiler.
 SERVES 4.

COOKED OR LEFTOVER FISH

CANADIAN SCRAMBLED FISH

1½ cups flaked cooked muskie
2 tbsps. butter
1 cup milk

1 tbsp. dry sherry
5 eggs, beaten

Brown the muskie in butter. Add milk and sherry to eggs. Pour over the muskie and cook until set but still soft, 3 to 5 minutes.
 SERVES 3 or 4.

ENGLISH FISH LOAF

2 cups flaked cooked sea bass
1 tbsp. lemon juice
1 cup medium white sauce
½ cup bread crumbs

½ cup minced celery
2 tbsps. minced parsley
1 tsp. grated onion
¼ tbsp. salt

Add lemon juice to fish flakes. Cool white sauce. Add the fish and remaining ingredients. Mix well. Shape into a loaf in a greased shallow pan and bake at 350° for 45 minutes.

SERVES 4 to 6.

HAWAIIAN FISH CASSEROLE

3 lbs. swordfish, steamed or poached
4 cups milk
½ cup flour
⅛ tsp. curry powder
½ large onion, sliced
¼ cup chopped parsley

salt and pepper
2 eggs, beaten
½ cup butter, cut into small pieces
dash of Tabasco
bread crumbs
grated Parmesan cheese

Cut fish into bite-size pieces. Make the sauce—heat milk, carefully add flour and curry powder, and stir until smooth. Add onion, parsley and salt and pepper to taste. Cook over low heat, stirring constantly, until thickened. Remove from heat and pour a bit of sauce into eggs. Stir eggs into remaining sauce and add butter and Tabasco. Strain sauce. Butter a casserole. Put in a thin layer of sauce, then a layer of fish, building alternating layers ending with sauce. Sprinkle with crumbs and cheese. Bake at 350° for 30 minutes.

SERVES 6.

CHAPTER FIVE

Recipes
for
Soft-Fleshed
Fish

Moist Fish

Undoubtedly the most popular fish in this group of moist soft-fleshed fish (from both the angler's and the eater's viewpoint) is the freshwater trout. Unlike all other fish species, there can be a great variety of basic quality in this fish: it can be a wild native, taken from a cold high mountain lake, or a fish newly released from a hatchery, which has been pellet-fed until only a day before. While other wild species will have a small difference in quality because of differences in feed available in different waters and water temperatures, the trout, even if caught by an angler, may not necessarily be prime. Yet it is still excellent fare, except, perhaps, to the most sophisticated palate.

SOUP

FRENCH FISH SOUP

4 lbs. mullet, boned and skinned
2 tbsps. olive oil
1 onion, chopped
2 celery ribs, chopped
4 raw potatoes, diced
2 tomatoes, chopped

1 small garlic clove, minced
sprig of fresh fennel
3 cups dry white wine
1 tsp. salt
¼ tsp. pepper
pinch of saffron

Cut fish into 3-inch squares. Heat the oil and brown the onion and celery. Add remaining ingredients. Simmer until tender, about 10 minutes.

SERVES 4 to 6.

ENTRÉES

ALSATIAN MATELOTE

2 to 2½ lbs. pike or pickerel, cut into rather thick slices
3 tbsps. oil
¼ cup brandy, warmed
3 or 4 shallots, minced
1 bottle dry rosé or white wine
large parsley sprig
1 bay leaf
pinch of dried thyme
2 tbsps. butter
2 tbsps. flour
½ cup heavy cream

Cook fish slowly in heated oil for about 3 minutes on each side. Add brandy and ignite it. Add shallots and cook briefly. Add wine and herbs. Cover casserole and cook very slowly until done. Remove fish; strain and reserve the juices. Make a sauce. Melt butter, stir in the flour, and cook briefly, stirring, without browning. Add reserved juices gradually, stirring. Simmer until reduced to about 1½ cups. Stir in cream, reheat without boiling, and spoon over fish.

SERVES 6.

ROAST PIKE
Adapted from *The Compleat Angler*

1 pike, 36 inches long

Clean the pike and reserve the liver. Make a stuffing. Finely shred the liver and season it with ¾ tsp. mixed dried thyme, marjoram and savory. Add ½ cup pickled oysters and 2 or 3 anchovies, chopped. Work this mixture into a pound of butter. Stuff the pike with this mixture; skewer or sew up the fish and chill well. Bake in a preheated 350° oven, basting frequently with ½ cup claret wine heated with 1 tbsp. butter and 1 mashed anchovy. Be generous with the basting wine and, for following bastings, remove the liquid from the bottom of the roaster with a bulb baster, squirting it back over the fish. Remove fish when done to a warm platter that has been rubbed with a cut clove of garlic; keep fish warm. Heat the pan juices with the juice of 2 or 3 oranges, and serve with the fish.

SERVES 4 to 6.

FRENCH QUENELLES

1½ lbs. pike fillets, skinned and trimmed of center line and cut into thin strips
2 eggs, separated
½ cup flour
¼ tsp. grated nutmeg

¾ tsp. salt
¼ tsp. fresh ground pepper
3 tbsps. melted butter
½ cup milk
1 cup heavy cream
4 cups salted water or fish stock

Combine egg yolks, flour, half of the nutmeg, salt and pepper in a saucepan and stir rapidly with a whisk. Add melted butter while stirring. Bring milk just to a boil and beat in with a whisk. Continue stirring and cooking rapidly until mixture pulls away from the sides of the saucepan. Spread in a shallow dish and chill very well in refrigerator. Pound the fillets, small amounts at a time, in a mortar until puréed; or purée in a blender. Season with salt and pepper and remaining nutmeg. Blend fish thoroughly with the first mixture, a bit at a time, with an electric beater at medium speed; put beater bowl over a bowl of cracked ice. When well blended, add the egg whites, a bit at a time. Beat in the cream gradually. Butter a large pan (17 by 12 and at least 3 inches deep). Dip 2 large dessert spoons (for main-course servings) or 2 teaspoons (for appetizers) briefly into hot water, then use to shape the mixture into egg-shaped balls. Arrange balls neatly, well separated, in the buttered pan. Dip spoons into hot water before shaping each quenelle. Butter a piece of wax paper slightly smaller than the pan and put buttered side down over quenelles. Pour boiling stock or salted water gently on the paper, letting the liquid run into the pan. Bring to a boil on top of the stove and let simmer for 10 minutes (5 minutes for small ones). Drain, and serve with a warm sauce of your choice.

SERVES 8 main courses, 16 appetizers.

KEYS BAKED BONEFISH

1 (5-lb.) bonefish, cleaned and opened flat
salt

1 large onion, thinly sliced
4 slices of bacon

Put fish, skin side down, in a greased pan. With an ice pick, puncture the flesh side of the fish with holes 1 inch apart. Sprinkle well with salt. Cover with onion rings and top these with bacon. Bake at 350° for 1½ hours.

SERVES 4 to 6.

KEYS BROILED BONEFISH

Bonefish, filleted but unscaled

Squeeze Key lime juice heavily over flesh side of fillets. Dust well with seasoned bread crumbs and grated Parmesan cheese; dot with butter. Broil 5 inches from the source of heat until golden, without turning.

BAHAMA BAKED BONEFISH

Clean fish and remove backbone. Put fish in a baking dish. Cover with strips of bacon. Smother with sliced onions and diced tomatoes. Add a bit of water to cover the bottom of the pan, or use sherry-flavored creole sauce. Bake at 350° for 1½ hours.

ITALIAN FISH WITH WHITE-WINE SAUCE

2 medium-size mullet
1 small onion, minced
  olive oil
1 tbsp. white-wine vinegar

¾ cup white wine
4 fresh mint leaves (2 per fish)
2 small pieces of garlic
  flour

Sauté onion in olive oil until softened but not brown; drain. Add vinegar and wine and simmer together until reduced by one third; cool. Put mint leaves and garlic in fish. Roll fish in flour and fry gently in hot oil. Drain and marinate in the cooled sauce for several hours. Chill.

SERVES 2.

ITALIAN FISH WITH PESTO

4 medium-size mullet
3 or 4 flat anchovy fillets
2 tbsps. olive oil
1 garlic clove, crushed

½ lb. tomatoes, peeled and chopped
salt and pepper
1½ tbsps. chopped fresh basil

Steam the mullet until tender, or sauté in oil and drain well. Rinse anchovies in vinegared water and chop. Heat olive oil with garlic. Add tomatoes and cook, stirring, for 5 minutes. Add the anchovies and salt and pepper to taste. At the last minute, stir in the basil and pour over fish.
SERVES 4.

ITALIAN BROILED FISH WITH FENNEL

Wash and dry whole mullet. Lay the fish on a bed of fennel leaves and branches in a pan. Brush with olive oil and broil until done. Ignite brandy (use 1 tbsp. per fish) and pour flaming over the mullet.

ITALIAN BROILED FISH

Use medium-size mullet, with the liver left in. Slash fish on the sides. Brush with olive oil and broil for 7 minutes each side.

FRENCH SAFFRON FISH

6 small (8 oz.) mullet, wiped dry
but not eviscerated
olive oil
3 or 4 tomatoes, peeled, seeded and
chopped
1 garlic clove, crushed
1 bay leaf, crumbled

2 or 3 pinches of saffron
several sprigs of fennel and thyme
dash of ground coriander
salt
pepper
white wine

Put fish in a shallow baking dish and sprinkle with oil. Surround with chopped tomato seasoned with all but the wine. Pour on wine to a depth of ¼ inch. Bake in 350° oven; when the liquid comes to a boil, bake for 10 minutes longer, or until done. This is best served cold, but is sometimes eaten hot.

SERVES 6.

ENGLISH FISH IN WHITE WINE

4 small mullet
¼ lb. fresh mushrooms, thinly sliced
1 cup chopped parsley

½ cup chopped fresh chives
white wine fish stock
bouquet garni

Butter a deep baking dish. Cover bottom with bed of mushrooms, parsley and chives. Add the fish. Cover 1½ inches deep with seasoned stock; add bouquet garni and cinnamon. Bake at 350° for 15 to 20 minutes.

SERVES 4.

ENGLISH BAKED FISH

4 white perch
4 tbsps. tomato sauce
4 tbsps. melted butter

3 tbsps. bread crumbs
1 tbsp. chopped parsley
salt and pepper

Place the fish in a buttered baking dish. Blend remaining ingredients with seasoning to taste and put on top of fish. Bake at 350° for 15 to 20 minutes, basting often.

SERVES 4.

ENGLISH MOUSSE

1 lb. seatrout, skinned, boned and cut into chunks
1 tbsp. minced onion
butter
pinch grated mace
½ tsp. dried thyme

dash cayenne
1½ cups milk, scalded
6 eggs
1 envelope unflavored gelatin
1½ cups heavy cream, whipped

Sauté the onion in 2 tbsp. butter until soft. Add the fish and mace, thyme and cayenne. Sauté quickly. Remove fish and force through a sieve. Save the pan juices and let them cool. When juices are congealed, pound with the sieved fish. Make a custard of the scalded milk and the eggs; while still warm, but not hot, add the gelatin and dissolve it. Cook custard over low heat until thickened; then put through a sieve and let it cool. Mix with the fish, then add the whipped cream. Put into a mold and chill until firm, about 2 hours.
SERVES 4 to 6.

HAWAIIAN FISH WITH COCONUT MILK

2 lbs. southern kingfish fillets, cut into serving pieces if necessary
½ tbsp. salt

4 tbsps. butter
¾ cup coconut milk

Sprinkle fish with salt. Sauté the fish in butter until barely done. Add the coconut milk, bring to a boil, and simmer for 2 minutes.
SERVES 4.

CANADIAN PLANKED FISH

1 (2½- to 3-lb.) lake whitefish, split down the back, but not separated
½ cup melted butter

2 tbsps. lemon juice
salt and pepper
Tabasco

Heat an oak plank thoroughly; brush with melted butter. Lay the fish on it, skin side down. Combine lemon juice and seasonings to taste with remaining melted butter and brush onto fish flesh. Bake at 425° for 35 minutes, basting frequently with seasoned butter.

SERVES 6.

CANADIAN BAKED FILLETS

2 lbs. lake whitefish fillets	½ tbsp. minced chives
salt and pepper	½ cup minced mushrooms
1 tsp. seasoned salt	½ cup dry white wine
pinch of cayenne	½ cup bread crumbs
3 tbsps. minced onion	4 tbsps. butter, diced

Put fillets in a greased baking dish, and season with salt and pepper. Blend seasoned salt, cayenne, onion, chives, mushrooms and wine and spread over the fish. Top with crumbs and butter. Bake at 350° for 25 to 30 minutes.

SERVES 4.

HUNGARIAN BAKED FISH

1 (2½- to 3-lb.) rockfish, backbone removed	salt and pepper
4 slices of bacon, diced	4 tomatoes, cut into ¼-inch slices
1 medium-size potato, cooked, peeled and cut into ½-inch slices	1 tsp. flour
	1 tsp. paprika
3 large green peppers, sliced and parboiled	1 cup dairy sour cream

Make crosswise incisions in the fish 2 inches apart. Fill slashes with bacon pieces. Grease a baking dish and lay in the potato slices. Cover with pepper slices and season with salt and pepper. Top with tomato slices and season lightly. Put fish on top, flesh up, and sprinkle with combined flour and paprika. Bake at 400° for 15 minutes. Spread sour cream over fish and bake for 5 minutes more, or until done.

SERVES 6.

SWISS FISH EN BLEU

4 trout
1 cup white-wine vinegar, warmed

court bouillon (p. 345)

Keep fish alive until just before cooking if at all possible. Kill the fish, gut as quickly as possible, and rinse lightly. Put in a glass dish, pour on the warmed vinegar, and let stand for 1 minute. Plunge into boiling court bouillon and simmer for 8 to 10 minutes depending on size (until eyes are opaque). Drain carefully and serve.

SERVES 4.

CANADIAN BAKED STUFFED FISH

1 (5 lb.) lake trout
2 cups bread crumbs
1 medium-sized onion, minced
1 celery rib, chopped
1 egg
½ cup butter

1 tsp. salt
⅛ tsp. dried thyme
⅛ tsp. dried sage
⅛ tsp. pepper
sliced bacon

Wipe the fish dry. Combine all but the bacon to make a stuffing. Fill cavity and secure. Put fish on a greased rack in a pan and lay bacon slices over the fish. Pour ½ cup water into the pan. Bake at 300° for 1 hour, basting from time to time.

SERVES 3.

FRENCH BAKED TROUT

6 trout fillets, cut into halves
4 slices of bacon
1 cup chopped onions
1 cup grated carrots
1 cup chopped mushrooms
2 tbsps. chopped celery
1 tbsp. minced parsley

½ cup diced cooked ham
2 tsps. salt
½ tsp. dried thyme
½ tsp. pepper
1 cup dry white wine
3 tbsps. butter

Half-cook bacon, drain well, and cut into small pieces. Sprinkle bacon in the bottom of a shallow casserole. Mix together vegetables, ham and seasonings. Spread half of the mix on the bacon, add the fish, and top with remaining vegetable mixture. Pour on the wine and dot with butter. Bake at 375° for 50 minutes.

SERVES 6.

FRENCH STUFFED FISH

6 to 8 medium-size trout, split and boned, but with head and tails on
1 tsp. minced shallot
dry white wine
lemon juice
½ tbsp. beurre manié

Stuffing:
1 cup warm milk

¾ cup flour
3 small eggs, beaten
1 scant cup boned trout meat
¾ tsp. minced shallot
½ tsp. minced chives
1 tbsp. minced parsley
2 or 3 canned mushrooms, minced
salt and pepper

Prepare a stuffing. Blend the milk gradually with the flour and one sixth of the eggs (or half of 1 beaten egg) and heat, stirring occasionally, until perfectly smooth and thickened. Let cool. Pound the cup of boned trout in a mortar until smooth; press through a sieve and combine with the cooled sauce. Add the rest of the eggs; blend well. Add ¾ tsp. shallot, plus chives, parsley and mushrooms. Season with salt and pepper to taste. Spread the stuffing on the side of each trout that still has the head and tail. Fold over the top side and reshape the fish. Generously butter a baking dish and sprinkle with 1 tsp. shallot pieces. Lay fish on top. Add enough dry white wine to half-cover the fish. Bake at 350° for 20 to 30 minutes. Remove to a serving dish and sprinkle with lemon juice; keep warm.

Make a sauce of the strained pan juices by reducing to 1¼ cups, if necessary. Adjust seasoning. Stir in the beurre manié and cook over low heat, stirring constantly, until sauce is blended and smooth. Pour sauce over trout.

SERVES 6 to 8.

COOKED OR LEFTOVER FISH

CANADIAN CUTLETS

2 cups flaked cooked pike
¼ cup butter
½ cup flour
2 cups milk
  salt and pepper

¼ tsp. dried tarragon
1 tsp. lemon juice
1 bay leaf
1 tsp. Worcestershire sauce
1 cup fine bread crumbs

Make a white sauce with butter, flour and milk. Add salt and pepper to taste and remaining seasonings. Cook in top of a double boiler for 15 minutes. Remove bay leaf and add fish; cool. Drop large spoonsful of mixture onto crumbs, coat well, and flatten into cutlets. Chill thoroughly. Bake at 425° until brown, about 15 minutes.

SERVES 4 to 6.

SMOKED FISH

BROILED SMOKED FISH

Freshen smoked mullet in cold water, if necessary. Drain, dry, and sprinkle well with oil. Put on a rack, flesh side up. Broil for 5 minutes; turn and broil on other side long enough to heat.

CANADIAN FILLETS IN CREAM

6 smoked whitefish fillets
1 onion, sliced
¼ tsp. dried thyme
  salt and pepper
1 large bay leaf

6 parsley sprigs
1 tall can (14 oz.) evaporated milk
⅓ cup grated cheese
  buttered crumbs

Put fillets in a buttered baking dish. Arrange onion slices on top. Season with thyme and salt and pepper to taste. Tie bay leaf and parsley together and add. Pour evaporated milk over the fish. Bake at 300° for 30 minutes. Discard bay leaf and parsley. If desired, sprinkle on grated cheese and buttered crumbs for last 15 minutes of cooking.

SERVES 6.

Oily Fish

Soft-fleshed fish with a good oil content, such as the ones in this group, of course smoke well and are particularly compatible to the tang of pickling.

APPETIZERS

ACAPULCO CEVICHE

Spanish mackerel cut into bite-sized pieces

Combine equal amounts of lemon, orange and Mexican or Key lime juice. Pour over and chill for several hours. Diced and seeded green pepper and tomato can be added as well as minced hot pepper to taste.

NEW ENGLAND PICKLED FISH

6 (1 lb.) mackerels, cut into chunks
2 tbsps. salt
2 tsps. pepper

¼ cup grated mace
oil
vinegar

Roll the fish chunks in blended salt, pepper and mace. Fry in 1 cup oil for

10 minutes. Cool and pack into glass jars. Cover with vinegar, and float a little oil on top. Cover and store refrigerated for 2 weeks before using.

SERVES 12 to 16.

LATIN AMERICAN PICKLED FRIED FISH

1 (1½-lb.) Spanish mackerel, filleted but with skin on
1 tsp. salt
freshly ground pepper
¼ cup olive oil
⅓ cup flour

Pickling mixture:
¾ cup water
⅓ cup white vinegar

⅓ cup olive oil
¾ cup thick onion rings
⅓ cup thinly sliced carrots
1 medium-size green pepper, cut into 1½-inch strips
4 medium-size garlic cloves, thinly sliced
1 tsp. salt
5 black peppercorns, slightly crushed
1 large bay leaf

Cut mackerel into 4-inch pieces. Wash the fish quickly under cold running water and dry well. Rub salt well into both sides; sprinkle with ground pepper and rub in. Combine pickling ingredients in an enamelware saucepan, stir gently together, and put over high heat. Bring to a rapid boil. Reduce heat as low as possible. Cover and simmer for about 15 minutes, or until vegetables are tender. Remove from heat and set aside, covered.

Heat the oil as hot as possible without smoking in a heavy skillet. Just before adding fish, coat fish with flour. Put fish, skin side down, in the hot skillet. Fry briskly for 2 or 3 minutes each side until just golden brown and not fully cooked. Transfer drained fish to a shallow glass or ceramic dish just large enough to hold it in a single layer. Immediately pour on hot pickling mix, spreading vegetables and spices evenly over the top. Let cool to room temperature. Cover dish and refrigerate for at least 24 hours. Will keep refrigerated for 1 week, but baste fish from time to time with pickling mix.

SERVES 8.

NEW ENGLAND POTTED FISH

12 tinker mackerel
½ cup salt
3 tbsps. whole cloves

2½ tbsps. whole allspice
cider vinegar

Roll the mackerel in salt and pack closely in an ovenproof pot such as a bean pot. Tie the whole spices in a cheesecloth bag and lay on top. Cover with cider vinegar; cover pot and bake at 350° for 6 hours. Cool the pot, cover, and refrigerate. Will keep for months.

SERVES 12.

SCANDINAVIAN HERRING IN MARINADE, BASIC RECIPE

24 herring fillets
2 whole herring
2 cups imported Swedish vinegar or cider vinegar
2 cups water

1 cup superfine sugar
1 cup chopped Bermuda onion
8 bay leaves
1 tsp. white pepper
½ tsp. ground allspice

Cut all the fish into 1-inch pieces. Combine marinade ingredients and bring to a boil. Simmer for 1 minute. Remove from heat and let stand until cool. Pour over prepared fish in a deep enamelware or glass dish. Marinate in a cool place for at least 6 hours. Use herring plain, or continue with following 7 recipes, after draining herring and gently pressing between the hands. Part of the marinating liquid is used in some of the recipes.

SERVES 56.

SCANDINAVIAN HERRING IN TOMATO SAUCE

marinated herring pieces from 4 fillets
1 cup ketchup
1½ tbsps. Danish mustard
6 tbsps. light brown sugar

⅓ cup imported Swedish vinegar or cider vinegar
⅓ cup freshly ground pepper
Tabasco
¾ cup chopped white onions

Combine ketchup and mustard and blend well. Combine sugar, vinegar, pepper and Tabasco to taste, and stir until sugar dissolves. Stir into ketchup mixture. Blend in onions and herring. Will keep for several weeks refrigerated.
SERVES 8.

SCANDINAVIAN HERRING IN SOUR CREAM

marinated herring pieces from 4 fillets
2 cups sour cream
1 medium-size Bermuda onion, quartered and thinly sliced
¼ cup chopped green part of scallions
salt
ground pepper
chopped chives for garnish

Combine all but garnish, stirring the herring in last, gently. Add salt and pepper to taste. Chill. When serving garnish with chives.
SERVES 8.

SCANDINAVIAN HERRING SALAD

marinated herring pieces from 4 fillets
1 lb. pickled beets, sliced
1 lb. potatoes, cooked and cooled
1 fresh apple, peeled, cored and quartered
½ cup canned sliced pie apples
1 cup pickled cucumbers
3 tbsps. chutney
1½ cups dairy sour cream
2 tbsps. Danish mustard
dash of red food coloring
salt and pepper
2 hard-cooked eggs, separated

Put herring, beets, peeled potatoes, fresh apple and canned apples, cucumbers and chutney through the fine blade of food grinder. Drain briefly in a large sieve and place in bowl. Add remaining ingredients except eggs and blend well. Season to taste and chill. Just before serving sieve egg whites and yolks separately and garnish the salad. Will keep for several weeks refrigerated.
SERVES 12 to 18.

SCANDINAVIAN HERRING IN MUSTARD SAUCE

marinated herring pieces from 4 fillets
½ cup mayonnaise
⅓ cup sour cream

¼ cup prepared mustard
3½ tbsps. Danish mustard
⅓ cup minced fresh dill
fresh dill sprigs for garnish

Combine all but garnish, adding herring last and folding it in gently. Chill. Garnish with dill sprigs.
SERVES 8.

SCANDINAVIAN HERRING IN DILL

marinated herring pieces from 4 fillets
¾ cup chopped Bermuda onion
⅔ cup marinating liquid

⅔ cup beet pickling juice (sugar, vinegar, salt and pickling spices)
onion rings
⅓ cup minced fresh dill

Arrange pieces on a shallow dish. Spoon chopped onion around fish and between pieces. Pour on the marinade, then the beet juice. Garnish with onion rings and dill. Chill.
SERVES 8.

SCANDINAVIAN CURRIED HERRING

marinated herring pieces from 4 fillets
5 shallots, coarsely chopped
2 tart pie apples, unpeeled, each cut into 8 pieces, cored
3 pieces of dried gingerroot
4 bay leaves
3 tbsps. curry powder

3 tbsps. chopped chutney in syrup
⅓ cup imported Swedish vinegar or cider vinegar
1¼ cups water
⅓ cup herring marinating liquid
½ cup chopped Bermuda onion
salt

Combine shallots, apples, gingerroot, bay leaves, curry powder, chutney, vinegar and water in an enamelware pan. Bring to a boil and simmer, stirring frequently and turning apple pieces, for 10 minutes. Let stand until thoroughly cool. Sieve mixture, pressing liquid from the solids. Discard solids. Add herring marinade, onion, and salt to taste to curry sauce. Stir in the herring. Chill. SERVES 8.

SCANDINAVIAN HORSERADISH HERRING

marinated herring pieces from 2 whole fish

10 thin round slices of fresh horse-radish

15 thin slices of carrot

1 red onion, thinly sliced into rings

¾ cup herring marinating liquid

Combine all well, but gently. Cover dish well and refrigerate for several days. SERVES 8.

DUTCH MARINATED FISH SALAD

marinated herring pieces from 3 whole fish, cut into smaller cubes

2 large tart apples, peeled and sliced thin

6 medium-size potatoes, boiled in their jackets

2 beets, cooked

2 cups minced cold roast veal or other meat

1 medium-size sweet onion, chopped

2 or 3 gherkin pickles, chopped mayonnaise

Marinate apple slices in a mixture of oil and vinegar for a few hours. Peel potatoes and cut into thin slices; marinate these also in oil and vinegar with a little salt and pepper. Peel beets and dice. Stir all together and add just enough mayonnaise to bind together. Chill. Serve on salad greens. Garnish with sliced hard-cooked eggs and whole gherkins. SERVES 8 to 10.

SCANDINAVIAN MARINATED HERRING WITH ROE

12 herring with roe, split
8 onions, thinly sliced
4 small lemons, cut into very thin slices

48 whole peppercorns
white wine or tarragon vinegar
sour cream

Lay 6 herring halves in a flat deep glass or ceramic dish. Spread over the fish a layer of one quarter of the onions, lemon slices and peppercorns. Repeat layers until all herring are used. Press the herring roes through a sieve and measure. Mix with an equal amount of vinegar and spoon evenly over fish. Top with a layer of sour cream. Cover dish with cheesecloth and marinate for at least 24 hours.

SERVES 6.

FRENCH MARINATED FISH

2 lbs. fresh herring, split
½ cup olive oil

Marinade:

1¼ cups white vinegar
1 cup dry white wine

2 medium-size onions, sliced
1 carrot, sliced
4 parsley sprigs, chopped
6 peppercorns
1 bay leaf

Brown the fish in the oil. Simmer marinade ingredients together until vegetables are tender. Pour marinade over fish and simmer for 15 minutes. Transfer to a deep dish and chill thoroughly.

SERVES 6.

CANADIAN PICKLED FISH

1½ lbs. herring fillets
1 tbsp. mustard seeds
½ tsp. dried dillweed
⅓ cup sugar

1 or 2 large onions, thinly sliced in rings
about 2 cups cider vinegar

Cut herring into 1-inch squares. Mix mustard seeds, dillweed and sugar. In a 6-cup glass jar make alternate layers of herring, onions and sugar mixture, making 3 layers of each and ending with sugar mixture. Pour in enough vinegar to cover. Chill, tightly covered, for at least 2 days. Will keep for months refrigerated. Drain with a slotted spoon to serve.

MAKES 4 to 5 cups.

CANADIAN CURRIED FISH

2 cups Canadian pickled herring
1 tsp. curry powder
¼ tsp. turmeric

⅛ tsp. ground coriander
dash of ground cinnamon
¾ cup mayonnaise

Drain the herring and onions from the pickling liquid. Blend seasonings into mayonnaise; mix gently with herring. Cover and chill well before serving.

SERVES 6 to 8.

ENTRÉES

AZORES GRILLED FISH

1 (2-lb.) mackerel, split

Broil skin side of fish first. Turn, cover with mayonnaise, and broil. Add freshly ground black pepper and serve. Can be done over coals in a rack basket.

SERVES 4.

ENGLISH POACHED FISH

Slice mackerel into 3- or 4-inch slices. Cook slowly in highly seasoned white-wine court bouillon, with a few sprigs of fennel added, for 10 to 20 minutes.

PORTUGUESE FISH WITH ORANGE

6 mackerel fillets, skinned
2 oranges
1 cup white wine
2 or 3 green onions, minced
7 tbsps. butter

salt and pepper
⅓ cup sherry, warmed
1 cup heavy cream
3 egg yolks

Peel oranges; cut rind into slivers; discard white pith and separate fruit into sections. In a saucepan combine orange rind with wine, green onions, 1 tbsp. butter and a little salt and pepper. Cook over high heat until reduced by half; strain. Put in top part of double boiler with 2 tbsps. melted butter and the sherry. Stir in the cream and adjust seasoning. Set pan over hot water and cook for 2 or 3 minutes. Beat yolks until they are light colored. Warm them with a bit of the hot sauce, then combine with balance of hot mixture. Cook over hot water, stirring constantly, for 2 or 3 minutes, or until sauce is smooth and thick. Remove sauce from heat and cover to keep warm. Heat remaining 4 tbsps. butter in a heavy skillet until it foams. Sauté mackerel fillets until golden brown. Remove to heated plates and garnish with orange sections. Serve sauce separately.

SERVES 6.

NEW ENGLAND TINKERS

Split 6-inch-long tinkers. Season with salt and pepper. Broil skin side down under a medium-hot broiler for 2 minutes. Serve with drawn butter. Or fry whole tinkers quickly, floured or not as you wish, in a buttered heavy skillet.

NEW ENGLAND SOUSED FISH

2 lbs. mackerel fillets
1 tsp. salt
1 tsp. pickling spices

½ cup water
1 cup vinegar

Skin the fillets and cut each one into halves. Put fish in an enamelware pan;

sprinkle with salt and spices. Pour on water and vinegar. Cover and simmer for 45 minutes. Serve hot or cold.

SERVES 4 to 8.

NEW ENGLAND OATMEAL-CRUSTED FISH

3 large or 6 small mackerel,
   filleted and skinned

Sprinkle fish with salt and pepper; roll in regular oatmeal. Sauté in ½ cup butter until crisp and cooked through.

SERVES 6.

NEW ENGLAND JELLIED TINKERS

4 tinker mackerel, split
2 tbsps. unflavored gelatin
¼ cup water
6 chicken bouillon cubes

4 cups boiling water
juice of 2 lemons
1 tsp. salt

Broil the tinkers, skin sides down, under a hot broiler very briefly, about 1½ minutes. Sprinkle the gelatin onto the cold water and soften. Dissolve the bouillon cubes in boiling water. Stir in the gelatin, lemon juice and salt. Pour one fifth of jellied bouillon into 4 individual serving dishes. Put one split tinker in each dish, skin side down. Gently pour on remaining gelatin mix. Chill until set.

SERVES 4.

GREEK STUFFED FISH

2 small mackerel, prepared for baking
12 green olives, pitted

1 tbsp. olive oil
½ cup Greek ripe olives, pitted
salt and pepper

Stuff each fish with 6 green olives. Place in a glass or ceramic baking dish that has been brushed with olive oil. Surround with ripe olives. Sprinkle lightly with salt and pepper. Bake at 350° for 30 minutes, basting frequently.
SERVES 4.

MAJORCAN FISH AND RICE CASSEROLE

6 serving slices of mackerel
½ cup olive oil
3 garlic cloves, minced
3 tomatoes, peeled, seeded and chopped
3 onions, thinly sliced
2 green peppers, cut into julienne strips

2 tsps. Spanish paprika
¼ tsp. ground saffron
1 tbsp. salt
1½ cups dry white wine
1½ cups water
¼ tsp. dried ground chile pepper
2 bay leaves
1½ cups raw rice

Heat half of the oil; in it sauté garlic, tomatoes and onions for 5 minutes. Mash with a fork and add green peppers, paprika and saffron. Cook over low heat, stirring frequently. Season fish with 1 tsp. salt. Heat remaining oil in a skillet and brown the fish on both sides. Add wine, water, 2 tsps. salt, the chile pepper and bay leaves to tomato mixture. Bring to a boil and add rice. Stir gently and add fish. Cover and cook over low heat for 25 minutes or until rice is done. Correct seasonings. Discard bay leaves before serving.
SERVES 6.

INDONESIAN FISH SAMBAL

4 mackerel fillets, skinned
¼ tsp. dried ground chile pepper
1 tsp. ground ginger
3 onions, sliced
4 garlic cloves, minced
½ tsp. ground saffron

½ tsp. ground cuminseed
4 tbsps. melted butter
½ tbsp. salt
2 tbsps. heavy cream
¾ cup coconut milk

Poach mackerel in lightly salted water for 10 minutes. Drain, and flake fish.

Sauté the chile pepper, ginger, onions, garlic, saffron and cuminseed in the melted butter for 10 minutes, stirring constantly. Add flaked fish and cook over high heat for 5 minutes, stirring constantly. Add salt, cream and coconut milk. Cook over low heat for 10 minutes, stirring frequently.

SERVES 6 to 8.

FRENCH CHILLED FISH

6 bluefish or mackerel fillets
2 cups thinly sliced onions
1 tbsp. peanut oil
3 garlic cloves
½ tsp. dried thyme
2 parsley sprigs
2 bay leaves

⅓ cup white vinegar
3½ cups dry white wine
salt and pepper
Tabasco
2 lemons, thinly sliced
1 carrot, thinly sliced

Cook onions in oil until barely wilted; do not brown. Add garlic, thyme, parsley, bay leaves, vinegar, white wine, and salt, pepper and Tabasco to taste. Simmer 15 minutes. Oil a shallow baking pan large enough to take fillets without overlapping. Put fillets in pan and pour hot sauce over. Arrange lemon and carrot slices over fish. Bring to a boil on top of the stove. Cover dish and bake in 350° oven for 20 to 25 minutes, until fish is done. Chill, covered.

SERVES 6.

NEW ENGLAND BAKED FISH

1 (3-lb.) bluefish, scaled

Rub fish with salt, pepper and paprika to taste and put into a buttered baking dish. Pour on equal parts of lemon juice and melted butter, mixed. Cover with buttered brown paper and bake at 350° for 30 minutes. Serve with sauce of your choice (New Englanders use a mustard sauce).

SERVES 4 to 6.

FRENCH FISH FLAMED WITH FENNEL

1 (3-lb.) bluefish, split for broiling
1 tsp. fennel seeds
1 tbsp. dried parsley
1 tsp. dried thyme
¼ cup brandy

Broil fish under medium heat, turning once, until done. Place on a heated platter and sprinkle with herbs. Heat brandy in a ladle over a match or candle; ignite brandy and pour gently over fish to flame it. Allow flames to die out by themselves.

SERVES 6.

FRENCH FISH BONNE FEMME

1 (3-lb.) bluefish, split from the back
½ cup sliced raw mushrooms
¼ tsp. minced shallot
¼ tsp. minced parsley
salt and pepper
½ cup white wine
½ cup fish stock
½ tsp. flour
2 tbsps. butter in small bits

Sprinkle a buttered baking dish with mushrooms, shallot and parsley. Put fish in, flesh side up. Season with salt and pepper. Add wine and stock slightly thickened with the flour. Cover with a sheet of buttered brown paper and bake at 350° for 25 minutes. Remove the paper and bake for 5 minutes more. Drain liquid from baking dish into a heated saucepan. Add the butter bits slowly to the saucepan, stirring. Pour back over fish and glaze quickly under the broiler.

SERVES 6.

PARISIAN SHIRRED INDIVIDUAL FISH

24 small smelts

Remove heads and tails from fish and split them from the back. Butter 6 individual oven dishes and put 4 fish in each dish. To each dish add 1 tbsp. fish stock and a few drops of lemon juice. Bake at 350°, basting frequently, for 25 minutes, or until liquid is nearly evaporated. Cover with Mornay sauce (p. 354) and glaze quickly under the broiler.

SERVES 6.

WHITEBAIT

Whitebait, the smallest of edible fishes, is a silverside and is netted. Wash the fish; there's no need to remove head or entrails. Dry; roll in seasoned flour or cornmeal. Fry until crisp in deep fat heated to 380°. Or deep-fry with chopped bacon slices or oyster crabs. Serve to be eaten as "finger food," or serve with rémoulade or tartar sauce (pp. 356 and 357).

SMOKED AND SALTED FISH

BELGIAN STUFFED SMOKED FISH

6 smoked herring
½ cup fine dry bread crumbs
  sherry
3 tbsps. butter
2 fresh mushrooms, chopped
1 tsp. minced parsley

1 tsp. minced shallot
1 tsp. minced onion
1 garlic clove, mashed
  black pepper
2 tbsps. chopped chives

Skin the herring, split lengthwise, and wipe with a damp cloth. Soak bread crumbs in sherry; gently squeeze out liquid. Make a stuffing with all ingredients except chives. Season with pepper to taste. Spread a portion of stuffing on half of each fish. Sprinkle with chopped chives and top with other halves of fish. Wrap each fish in oiled brown paper. Bake at 350° for 30 to 35 minutes.

SERVES 6.

POLISH FISH CREAM

4 large salt herring with milt and roe
2 hard rolls, softened in milk
2 tbsps. butter
2 eggs, separated
3 tbsps. dairy sour cream

1 onion, grated
3 tbsps. grated Parmesan cheese
grated nutmeg
salt and pepper
bread crumbs

Put fish and rolls through finest blade of a food grinder. Cream the milt and roe with 1 tsp. butter and the egg yolks. Add sour cream, onion, cheese, and fish mixture. Season to taste and mix well. Beat egg whites stiff and fold in. Pour into a greased baking dish, top with crumbs, and dot with butter. Bake at 400° for 30 minutes.

SERVES 5 or 6.

FINNISH PICKLED SALT FISH

4 salt herring, freshened
3 onions, sliced
½ cup hot water
1½ cups vinegar

¼ cup sugar
2 tbsps. pickling spices
2 bay leaves

Drain fish and cut into 4 pieces. Put in layers with onion slices in a jar. Combine water, vinegar, sugar, spices and bay leaves. Dissolve sugar and pour liquid over fish. Cover and refrigerate for at least 24 hours.

SERVES 8 to 10.

ENGLISH KIPPERS

6 kippers

Arrange kippers in a single layer on broiler foil. Dot generously with butter. Broil 4 inches from the source of heat until butter is golden and kippers thoroughly hot. Carefully transfer to heated platter and sprinkle generously with lemon juice. Garnish with lemon and parsley.

SERVES 6.

ENGLISH KIPPER SALAD

½ lb. kippered herring, chopped fine   salt and pepper
2 cups chopped celery   paprika
½ cup French dressing   1 green pepper, chopped

Toss all together, adding seasonings to taste.
  SERVES 2 to 4.

Dry Fish

The majority of the fish in this group of relatively dry soft-fleshed fish are most familiar to our northeastern coast, where for generations salt cod has been a staple. These fishes take well to salting; the process firms the soft meat. However scrod, which is a juvenile cod weighing up to 2 pounds, is a delicacy and is seldom treated in that way.

The large sharks that make up a good percentage of this group are rarely used for human food in this country, but the Soviet commercial fishing fleets are processing them, up to and including drying the fins, which, of course, have been an ingredient in Oriental cuisine for many, many years. If you're tempted to try drying your own, scrub the fins well with a hard brush in salt water, then soak them in a saturated brine for an hour to allow the salt to penetrate the meaty base. Rinse them in fresh water and hang by strings threaded through the meaty part to dry. Correctly dried, the fins have a relatively straight, dull surface without folds or bends and the meaty base is dry throughout. The thin parts are resilient and elastic, without being brittle. Shark, incidentally, smokes fairly well and has been called "delicious" in England.

APPETIZERS

CANADIAN DELICACIES

Codfish tongues and cheeks. Poach in court bouillon and serve with cream sauce and chopped hard-cooked egg. Also roll in cornmeal and fry quickly. Also scramble with potatoes in a hash.

SCANDINAVIAN SPICED APPETIZER

3 lbs. boned cod, cut into serving pieces
salt and pepper
½ cup salad oil
3 onions, thinly sliced

1 garlic clove, minced
2 cups vinegar
2 bay leaves
1 tbsp. mixed pickling spices

Season fish lightly and fry in hot oil until light brown. Place in a baking dish. Brown onions and garlic in oil, season, and spread on the fish. Scald vinegar with bay leaves and pickling spices and simmer for 5 minutes. Pour over fish. Bake at 325° for 45 minutes. Chill. Will keep for a week refrigerated.
SERVES 24.

JAPANESE APPETIZER

1½ lbs. cod fillets, cut into thin strips
½ cup soya sauce
2 tbsps. sherry

3 tbsps. sugar
½ tsp. ground ginger
1 garlic clove, mashed

Combine soya sauce, sherry, sugar, ginger and garlic. Marinate fish strips in the mixture for 30 minutes. Thread on skewers and broil over a hibachi.
SERVES 6.

GREEK MARINATED FISH

2 lbs. halibut steaks
  flour seasoned with salt and pepper
⅓ cup olive oil

3 garlic cloves, minced
½ tsp. dried rosemary
½ cup white-wine vinegar

Dip fish into seasoned flour, coating well. Fry fish on both sides in hot oil. Remove fish to a heated platter. Drain oil from pan and reserve. Add garlic, rosemary and vinegar. Bring to a boil and let simmer for a few minutes, pour over fish. Serve fish hot, or cool and serve chilled.
SERVES 8.

JAPANESE EGG ROLL

5 oz. halibut fillet, shredded
¼ tsp. salt
4 tbsps. sugar
6 eggs, beaten
5 tbsps. dashi

3 tbsps. soya sauce
2 tbsps. mirin or sherry
½ tsp. sesame oil
2-inch piece of daikon (radish) or
  turnip, grated

Add salt to fish and pound well. Add sugar and mash well. Add eggs, *dashi*, 2 tbsps. soya sauce and *mirin;* stir well. Divide into 6 portions and fry in oil. Immediately upon taking from skillet, place on a bamboo mat (or napkin) and roll. Let stand to set, then cut into ½-inch lengths. Serve with grated radish mixed with 1 tbsp. soya sauce as a dip.
SERVES 6.

PERUVIAN CEVICHE

1-lb. haddock fillet, skinned
3 long, hot green chile peppers
3 long, hot red chile peppers or 1
  tsp. dried hot red pepper flakes

1 medium-size onion
1 cup Key or Mexican lime juice
1 tsp. salt
  fresh coriander (Chinese parsley)

Slice haddock into thin strips. Seed the whole peppers and cut into thin strips. Cut onion into wafer-thin slices. Combine all but coriander well and chill overnight. Sprinkle with coriander before serving.

SERVES 4 to 6.

SOUPS

CHINESE SHARK'S FIN SOUP

¾ lb. dried shark's fins

½ lb. canned or cooked crab meat, flaked

1 tbsp. cooking oil

2 tbsps. sliced gingerroot

¼ cup sliced scallions

1 tbsp. dry sherry

3 qts. stock

2 tbsps. cornstarch

¼ cup water

1 tsp. soya sauce

½ tsp. MSG

Wash the fins, cover with cold water, and drain. Re-cover with cold water, bring to a boil, and boil for 3 hours. Drain, cover again with fresh water, and boil for another 3 hours. Drain, pat dry, and dice. Heat the oil and in it sauté the gingerroot and scallions for 3 minutes. Add the sherry, 1 qt. of the stock and the diced fins. Cook over high heat for 10 minutes. Drain off remaining liquid. Add 2 qts. stock and bring to a boil. Mix together into a paste the cornstarch, water, soya sauce and MSG. Stir into the soup with the crab meat and heat to thicken somewhat.

SERVES 8 to 10.

FRENCH FISH SOUP

2½ lbs. halibut, in 1½-inch cubes

2 qts. water

fish bones and trimmings

3 garlic cloves

1 whole onion

1 parsley sprig

1 tbsp. salt

½ cup olive oil

1 cup minced onion

1½ cups stewed tomatoes

1 to 2 tbsps. lemon juice

salt and pepper

¼ cup minced parsley

4 slices French bread, toasted

Make stock of water, bones and trimmings, 1 garlic clove, the whole onion, parsley sprig and salt. Bring to boil and simmer for 30 to 40 minutes. Reduce stock over high heat for 5 minutes. Strain, measure, and reserve 6 cups stock. Sauté fish in olive oil until delicately colored on all sides. Add minced onion, remaining garlic, chopped and stewed tomatoes. Add lemon juice and season with salt and pepper to taste. Add reserved stock and simmer for 10 to 12 minutes. Correct seasonings and add minced parsley. Put a slice of toast in bottom of a soup bowl; add soup.

SERVES 4.

GREEK FISH SOUP

1½-lb. piece of halibut	1 celery rib, sliced
1½ qts. salted water	⅓ cup olive oil
12 small new potatoes	¼ cup lemon juice
12 small white onions	salt and pepper
2 green onions, minced	2 tbsps. minced parsley

Simmer halibut in salted water for 20 to 30 minutes, until tender. Drain, reserving the liquid, and skin and bone the fish; keep fish warm. Strain fish cooking liquid, bring to a boil, and add potatoes, white and green onions and celery. Cover and simmer for 20 minutes, or until vegetables are tender. Mix together the oil, lemon juice, and salt and pepper to taste. Pour half of this over the fish and stir remainder into the soup. Sprinkle parsley on the fish and serve the fish as a side dish to the soup.

SERVES 4 to 6.

ITALIAN FISH SOUP

2 lbs. haddock, cut into 1½-inch cubes	1 tbsp. chopped fennel tops
2 garlic cloves, crushed	1 tbsp. chopped parsley
¼ cup olive oil	½ tsp. dried orégano
3 cups water	pinch of Italian red pepper

Sauté garlic in oil for 1 minute. Add remaining ingredients. Simmer until fish is tender. Adjust salt to taste.

SERVES 4 or 5.

NEW ENGLAND FISH CHOWDER

---

1 (4-lb.) cod, skinned and boned
fish bones and trimmings
2 cups cold water
1 bay leaf
6 parsley sprigs
4 celery ribs
1½ oz. salt pork, cut into small dice

3 onion slices
4 cups milk, scalded
salt and pepper
4 tbsps. cold butter, cut into pieces
6 pilot crackers, moistened with a little cold milk

Cut fish into 2-inch pieces. Put fish trimmings into the cold water with bay leaf, parsley and celery. Bring to a boil and simmer for 25 minutes. Strain stock into soup kettle. Render the salt pork dice with the onion slices. Strain the fat into the kettle. Add fish to kettle and cook over low heat for 5 minutes. Stir in the scalded milk and simmer for 15 minues. Season to taste and stir in the butter pieces. Put a cracker in the bottom of each soup bowl, pour on the chowder.

SERVES 6.

NEW ENGLAND FISH CHOWDER, BAKED

Put alternate layers of cod slices, sliced onions, and sliced potatoes in a deep baking dish, dotting each layer with butter and seasoning with salt and pepper. Cover with milk 1 inch over top layer. Bake covered at 350° for 1 hour.

ENTRÉES

BASQUE STYLE STEAKS

4 individual halibut steaks
  juice of 1 lemon
  salt and pepper
1 egg, beaten until frothy

  flour
3 to 4 tbsps. olive oil
2 garlic cloves

Squeeze the lemon juice over the steaks and let stand for 10 minutes. Sprinkle with salt and pepper. Dip steaks into beaten egg, then into flour, shaking off excess. Heat oil with garlic and cook until garlic begins to brown. Remove garlic and cook steaks in oil over medium high heat until lightly browned on both sides, about 8 to 10 minutes.

SERVES 4.

BENGAL FISH CURRY

2 lbs. halibut
  salt
  juice of ½ lemon
¾ cup oil
2 cups shredded fresh coconut
8 tsps. curry powder
8 tsps. ground cuminseed
4 tsps. chile powder
4 green chiles, seeded and ground
½ tsp. mashed garlic

3 tomatoes, peeled, seeded and chopped
1 green chile, halved and seeded
1 tsp. minced fresh coriander leaves
¾ cup water
5 tbsps. ground peas or lentils, or 2 tsps. potato flour mixed with a little water
  lemon juice

Rub fish with a little salt and juice of ½ lemon. Heat oil and sauté coconut in it until brown. Add curry powder, cuminseed, chile powder, ground green chiles and mashed garlic; sauté until brown. Add tomatoes, halved green chile, coriander leaves and water. Simmer for 5 minutes to blend flavors. Add ground peas or flour mixture with water to sauce. Add fish to sauce; season with salt and more lemon juice to taste. Let sauce boil up a few times until fish is tender.

SERVES 6.

SPANISH FILLETS WITH WINE

4 halibut fillets, skinned
  salt and pepper
1 wineglass of dry white wine
1 wineglass of boiling water

1 sweet red pepper, diced
1 cup medium white sauce
2 tbsps. buttered crumbs
2 tbsps. grated cheese

Tie or skewer the fillets in rolls; put in a buttered baking dish. Season. Mix wine and water and pour over the fish. Cover and bake at 400° for 25 minutes. Mix red pepper with white sauce and pour over fish. Sprinkle with crumbs and cheese and brown under the broiler.

SERVES 4.

SPANISH BAKED FISH WITH NUT SAUCE

1 (2-lb.) piece of halibut
  salt
¼ cup olive oil
1 garlic clove
¼ cup pine nuts or blanched
  almonds

¼ cup minced parsley
2 large onions, chopped
1 (1-lb.) can tomatoes
  pepper
½ tsp. sugar

Sprinkle both sides of fish with salt and put in a shallow baking dish. Heat oil and add garlic and nuts; sauté until golden. Remove garlic and nuts from oil and crush them into a paste, gradually adding parsley with a bit of oil from skillet. Add onions to oil and sauté until golden. Add tomatoes to onions and simmer for 5 minutes. Stir in nut paste. Season with salt and pepper. Add sugar and pour over fish, covering it completely. Bake at 350° for 30 minutes.

SERVES 6.

ENGLISH FISH AND CHIPS

2 to 2½ lbs. halibut or haddock fillets
1 cup flour
½ tsp. paprika
¼ tsp. salt

⅛ tsp. pepper
¾ cup beer
  oil for deep-frying

Skin the fillets and cut into slices ½ to ¾ inch thick; then cut slices into chunks 3 by 5 inches. Make a batter by mixing dry ingredients and slowly stirring in the beer. Beat until smooth. Heat oil in a deep-fryer to 375°. Dip each piece of fish into batter, drain briefly. Deep-fry a few pieces at a time until golden brown, turning as needed, for 3 to 4 minutes. Drain. Serve with malt vinegar, salt and lemon wedges on the side. The "chips" are French fried potatoes, yours or frozen and cooked.

SERVES 4 to 6.

CANADIAN FISH STEAKS

2 lbs. halibut steaks
juice of 1 lemon
½ tsp. salt
⅛ tsp. pepper
½ tsp. dried marjoram

½ cup thinly sliced green onions
½ cup chopped celery
2 tbsps. butter
½ tbsp. caraway seeds
½ cup white wine

Put halibut steaks in a shallow baking dish. Squeeze on the lemon juice. Season with salt, pepper and marjoram. Let marinate for 1 hour, turning once. Sauté green onion slices and celery in the butter for 5 minutes, or until tender. Spread over fish steaks. Sprinkle on caraway seeds. Bake at 400° for 10 minutes. Pour on the wine and bake for 10 minutes more.

SERVES 6.

GREEK BAKED STEAKS WITH VEGETABLES

2 lbs. halibut steaks, 1¼ inches thick
1 medium-size onion, minced
1 bunch of scallions, chopped
¼ cup olive oil
4 celery ribs, minced
3 carrots, sliced

1 lb. spinach, chopped
½ cup minced parsley
1 cup canned tomatoes
5 mint leaves, chopped
2 garlic cloves, minced
salt and pepper

Sauté onion and scallions in oil until limp but not browned. Add celery, carrots, spinach, parsley, tomatoes, mint, garlic, and salt and pepper to taste;

simmer for 15 minutes. Spoon half of the vegetable mixture into a buttered baking dish. Cover with fish steaks and spoon on rest of mixture. Cover and bake at 325° for 1 hour.

SERVES 6 to 8.

FRENCH FISH STEAKS

2 lbs. halibut steaks, 1 inch thick
½ lb. mushrooms, thinly sliced
3 tbsps. butter
2 small tomatoes, peeled, seeded and
    chopped

1 garlic clove, minced
salt and pepper

Sauté mushrooms in butter until just limp. Add tomatoes and garlic. Heat through and season to taste. Put fish in a fairly close-fitting baking dish. Sprinkle with salt and pepper and spoon mushroom sauce on top. Bake, uncovered at 400° for 25 to 30 minutes. Serve as is, or with shrimp sauce.

SERVES 4 to 6.

NORWEGIAN FISH PUDDING

2 lbs. fish, preferably half cod and
    half haddock
4 egg whites
2 tsps. potato flour, or 1 tsp. corn-
    starch

little cold milk
salt and white pepper
grated nutmeg
3 cups cold milk
1 cup cold heavy cream

Skin and bone the fish. Put fish twice through the finest blade of food chopper. Add 2 egg whites and put through the chopper twice again. Add 2 more whites and put through the chopper twice again. Rub mixture through a fine sieve, adding flour or cornstarch moistened with a little cold milk at the same time. Season to taste. Beat with an electric mixer for 20 minutes, gradually adding 3 cups cold milk and the cream. Pour into a buttered baking dish. Bake at 300° for 1 hour, or until firm and dry enough to slice.

SERVES 6.

SCANDINAVIAN INDIVIDUAL FISH PUDDINGS

1½ lbs. cod or haddock
1½ cups heavy cream
1 tbsp. cornstarch

salt and white pepper
fresh bread crumbs
fresh dill sprigs

Divide fish into 2 or 3 parts and purée with the cream, cornstarch and seasonings to taste in a blender, 1 part at a time, until smooth. Butter well 6 individual molds and coat with bread crumbs. Fill molds almost to the top with the fish mixture and cover securely with foil. Set in a baking pan and fill pan with enough water to come halfway up the sides of the molds. Bake at 325° for about 45 minutes, or until puddings are firm. Don't let water boil, and add more heated water if needed. Serve with a sauce of your choice. Garnish with fresh dill.

SERVES 6.

DUTCH FISH CASSEROLE

4 individual cod fillets
2 cups court bouillon
4 tbsps. butter
3 tbsps. flour
¼ cup Dijon-style mustard
¼ tsp. paprika
  salt and pepper

1 large onion, thinly sliced
1½ lbs. potatoes
  milk and butter for potatoes
¼ tsp. grated nutmeg
5 tsps. lemon juice
½ cup buttered bread crumbs
½ cup grated mild cheese

Poach codfish in court bouillon. Drain fillets and reserve the court bouillon. Make a mustard sauce as follows: Melt 3 tbsps. butter; stir in flour smoothly. Gradually add reserved court bouillon, stirring to make a smooth sauce. Bring to a boil, stirring constantly. Season with mustard, paprika, and salt and pepper to taste. Sauté onion in remaining tbsp. butter until soft and transparent. Boil potatoes until tender; peel and mash, mixing with enough hot milk and butter to give a fairly soft consistency. Season with nutmeg. Butter a shallow baking dish and build layers of half of the fish, half of the onion slices, half of the lemon juice, half of the mustard sauce and half of the potatoes. Repeat layers, topping with potatoes. Sprinkle top with crumbs and cheese. Bake at 350° for about 30 minutes; slide under the broiler until top is brown and bubbly.

SERVES 4 to 6.

FRENCH STEAKS

6 cod steaks
  salt and pepper
1 cup sliced mushrooms
3 tbsps. butter
1 onion, chopped
1 garlic clove, crushed

2 tbsps. chopped parsley
  pinch of dried thyme
2 tomatoes, peeled, seeded and
  chopped
1 cup white wine

Season cod steaks with salt and pepper and place in a buttered baking dish. Sauté mushrooms in 2 tbsps. butter until tender. Sprinkle fish with onion, garlic, parsley, thyme, tomatoes, mushrooms and wine. Bring mixture slowly to a boil and simmer for 15 to 20 minutes, or until tender. Remove the fish and keep warm. Reduce the liquid in the pan by half by boiling. Add remaining 1 tbsp. butter. Pour sauce over fish.

SERVES 6.

SPANISH BAKED FILLETS

2 lbs. cod fillets, skinned and cut
  into 6 serving pieces
¼ cup olive oil
1 onion, sliced
2 tbsps. flour

salt
1 cup asparagus tips
2 cups sliced tomatoes
2 tbsps. butter
2 tbsps. grated Romano cheese

Put half of the oil in a shallow baking dish and cover with onion. Dust fish with flour and salt. Arrange on the onion. Arrange asparagus tips on top, then top with sliced tomatoes. Dot with butter and sprinkle with cheese. Bake covered at 350° for about 30 minutes, or until done.

SERVES 6.

SPANISH BAKED STEAKS

4 cod steaks, ¾ inch thick
  pepper
  salt
2 tbsps. lemon juice

4 tbsps. butter
2 onions, sliced
2 (1-lb.) cans tomatoes
¼ tsp. dried orégano

Lay steaks in a single layer in a buttered baking dish. Sprinkle with pepper, salt and lemon juice, and dot with 2 tbsps. butter. Bake at 350° for 25 minutes. Make a sauce. Sauté onions in 2 tbsps. butter; add tomatoes, orégano and 1 tsp. salt. Simmer uncovered for 30 minutes. Pour sauce over fish and bake for 5 minutes longer.

SERVES 4.

PORTUGUESE STEAKS

4 individual cod steaks
  salt and pepper
⅛ tsp. dried thyme
1 garlic clove, mashed
1 onion, chopped

2 tsps. chopped parsley
2 large tomatoes, sliced
1 cup Portuguese white wine
½ tbsp. butter
½ tbsp. flour

Sprinkle cod with salt and pepper. Put steaks side by side in a casserole. Sprinkle with thyme, garlic, onion and parsley. Cover with tomato slices. Add wine to baking dish. Cover and bake at 350° for 25 to 30 minutes, or until cod is tender. Remove fish to a heated platter and keep warm. Reduce pan juices by half by rapidly boiling. Make *beurre manié* with butter and flour and stir into pan juices; cook over low heat, stirring constantly, until sauce is thickened. Pour over fish.

SERVES 4.

SPANISH FISH WITH GREEN SAUCE

2 lbs. haddock fillets, cut into 6 serving pieces
¼ cup olive oil
1 garlic clove
½ cup minced parsley
2 tbsps. flour

½ tbsp. salt
¼ tsp. ground cuminseed
dash of pepper
¾ cup fish stock
2 tbsps. light cream

Brown fish slowly on both sides in hot oil. Remove to a platter and keep warm. Add garlic to oil and sauté until golden. Remove garlic and crush in a mortar. Slowly work the parsley into the garlic, then blend in flour, salt, cuminseed and pepper. Pour off all but 1 tbsp. oil from skillet. Add parsley mixture to oil in pan and blend well. Add stock and cream and cook, stirring, until thickened. Pour over fish.

SERVES 6.

SINGAPORE STEAMED FISH

1½-lb. haddock fillet
3½ tbsps. salted black beans (from Chinese market), or canned black beans
2 garlic cloves, crushed, or 2 (½-inch-thick) slices of fresh gingerroot

1 tbsp. oil
1 tbsp. wine vinegar
½ tsp. sugar
salt and pepper

Soak Chinese black beans in water to cover for 15 minutes; drain. Mash half of the beans with garlic or gingerroot and make a paste with the oil. Add vinegar and sugar. Put fish into an oiled baking dish and season lightly with salt and pepper. Spread on the bean paste and let stand for 30 minutes. Sprinkle on the reserved beans. Cover dish tightly and set in a pan half filled with simmering water. Steam in 200° oven for 20 minutes.

SERVES 4.

SCANDINAVIAN FISH PUDDING

1¼ lbs. haddock, skinned and boned
4 tbsps. chilled butter
¾ tsp. salt

¼ cup heavy cream
2 egg whites, beaten stiff

Put fish and butter through the finest blade of a food chopper twice. Pound smooth. Add salt and cream gradually. When well blended, fold in egg whites. Turn into a buttered mold, filling three quarters full. Set in a pan of hot water, cover, and cook at 325° until set, about 1 hour. Unmold and serve with a sauce.

SERVES 4.

JAPANESE SKEWERED FISH

1½ lbs. haddock fillets, skinned
½ cup soya sauce
2 tbsps. sherry

3 tbsps. sugar
1 garlic clove, mashed
½ tsp. ground ginger

Make a marinade of all ingredients except fish. Slice fish into thin strips and marinate for 30 minutes. Thread on skewers and cook in a broiler under medium heat until done; or guests can cook on individual skewers over a hibachi.

SERVES 6.

INDIAN POACHED FISH

3 lbs. fillets of haddock, washed and dried
½ tbsp. turmeric
fresh ground pepper
6 cups buttermilk

1 tbsp. lemon juice
1 tsp. salt
1 tbsp. ground cuminseed
3 tbsps. chopped green pepper
5 tbsps. butter

Rub fish with turmeric and black pepper. Poach in buttermilk for 5 minutes. Remove fish and keep warm. Add lemon juice and salt to liquid in pan and simmer until reduced by half. Replace fish and add cuminseed and green pepper. Simmer for 10 minutes. Brown the butter and pour over the fish.

SERVES 6.

DUTCH FISH AND POTATOES

2½-lb. piece of cod or haddock
3 lbs. potatoes

salt and pepper
½ cup melted butter

Generously butter a deep baking dish. Peel potatoes and cut into ⅛-inch slices. Cover bottom of dish with about 3 layers of potato slices; use only half of the 3 pounds; stagger potatoes so they overlap; season to taste. Put the piece of fish in the center of potatoes and layer remaining potatoes around fish; season to taste. Pour on the melted butter. Bake at 375° for 1 to 1¼ hours, basting every 15 minutes with a bulb baster to draw up juices from the bottom of the dish. Add additional melted butter if necessary.

SERVES 6.

SPANISH FISH STEW

1 (1½-lb.) cusk, boned and cut into
    chunks
4 large potatoes, thickly sliced
2 onions, sliced
6 cups hot water
4 tbsps. raw rice

½ cup diced salt pork
1 green pepper, diced
    salt and pepper
2 tbsps. minced parsley
2 pilot crackers, broken

Bring fish, potatoes, onions and water slowly to a boil, covered. Sprinkle in the rice, salt pork and green pepper, and simmer until tender. Season to taste. Add parsley and broken crackers. (Leftover vegetables can be added here, if desired.) Heat and serve.

SERVES 4 to 6.

SCANDINAVIAN BAKED FILLETS

2 lbs. cusk fillets
4 tbsps. flour
2 tsps. salt
¼ tsp. pepper
1 cup milk

2 cups coarse soft bread crumbs
4 tbsps. butter
1 tsp. dried dillweed
1 cup dairy sour cream

Coat fillets with seasoned flour. Arrange in a single layer in greased baking dish. Pour on milk. Bake at 350° for 45 minutes. Toast crumbs lightly in butter. Stir dill into sour cream. Spoon sour-cream mixture over the fish; top with crumbs. Bake for 10 minutes longer, or until cream is set.
   SERVES 6.

CHINESE GRILLED STEAKS

1½ lbs. individual pollock steaks
¼ tsp. salt
¼ tsp. pepper
   dash of garlic powder

½ tsp. ground ginger
6 tbsps. peanut oil
3 tbsps. vinegar
1 tbsp. soya sauce

Make a basting sauce of salt, pepper, garlic powder and ginger with 1 tbsp. of the oil and 1 tbsp. vinegar. Beat with a wire whisk. Add 2 tbsps. oil and 1 tbsp. vinegar and beat again. Add remaining oil and vinegar and the soya sauce and beat until well mixed. Arrange pollock steaks on a greased broiler pan and brush liberally with sauce. Broil for about 5 minutes per side, brushing frequently with the sauce.
   SERVES 6.

COOKED AND LEFTOVER FISH

SCANDINAVIAN FISH SOUP

2 lbs. cod fillets, poached
1 cup chopped onions
½ cup chopped green pepper
3 tbsps. olive oil
1 (1-lb.) can tomatoes
2 cups cooked or canned lima beans

1 (8-oz.) bottle clam broth
2 cups court bouillon or fish stock
2 tsps. salt
¼ tsp. black pepper
¼ cup chopped parsley

Flake the fish. Sauté onions and green pepper in olive oil until tender. Add tomatoes and simmer for 10 minutes. Add limas, tomato mixture and clam broth to the court bouillon or fish stock. Add salt and pepper. Bring to a boil, reduce heat, and add flaked fish. Heat through. Sprinkle with parsley and serve.

SERVES 6.

KEDGEREE, ENGLISH VERSION

1½ lbs. cod, haddock or hake, boiled

Bone and flake the fish. Boil 4 tbsps. raw Patna rice in salted water until tender. Drain rice and rinse well. Let stand a while. Place rice on a cookie sheet and dry gradually in a slow 250° oven. Mince 3 hard-cooked eggs. Mix fish, rice and eggs; season well with salt and pepper. Melt 4 to 6 tbsps. butter, add fish and stir until hot.

SERVES 4.

Variation:

2 lbs. cod
1½ cups salted water
　salt
　cayenne pepper
½ cup butter

2 tbsps. minced parsley
1 tbsp. minced chives
3 cups cooked rice
3 hard-cooked eggs, separated

Bring salted water to a boil; add fish. When water returns to a boil, reduce heat and simmer until fish flakes, about 3 minutes per pound. Remove fish, reserving broth. Strain broth and season with salt and cayenne pepper to taste. Bone and flake fish and return to broth. In a skillet melt the butter; add parsley, chives and rice. When heated through, add to the broth. Return to a boil again and simmer for 5 minutes. Chop egg whites and add to kedgeree. Garnish with sieved egg yolks just before serving.

SERVES 6.

KEDGEREE, SOUTHERN VERSION

2 cups flaked cooked cod or haddock
1 onion slice, minced
3 tbsps. butter
2 cups cooked rice

⅓ cup cream or evaporated milk
½ tsp. curry powder
salt and pepper
2 hard-cooked eggs, sliced

Cook the onion in butter until softened and clear. Add rice and fish, then the cream and curry powder. Season to taste. Heat, stirring from time to time. Bring to a boil, add eggs, and serve.

SERVES 6 to 8.

CANADIAN FISH MOUSSE

1½ cups well-packed flaked poached
    halibut fillet
1½ cups cool but liquid fish aspic
    (p. 362)
1 envelope unflavored gelatin

2 tbsps. cold water
½ cup white wine
6 heaping tbsps. whipped cream
    salt and pepper

Set a small fish mold (about 6-cup size) on a bed of cracked ice. Line the inside with some of the aspic. Decorations can be set in the aspic and sprinkled with more liquid aspic to hold them in place. When lining and decorations are set, pour in more aspic ½ inch deep; chill again. Soften the gelatin in the cold water and dissolve over hot water. Force the fish through a sieve and mix with dissolved gelatin. Add wine and whipped cream;

season to taste. Either gently heap fish mix into the mold with a large spoon, or put the mix through a pastry bag with large tube into center of mold, not taking it to the sides. Chill until mousse is set. Fill the space around the edges of mold with cool liquid aspic, and chill again until aspic is firm. Unmold and serve on a cold platter.

SERVES 4 to 6.

SCANDINAVIAN DILLED SALAD

1½ cups flaked cooked and boned haddock, cold
4 or 5 red-skinned potatoes, cooked
4 large tomatoes
1 red onion
1 tbsp. capers, finely chopped

6 tbsps. olive oil
2 tbsps. tarragon vinegar
¼ tsp. prepared mustard
salt and pepper
minced fresh dill

Peel and slice potatoes and tomatoes; cut onion into thin slices. In a deep bowl arrange alternate layers of haddock, potatoes, tomatoes and onion. Sprinkle with capers. Make a dressing of oil, vinegar and mustard; add salt and pepper to taste. Toss salad gently with dressing, chill. Garnish well with minced fresh dill.

SERVES 4.

SMOKED AND SALTED FISH

BASQUE-STYLE STEW

1 lb. salt cod, freshened
¼ cup olive oil
1½ cups chopped onions

2 tbsps. minced garlic
1½ cups peeled chopped tomatoes
⅛ tsp. pepper

Heat oil; cook onions and garlic over low heat for about 3 minutes. Add the fish; cover tightly and simmer for 25 minutes. Add tomatoes and simmer, covered, until fish is flaky, about 10 minutes longer. Season with pepper. Serve with boiled potatoes or rice.

SERVES 6.

BERMUDA BREAKFAST (but better for supper!)

2 lbs. salt cod
6 potatoes, peeled
⅓ cup butter or olive oil
½ tsp. Tabasco
½ tsp. prepared mustard

1 hard-cooked egg, minced
3 bananas, sliced
1 avocado, peeled and sliced
2 tbsps. chopped parsley

Put fish in a pan with water to cover and cook over medium heat for 2 hours. Drain; remove skin and bones and return fish to pan. Add fresh water to cover the potatoes. Cook at medium heat until potatoes are tender, about 30 minutes. Drain well and keep warm. Combine butter, Tabasco, mustard and egg. Bring to a boil and remove from the heat. Arrange fish on a platter with potatoes; garnish with bananas and avocado, and pour the sauce over all. Top with parsley.

SERVES 6.

BRANDADE DE MORUE (PROVENÇAL COD PURÉE)

2 lbs. salt codfish
1 or 2 garlic cloves, mashed

1 cup heavy cream
1 cup olive oil

Soak codfish in water overnight. Drain and rinse well. Put fish in a saucepan, cover with fresh cold water, and bring to a boil. Remove from heat, drain fish, and bone and flake it. Put in a saucepan with mashed garlic. Over low heat, beat in alternately the heavy cream and olive oil, only a spoonful at a time, beating constantly until purée has the desired consistency. Less cream and oil makes a thicker, more spreadable paste; 1 cup each of cream and oil gives the consistency of thick cream, good for using as a dip. May also be puréed in a blender in small doses. Serve warm or room temperature, not chilled. Can be used as a sauce for boiled potatoes as well.

MAKES 5 or 6 cups.

FRENCH SALT FISH, MEDITERRANEAN STYLE

1½ lbs. salt cod
4 tbsps. butter
½ cup olive oil
3 onions, minced
3 garlic cloves, minced
3 tomatoes, peeled, seeded and
    chopped
2 cups red wine

3 tbsps. tomato paste
1 tsp. dried rosemary
1 bay leaf
½ cup pine nuts
¾ cup black olives, pitted
3 tbsps. capers
    flour
    salt and pepper

Soak codfish in water overnight. Drain, and cut into serving pieces. Heat three fourths of the butter and oil. In it, sauté the onions and garlic until soft but not browned. Add tomatoes, wine, tomato paste, rosemary and bay leaf; cook the mixture until reduced and thickened. Add pine nuts, olives, capers, and salt and pepper to taste. Simmer for 30 minutes. Remove the bay leaf. Roll fish in flour, shake off excess, and brown in mixture of remaining butter and olive oil. Arrange on a heated platter and pour on the sauce.
SERVES 6.

FRENCH WARM SALAD

1½ lbs. salt cod, freshened
12 small potatoes
¼ cup white wine
½ cup minced onion
3 or 4 shallots, minced
3 tbsps. minced parsley, chervil and
    chives, mixed

¼ cup white-wine vinegar
2 tbsps. olive oil
¼ garlic clove, mashed
1 tsp. Dijon-style mustard
    ground pepper

Cover fish with fresh cold water and bring just to a boil. Drain. Cover with fresh cold water and simmer over very low heat for 30 minutes. Cook potatoes in water to cover until half done. Add fish to potatoes and cook until potatoes are tender and fish somewhat broken. Skin and bone the fish; peel and slice potatoes. Put both in a large salad bowl; sprinkle with wine, minced onion and shallots and mixed herbs and toss. Make a dressing of the vinegar, oil, garlic, mustard and pepper to taste; mix lightly into the fish and potatoes.
SERVES 6.

HAITIAN MIX

½ lb. salt cod

Tear fish into strips and soak in cold water for 3 hours. Boil in the same water for 1 hour. Cook 2 cups rolled oats until done; keep warm. Boil 2 potatoes; peel and dice while still hot. To the oatmeal add hot diced potatoes; 1 (4-oz.) can of pimientos drained and cut into strips; 1 avocado, sliced; 1 garlic clove, mashed; and the fish. Mix well and serve with French dressing.
SERVES 6.

ITALIAN FISH STEW WITH HERBS

2 lbs. salt cod, freshened
½ cup chopped scallions
½ cup sliced mushrooms
¼ cup chopped fresh basil

¼ cup chopped parsley
½ cup olive oil
2 cups tomato purée
freshly ground black pepper

Drain cod. Remove bones and shred fish. Sauté the scallions, mushrooms, basil and parsley in oil until lightly browned. Add tomato purée and fish shreds and simmer, stirring occasionally, over low heat for 40 minutes. Season with freshly ground black pepper to taste. Serve with polenta or pasta.
SERVES 6.

NEW ENGLAND SALT FISH CHOWDER

½ lb. salt cod, freshened
4 onions, thinly sliced
3 potatoes, peeled and cubed
½ tbsp. butter

1 tbsp. chopped parsley
1 qt. milk
¼ tsp. pepper
salt

Flake the fish. Pour just enough boiling salted water over onion slices to barely cover. Simmer gently until half done, about 15 minutes. Add potatoes and enough boiling water to cover them. Cook for 10 minutes. Add the fish flakes and cook for 10 minutes longer. Add butter, parsley, milk and pepper and cook for 5 minutes. Add salt, if needed. Serve with plain crackers or lightly buttered soda crackers.

SERVES 8 to 10.

NEW ENGLAND SALTED FISH CAKES

1 lb. salt codfish, freshened
2 cups peeled and diced raw potatoes
1 egg, beaten

fresh ground black pepper
fat for frying

Drain fish and cut into coarse dice. Simmer potatoes and fish in water until tender. Drain thoroughly. Beat potato and fish mixture until light. Add egg and pepper to taste and beat together. Form into cakes. Fry on both sides in unflavored cooking oil until browned on both sides. For fish balls drop paste by spoonfuls into deep fat heated to 375° and fry until browned; drain well.

SERVES 6.

NEW ENGLAND CREAMED FISH

Strip salt cod into small pieces. Put in cold water and allow to come to a boil. Drain off water and add 2 cups or more of milk, according to the amount of fish used. Boil slowly for 15 minutes, then add 1 tbsp. butter and a dash of pepper. Thicken with enough flour blended with cold water to make a cream. Stir well and cook for 5 minutes longer. Add 1 well-beaten egg and serve.

NEW ENGLAND FRIZZLED FISH

2 cups shredded salt cod, freshened
3 tbsps. salt pork or bacon fat

1 small green pepper, minced
1 onion, thinly sliced

Squeeze the fish dry. Melt fat and cook fish in it for 5 minutes, stirring constantly. Add onion and pepper and cook for 5 to 10 minutes, stirring, until mixture is light golden in color.

SERVES 4.

NEW ENGLAND OLD-FASHIONED SALT COD DINNER

Strip salt cod into small pieces or flakes. Put into a saucepan with cold water to more than cover. Let come just to a boil; drain, cover again with cold water, and let come to a boil. Render finely diced pork fat in a skillet; serve with pan juice in a side bowl. Always served with boiled potatoes and boiled beets, sometimes with boiled onions as well.

SPANISH SALT FISH WITH HERBS

2 lbs. salt cod fillets, freshened
6 garlic cloves, chopped
3 large onions, chopped
⅔ cup olive oil
1 fennel bulb, including stems, minced
2 bay leaves, crushed
1 tsp. dry mustard

pinch of dried rosemary
pinch of dried thyme
½ cup capers
½ cup chopped black olives, pitted
½ cup red wine
2 cups tomato purée
½ cup pounded or ground walnuts

Sauté garlic and onions in oil until just soft but not browned. Add fennel, bay leaves, mustard, rosemary, thyme, capers, olives and wine. Simmer for 20 minutes. Add tomato purée and walnuts and cook for 5 minutes longer. Add drained fish and cook until fish is done.

SERVES 6.

SPANISH FRIED PUFFS

½ lb. dry salt cod
1½ cups flour
¾ tsp. salt
1 tsp. baking powder

1½ cups water
1 garlic clove
4 peppercorns
fat for deep frying

Wash cod and bring to a boil in water to cover. Drain and wash in cool water several times. Skin and bone. Shred fish and let stand in water for 1 hour. Combine flour, salt and baking powder. Stir in water to make a batter. Add garlic and peppercorns pounded together. Drain fish and add to batter. Drop by spoonfuls into deep fat heated to 390°. Use teaspoons for appetizers, tablespoons for main-course servings. Make doubles by dropping one on top of another, if desired. Fry until golden; drain.

MAKES 240 single appetizer puffs or
120 double appetizer puffs or
main course puffs, singles, for 16.

GLOUCESTER STYLE SALT FISH BALLS

2 cups flaked poached salt codfish
4 cups cold mashed potatoes
butter
salt and pepper

1 egg yolk, beaten
fine dry bread crumbs
fat for deep frying

Whip the fish flakes and potatoes together until smooth; season with butter and salt and pepper to taste. Add well-beaten yolk. Form into cakes, and roll in crumbs. Fry in deep fat heated to 375° until a rich brown.

MAKES 12 to 16 cakes.

NEW ENGLAND PINK HASH

Dice leftover salt cod, potatoes and beets from New England Old Fashioned Salt Fish Dinner together. Heat leftover pork fat scraps and grease. Press hash firmly together and fry in pork fat to a good brown on both sides.

ITALIAN FISH STEW WITH VEGETABLES

2 lbs. salt cod, poached
2 bunches of Swiss chard
¾ cup olive oil
2 large onions, chopped
8 leeks, including tender green part, thinly sliced

½ small head of cabbage, chunked
1½ cups dry white wine
1 (1-lb.) can Italian plum tomatoes, broken up
3 (8-oz.) cans tomato sauce
1 (14-oz.) can chicken broth

Skin and bone the poached cod and cut into serving pieces. Chop white and green parts of Swiss chard separately; measure 2 cups of the chopped green part and set aside. Make a sauce. Heat oil; add chopped Swiss chard (except reserved 2 cups), onions, leeks and cabbage. Cook over high heat, stirring frequently, until vegetables are soft. Blend in wine, tomatoes, tomato sauce and broth. Cover and simmer for 1½ to 2 hours, stirring occasionally. Add fish and simmer gently for 30 minutes to 1 hour, or until done. Immerse reserved Swiss chard greens in boiling salted water and cook for 5 minutes. Drain well and stir into fish mixture. Serve on polenta or rice.

SERVES 8 to 10.

Finnan haddie is smoked haddock, to be proper about it, although markets have gotten away with selling artificially colored smoked pollock as the real Scottish item. A proper finnan haddie has a gray-colored skin on one side and a strong smoky odor.

POACHED FINNAN HADDIE

The best way to prepare finnan haddie to prevent stringiness (to which it is subject) is to soak it in cold water for 30 minutes. Heat poaching water with 1 tbsp. sweet butter for 1½ cups of water. When the water is hot and the butter melted, add the drained fish and let it just heat through without boiling, about 10 to 12 minutes.

ENGLISH FISH SCRAMBLE

½ lb. finnan haddie
12 eggs
½ cup light cream

pepper
4 tbsps. butter

Put finnan haddie in a baking dish and broil flesh side up for about 10 minutes, or until fish begins to take on color. Turn off heat, cover fish with boiling water, and let stand in the oven for 15 to 20 minutes. Drain and break into small pieces. Beat eggs with cream and pepper to taste; stir in fish. Melt butter over low heat; cook fish and egg mixture for a minute or two, until it begins to set. Gently stir egg mixture until set but still soft.

SERVES 6.

FRENCH CREAMED FINNAN HADDIE

2 lbs. finnan haddie
6 tbsps. melted butter
1½ tbsps. flour

1 tsp. dry mustard
1½ cups milk
¾ cup bread crumbs

Steam fish over low heat for 15 minutes. Remove skin and cut into serving pieces. Put in a greased shallow baking pan. Heat 4 tbsps. butter; blend in flour and dry mustard. Slowly add milk and cook, stirring, until thickened. Pour over fish. Mix crumbs and remaining melted butter; sprinkle on top. Bake at 350° for 20 minutes.

SERVES 6.

FINNAN HADDIE SOUFFLÉ

¾ lb. finnan haddie
sweet butter
white pepper
½ cup milk

½ cup heavy cream
4 tbsps. sweet butter
½ cup flour
4 eggs, separated

Dry fish with paper towel. Dot a long narrow dish with butter and arrange fish on it. Sprinkle with pepper. Cover with milk, cream and several pats of butter. Bring just to a boil, reduce heat as low as possible, and barely simmer for 25 minutes. (Fine to eat right now!) Drain fish, reserving cooking liquid. Skin and bone fish, and mash with a fork. Melt the 4 tbsps. butter, blend in flour, and cook for 2 minutes without browning. Add about 1 cup of the cooking liquid to make a very thick sauce. Thoroughly mix in fish. Beat egg yolks and mix well into fish. Beat egg whites stiff and gently fold into fish mixture. Pour into a lightly buttered and warmed 6-cup soufflé dish. Bake at 350° for 20 to 25 minutes. Best served while still a bit creamy in the bottom, rather than highly puffed and dry at the bottom.

SERVES 4 to 6.

FINNAN HADDIE SCOTS STYLE

1½ lbs. finnan haddie	1 tbsp. cornstarch
2 tbsps. butter	1 cup milk
dash of pepper	

Skin the fish and cut into bite-sized pieces. Melt butter and add fish. Sprinkle with pepper. Cover tightly and cook very gently for 5 to 10 minutes. Blend cornstarch and milk and cook, stirring until thickened. Pour over fish; cover and simmer for 5 minutes. Serve with boiled or baked potatoes.

SERVES 4 to 6.

SCOTCH FLAN

1½ lbs. smoked fish, soaked if needed	2 egg yolks
1 cup milk, approximately	3 medium-size baking potatoes,
½ cup minced leek	boiled, peeled and riced
2 tbsps. butter	salt
2 tbsps. chopped parsley	6 tbsps. grated Gruyère cheese
pepper	1 baked pastry shell (8 or 9 inches)
1 cup medium white sauce	2 hard-cooked eggs, sliced

Put fish in a pan to fit, and pour in milk until fish is three fourths covered. Bring to a simmer, cover, and simmer gently for 8 to 10 minutes, or until fish flakes. Remove fish; strain milk and reserve 1 cup. Remove skin and bones from fish and flake; there should be about 2 cups fish. Sauté leek in butter until tender but not browned. Stir in fish and parsley. Season with pepper to taste. Keep warm while preparing the white sauce.

Beat egg yolks into hot riced potatoes; season with salt and pepper to taste and add 4 tbsps. of the cheese. Put leek and fish mixture into bottom of baked pastry shell. Arrange egg slices on top. Pour on the white sauce. Pipe the potato mixture decoratively onto the top. (If refrigerated, reheat at 375° for 20 to 30 minutes.) Sprinkle with remaining cheese. Brown under the broiler. SERVES 4.

SCOTTISH SMOKED FISH SOUP

1 lb. smoked haddock
1 medium-size onion, minced
2 cups boiling water
½ cup cold mashed potatoes

1 cup milk
salt and pepper
butter

Cover the fish and onion with the boiling water and simmer, covered, for 10 minutes. Remove from heat and, when cool enough to handle, remove bones and skin from the fish and return these to the broth. Cover and simmer this for 30 minutes. Flake the fish. Strain the broth and add mashed potatoes to it. Bring to a boil, stirring constantly, and stir in milk. Heat gently but thoroughly. Add fish and seasonings to taste. Serve with a small piece of butter floating on each serving. SERVES 4.

FINNAN HADDIE MOUSSE

1 lb. finnan haddie, poached and flaked
1 cup bottled clam broth
juice of ½ lemon
1 small onion, sliced

1 egg white, lightly beaten
1 envelope unflavored gelatin
2 tbsps. cold water
1 cup mayonnaise
1 cup heavy cream, whipped

Make easy aspic. Combine clam broth, lemon juice, onion and egg white. Simmer all together for 10 minutes. Let stand for 20 minutes and strain through cheesecloth to clarify. Sprinkle the gelatin over the cold water in a custard cup to soften. Set custard cup in simmering water and heat, stirring, until gelatin is thoroughly dissolved. Stir into clarified broth and pour a thin layer of the aspic into bottom of a 1-qt. soufflé dish or mold. Decorate as desired. Chill until firm. Chill remaining aspic but keep it still liquid. Mix flaked fish with mayonnaise and liquid aspic, then beat thoroughly. Fold in the whipped cream. Spoon onto the set layer of aspic in the mold. Chill until firm.

SERVES 8 to 10.

ENGLISH TOASTS

---

1 cup flaked poached finnan haddie
2 tbsps. butter
2 tbsps. flour
⅔ cup light cream

lemon juice
salt and pepper
toast points
buttered fresh bread crumbs

Melt butter; blend flour in smoothly. Cook for 2 or 3 minutes without browning. Add cream and cook, stirring constantly, until thickened. Mix in the flaked fish; add lemon juice and seasoning to taste. Spread mixture on toast points; top with buttered crumbs. Broil until hot and golden.

SERVES 6.

NEW ENGLAND NEWBURG

Warm bite-size pieces of poached finnan haddie in a rich Newburg sauce.

CHAPTER SIX

Coarse-Fleshed Fish

Moist Fish

A relatively small group of fishes with generally soft flesh have the additional characteristic of being coarse. As a result, virtually all of these fish can be used in the recipes found in the immediately preceding section. Yet there are a few that merit special mention.

Among the few firm-fleshed fish in this group that are—or at least have been—considered edible, is the tarpon, the silver king that makes a fly-fisherman's heart jump into his throat. The majority of anglers nowadays believe the tarpon has no food value, yet that is not the case.

In the records of the early days of tarpon fishing in Boca Grande Pass, Florida, there is mention that the tarpon roe "is excellent food" and that the flesh of the tarpon, when salted and dried as the New Englanders do with cod, provided "New England dinners in the subtropics."

It might be that its close resemblance to New England salt cod was so close that, when distribution of the cod broadened, there was no longer the interest in providing a local substitute.

There are some people who even yet eat tarpon; these are mainly the natives of the Keys. Far from using the whole fish, they cut out the section from halfway along the belly up at an angle to behind the dorsal fin, then down somewhat short of the back end of the anal fin. This gives them a good chunk of meat, which they will simmer or moist roast. The leftovers are excellent in a salad, as I can witness.

The smooth dogfish, the sand shark of the Atlantic Coast (*not* the so-called sand shark of the Pacific, which is a shovelnose shark) is a fish which surf-casters too often consider nothing but a nuisance. Many years ago, however, I learned on the beach from a fellow fisherman of Italian extraction that dogfish are not to be sneered at. A smooth dogfish about 18 to 20 inches long always went home with Del if he caught one. The flesh is white and somewhat resembles halibut. There is only one long bone which is easily removed; it is best to skin the fish and cut it into 1¼-inch steaks. These can be coated and fried, or take well to stewing slowly in a well-flavored stock or tomato-based liquid.

Oily Fish

Coarse oily fish seem to have the roe that is most prized; in this group are the shads and sturgeon. Sturgeon roe, of course, becomes the fine-grained, gray to black caviar that commands a premium price. Shad roe, too, commands a goodly price—in the market or on the menu as a main course. Roes, generally, however, are treated with in Chapter VIII. The flesh of these fishes—sailfish as well as shad and sturgeon—is excellent smoked, of course. The shad that is prized for eating, incidentally, is the American shad.

ENTRÉES

SUSQUEHANNA PLANKED SHAD

1 (4- to 5-lb.) shad, boned, with
    skin left on
1 tsp. salt

¼ tsp. pepper
melted butter

Lay shad skin side down on an oiled, preheated oak plank. Season flesh with salt and pepper; brush with melted butter. (Roes can be used, too; butter one side of each pair, sprinkle with salt, and lay them beside the shad.) Bake at 350° for 25 minutes. (If roes have been used, at this point turn them and brush with melted butter.)

If desired, at this point add 6 small tomatoes with tops removed and a slice cut from the bottoms so they will stand upright. Arrange around fish. Sprinkle tomatoes with salt and pepper and sugar. Combine 2 tablespoons soft butter with 1 tablepsoon prepared mustard and spread over the tomatoes. Sprinkle a little basil on the top. Duchess potatoes can then be piped around the fish and tomatoes. Put plank under the broiler for 10 minutes to finish.

SERVES 6.

INDONESIAN BAKED SHAD

1 (4-lb.) shad, split and boned
salt
pepper
2 garlic cloves, minced

½ cup melted butter
3 tbsps. lemon juice
¼ cup soya sauce
¼ tsp. ground dried chile pepper

Rub fish inside and out with mixed salt, pepper and garlic. Put fish in a buttered baking dish and bake at 375° for 10 minutes. Combine melted butter, lemon juice, soya sauce and chile pepper; mix well. Pour one third of this over fish. Bake fish for another 25 minutes, turning once and basting several times. Heat remaining sauce and pour over fish when serving.
    SERVES 6.

PORTUGUESE STURGEON STEAKS

6 individual sturgeon steaks
3 tbsps. butter
1 cup water
1 cup Madeira
1 bay leaf
3 parsley sprigs

1 dill pickle, thinly sliced
salt and pepper
1 tbsp. beurre manié
1 tbsp. minced capers
1 tbsp. shredded olives

Scald steaks by pouring boiling water over them. Drain and dry well. Melt the butter and add water and wine, bay leaf, parsley and half of the pickle. Bring to a boil and add the steaks with a good pinch of salt and pepper. Lower the heat, cover, and simmer for 15 minutes. Remove steaks, drain, and keep warm. Strain broth into saucepan and thicken by adding beurre manié slowly. Bring to a boil. Add capers and olives and remaining pickle. Pour sauce over the fish.
    SERVES 6.

POLISH STURGEON STEAKS

6 individual fresh sturgeon steaks
  flour
1 or 2 eggs, beaten
1 or 2 tbsps. milk
  fine dry bread crumbs
5 tbsps. butter

5 tbsps. oil
  salt and pepper
½ cup minced fresh dill
½ cup minced onion
½ cup minced parsley
1 to 1½ cups dairy sour cream

Dip steaks into flour, then into eggs and milk beaten together, then into dry crumbs. Heat butter and oil and gently sauté fish until browned and done. Season with salt and pepper to taste and arrange in a shallow baking dish. Mix dill, onion and parsley; sprinkle over fish. Cover with sour cream. Put under broiler flame or in 450° oven to brown lightly.
    SERVES 6.

RUSSIAN SALT-DRIED STURGEON

Put pieces of sturgeon in a tub, not touching. Cover with a thick layer of salt and a light sprinkle of saltpeter. After 9 to 12 days remove fish and soak in fresh water until all signs of salt disappear. Then dry completely in the sun. Remove to an airy, shady place until fish begins to develop a slight mold, showing it is cured (1 month to 6 weeks). Much like smoked salmon.

MIDWESTERN PADDLEFISH

This oddity left over from much earlier ages is delicious and a valuable food fish. Witness to this is that the roe is used commercially to make caviar; the flesh is often smoked and has been sold as sturgeon. It is technically boneless, since it has a single cartilage which should be removed. This is a fish which should be taken care of just as soon as it is beached: gut it, remove the head, and bleed it. To prepare it for cooking, skin it and remove the dark red meat along the vertical line. Some ways of preparing it are to butter and broil it, or to roll it in egg, then flour and fry. Chunks are smoked, and bite-sized pieces are pickled.

ITALIAN STUFFED SARDINES

fresh sardines, split from the back

Make a stuffing of equal parts of grated bread crumbs and Parmesan cheese, with chopped parsley and beaten egg to moisten. Stuff sardines; season with salt and pepper. Place in a greased shallow pan and fry lightly. Add barely enough water to cover bottom of pan. Cover and simmer for 10 minutes.

Dry Fish

The catfish family, which falls into the category of coarse dry-fleshed fish, is perhaps one of the largest, and has the broadest range from nil food value (as in the saltwater seacat) to popular fare in many freshwater areas. However, even here there's a broad spectrum of acceptance: if the cat has been scavenging—which is their feeding pattern—in an unpleasant muddy bottom, its flesh will reflect it.

APPETIZER

AUSTRIAN SPICED CARP

3 lbs. carp, boned and cut into bite-size pieces
2 cups vinegar
1 bay leaf
2 tbsps. pickling spices
2 onions, thinly sliced
1 lemon, thinly sliced

Steam fish until just tender, about 10 minutes. Scald vinegar with bay leaf and spices. Put fish in a shallow dish and cover with scalded vinegar. Arrange thin slices of onion and lemon over the top. Cover and refrigerate overnight, basting or turning.
Serves 12 to 18.

SOUPS

CENTRAL EUROPEAN FISH CHOWDER

3 lbs. tautog, skinned and cut into chunks
10 peppercorns
3 bay leaves
¼ lb. salt pork, sliced
2 medium-size onions, chopped

2 carrots, sliced
1 or 2 celery ribs, chopped
6 cups cubed raw potatoes
2 tbsps. minced parsley
salt and pepper
2 tbsps. beurre manié

Put fish, peppercorns and bay leaves in water almost to cover. Boil for about 10 minutes, or until flesh comes off the bones easily. Set aside to cool. Fry sliced salt pork slowly in a soup kettle. Add onions and cook for 5 minutes. Add carrots, celery, potatoes and boiling water to cover. Add parsley, and salt and pepper to taste. When potatoes are almost cooked, add boned fish and strained fish cooking liquid. Add beurre manié and blend in, stirring, until slightly thickened. Cook for about 5 minutes more.

SERVES 12.

EARLY AMERICAN CHOWDER

2 lbs. catfish
2 cups water
1 cup cream
large lump of butter

1 onion, sliced
1 tsp. prepared mustard
½ tsp. walnut catsup
salt and pepper

Wash catfish in warm water. Boil in water just to cover until flesh is tender and bones slip out easily. Remove larger bones and chop the fish. Mix fish with remaining ingredients in a kettle and stew slowly until quite thick. Season with salt and pepper to taste.

SERVES 4.

ENTRÉES

CENTRAL EUROPEAN FRIED FISH

2 (¾-lb.) catfish
1 qt. milk
1 tsp. seasoned salt
½ tsp. white pepper
¼ cup flour
½ tsp. salt
¼ tsp. black pepper

1 cup oil
½ cup margarine
1 tbsp. minced chives
1 lemon, cut into halves
½ cup sweet butter
1 tsp. minced parsley

Soak fish in milk with seasoned salt and white pepper for 24 hours. Drain and roll in flour mixed with salt and black pepper. Heat oil to 165°. Cook fish for 5 to 10 minutes, until browned. Pour oil from the pan; add margarine and chives. As fish are turned sprinkle with lemon juice. Simmer over low heat for 25 minutes. Drain off margarine. Melt the butter in the skillet, add parsley and sprinkle on the fish just before serving.

SERVES 2.

CREOLE FISH STEW

2 lbs. catfish, cut into bite-size pieces
2 onions, minced
1 green pepper, minced
6 celery ribs, minced
4 tbsps. bacon grease
1 14–16-oz. can tomatoes, chopped

2 (6-oz.) cans tomato paste
1 tomato can water
¼ lemon, thinly sliced
1 garlic clove, minced
1 tbsp. salt

Brown onions, green pepper and celery in bacon grease. Add tomatoes, tomato paste, water, lemon slices, garlic and salt. Stew very slowly for 2 hours. Add fish and cook without stirring for 20 minutes. Pour over cooked rice in deep bowls. (If rice is cooked in the stew, it's jambalaya.)

SERVES 4.

CHINESE BRAISED FISH

1 (3-lb.) gafftopsail catfish
1 tsp. salt
¼ cup oil
2 tsps. minced gingerroot
6 scallions, sliced
1 garlic clove, minced

1 tbsp. Chinese oyster sauce
2 tbsps. soya sauce
2 tsps. Tabasco
1 tsp. sugar
1 cup hot chicken stock
1 lb. bean curd

Rub fish with salt. Heat oil; stir in gingerroot, scallions, garlic, oyster sauce, soya sauce, Tabasco and sugar. Cook for 1 minute. Brown fish on both sides. Add stock, cover, and cook over low heat for 15 minutes, or until done. Cut bean curd into 1-inch squares and cook in boiling water for 15 minutes. Drain and arrange around cooked fish.

SERVES 4.

FRENCH FISH WITH HERBS

1 (4-lb.) carp, cut into 1-inch slices
½ cup chopped parsley
2 tbsps. chopped fresh chervil, or 1 tbsp. dried
1 tbsp. chopped garlic
1 tsp. dried thyme
1 bay leaf, crumbled

1 tsp. salt
¼ tsp. pepper
2 onions, minced
3 tbsps. olive oil
1 tbsp. flour
1 cup water
2 cups dry white wine

Put fish in a shallow dish. Cover with mixture of parsley, chervil, garlic, thyme, bay leaf, salt and pepper. Chill for several hours. Cook onions in oil until golden. Add flour and blend; cook for 3 to 4 minutes. Add water and wine and bring to a boil. Reduce heat, add fish, and cook over very low heat for about 45 minutes. Remove fish to a platter and keep warm. Sieve the sauce, or purée in a blender, and pour over the fish. Serve hot at once, or else cover and chill overnight and serve cold with highly seasoned mayonnaise.

SERVES 6 to 8.

CHINESE FRIED FISH

1 (3-lb.) carp, boned
3 tbsps. minced onion
1 tbsp. chopped gingerroot
1 tsp. soya sauce
½ tsp. salt

¼ tsp. pepper
1 tsp. sherry
½ cup cornstarch
fat for deep frying

Cut fish into serving pieces. Mix onion, gingerroot, soya sauce, salt, pepper and sherry; rub well into fish. Let stand for 30 minutes. Roll fish in cornstarch and let stand for 5 minutes. Fry in deep fat heated to 350° until done; don't let the pieces of fish touch while frying. Drain and cover with sweet and sour sauce.

SERVES 4.

CHINESE FISH TILES

2 lbs. carp, split along backbone line
¼ cup flour
6 tbsps. soya sauce
1 tbsp. sherry
    oil
1 tbsp. minced scallion

1 tsp. minced gingerroot
1 garlic clove, minced
½ tsp. sugar
½ cup vinegar
½ cup water
2 tbsps. cornstarch

Cut carp into 2-inch tile sections. Mix flour, 2 tablespoons soya sauce and sherry into a paste. Spread on tiles and let stand for 10 minutes. Heat oil in a skillet. Add tiles carefully so they do not touch. Fry until browned, 5 minutes on one side, 3 minutes on the other. Drain and keep warm. Pour off all but 2 tablespoons oil. Add scallion, gingerroot and garlic. Stir a few times; do not let brown. Add sugar, vinegar, remaining soya and the water. Cook stirring until sugar is dissolved. Mix cornstarch with an equal amount of water and stir into sauce. Cook until thickened and clear, stirring. Return tiles to pan and coat with sauce. Do not overcook.

SERVES 4.

CENTRAL EUROPEAN POTTED FISH

4 carp fillets
4 carrots, peeled and sliced thin
8 gingersnaps
½ cup sherry

flour
butter
salt and pepper

Cook carrots gently in as little boiling water as possible until just tender. Soak gingersnaps in sherry. Dredge fillets lightly with flour. Butter a skillet. Arrange carp fillets in skillet; season. Add the carrots and cooking water, gingersnaps and sherry. Cover tightly; bring to a boil. Lower heat and simmer gently for 15 to 20 minutes, or until tender.

SERVES 4.

HUNGARIAN FISH AND VEGETABLES

6 carp steaks
1 cup oil
2 carrots, sliced
2 medium-size potatoes, diced
2 onions, chopped
2 tomatoes, chopped
½ small eggplant, peeled and diced
1 green pepper, thinly sliced
½ lb. okra, sliced

½ lb. fresh peas
¼ lb. fresh green beans
1 cup shredded cabbage
2 garlic cloves, minced
1 bay leaf
⅛ tsp. dried thyme
1 tbsp. salt
½ tbsp. pepper

Bring oil to a boil in a deep baking dish. Combine vegetables, garlic and seasonings and add to oil. Bake at 350° for 30 minutes. Place fish slices on top and bake for 30 more minutes, or until done.

SERVES 6.

HUNGARIAN FISH

1 (4- to 5-lb.) carp
  salt pork for larding
  dash of salt
1 tbsp. paprika
3 medium-size tomatoes, sliced

2 or 3 parsnips, sliced
1 onion, sliced
1 cup melted butter
1 cup sour cream

Cut larding salt pork into thin strips and lard the back of the fish. Put fish in a buttered baking dish. Sprinkle with salt and paprika. Arrange vegetables on top. Sprinkle with melted butter and spread on sour cream. Bake at 350° basting frequently, until tender, about 45 minutes.

SERVES 6 to 8.

POLISH STUFFED CARP

1 (3- to 4-lb.) male carp, with milt
  and liver
2 truffles
4 to 6 mushrooms
1 tbsp. minced parsley

salt and pepper
1 tbsp. butter
2 eggs, separated
1 hard roll, moistened in milk

Soak fish in cold water overnight. Chop milt, liver, truffles, mushrooms and parsley together. Season. Cream butter with egg yolks and add the roll, chopped. Add milt mix and blend thoroughly. Fold in beaten egg whites. Stuff fish with mixture; close. Roll fish in buttered parchment paper. Bake in 400° oven for about 40 to 50 minutes, basting frequently.

SERVES 6 to 8.

POLISH FISH AND RED CABBAGE

3 lbs. drum, cut into serving pieces
1 head of red cabbage, shredded
1 onion, minced
1 tbsp. butter
½ tbsp. flour

1 cup red wine
  salt and pepper
  juice of ½ lemon
1 tsp. sugar

Blanch the fish in boiling water. Drain. Blanch the cabbage in boiling water and drain. Brown the onion in butter. Add flour and blend. Slowly stir in the wine. Season cabbage and sprinkle with lemon juice. Add cabbage to wine, add sugar. Cover tightly and steam until almost done, about 30 minutes. Add fish and cover with cabbage. Cover and steam for 30 minutes longer.

SERVES 6.

MIDWESTERN FRIED FISH

1 (2-lb.) gar, filleted and cut into halves

Sprinkle fillets with salt and let stand for 10 minutes. Rinse and dry. Roll in seasoned flour; dip into 1 egg beaten with 1 tbsp. water, then into dry bread crumbs. Fry in butter until brown.

SERVES 4.

COOKED AND LEFTOVER FISH

CANADIAN FISH SCRAPPLE

½ cup flaked cooked carp
1 cup cornmeal
1 tbsp. flour
1 tsp. salt

¼ tsp. pepper
1 cup cold water
3 cups boiling water

Mix cornmeal, flour, salt and pepper with cold water. Add in a slow stream to boiling water in top of a double boiler, stirring constantly. Cover and cook over high steam for 2½ hours, stirring frequently. Add fish and cook for 30 minutes. Pour into a buttered bread tin (9 x 5 x 3 inches). Cover with wax paper, cool, and chill. Slice and fry in butter.

SERVES 10 to 12.

ENGLISH DEVILED FISH

4 cups flaked cooked black drum
2 cups medium-thick white sauce
2 tsps. Worcestershire sauce
2 tbsps. minced parsley
1 tbsp. grated onion

½ tbsp. salt
1 tsp. curry powder
¼ tsp. paprika
½ cup buttered crumbs

Combine all ingredients except crumbs, blending with a fork. Turn into a buttered baking dish and top with crumbs. Bake at 400° for 30 minutes.

SERVES 4.

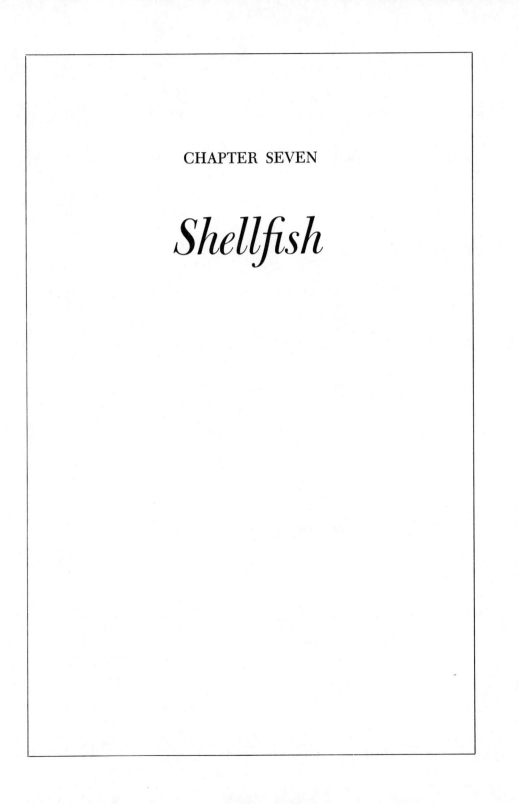

CHAPTER SEVEN

Shellfish

Shellfish, for our purposes, divide mainly into two categories: bivalves, those creatures enclosed by two shells, and crustaceans, those that live in a shell and are equipped with legs or claws that make them mobile. Keep in mind that practically all of these are protected in one way or another—permits, seasons, limits—which is perhaps just as well. When you stay legal and apply for a permit, you'll be *told* if the waters are clean, and that's important, particularly with bivalves that "bed." Most bivalves are taken by raking, with the tines of the fork spaced so as to leave the undersized ones undisturbed. Also, don't forget that any mollusk may raise a "pearl." It's nothing more than a concretion formed over an irritation . . . but gem pearls come only from tropical pearl oysters.

There are several exceptions to the categories given above. Two are considered delicious by the few people who have tried them, mostly residents along the coast of Maine.

The periwinkle is a freshwater or littoral snail, which can be eaten raw or cooked. (The escargot, of which the French are so fond, is a land snail.) A bent pin or wire makes a good tool to pull the soft meat out of the periwinkle shell. Do not eat the tough outer seal. These can be served raw with cocktail sauce, oil and vinegar, or just plain lemon juice. To cook them, cover with fresh water and add ½ cup of salt per quart of water. Bring to a boil and cook until the outer seal loosens and the "winkle," as the meat itself is called, protrudes; about 20 minutes. Drain and serve either in or out of the shell, either hot with garlic butter dotted on or cold, as above.

Sea urchins, which most people avoid because of the discomfort involved in close association, are another source of food known to Maine coasters. Perhaps they got the idea from the Orient or Mediterranean, where they have been eaten for many years. At any rate, here's the trick to getting to the meat: use a heavy glove; hold the urchin upside down (the white center up) and with small scissors or sturdy knife cut a large hole in the top; empty the shell of loose contents. To eat raw, pick out the meat and orange coral with a small seafood fork and dip into fresh lemon juice. The Maine way of cooking them is to boil them, unopened, in a large pan of water for 3 minutes. They are then opened and cleaned as the raw ones are. Some other uses are to add the sieved cooked meat to fish sauces, or to add a purée of the raw meat to mayonnaise or seafood bisques.

Two other exceptions to the main categories are considerably larger than periwinkles or urchins, but need even more special attention before eating. One is the conch, the spirally horned shell that hides a solid mass of meat; this creature has given its name to Keys natives. The trick to getting the conch out of his shell is to break into his house by driving a nail through the largest of the "horns" that stick out *below* the tip of the shell. This breaks the creature's grip on the shell and it can be drawn out. At this point, trim off the colored edges and the tough muscle and discard them. Unless the meat is to be cut into a dice, at this point it is wise to pound it well with something like a potato masher to tenderize it. With larger specimens, pound it after cutting into steaklike slices.

The West Coast abalone is another single-shelled saltwater creature that requires special techniques. Where the conch can be picked up with no difficulty, the abalone requires an iron to pry it loose from its home rock. Abalones can be kept alive for a day or two, incidentally, if they are kept in a sea-soaked burlap sack in a cool, damp place.

After the abalone has been allowed to rest and relax overnight, it is ready for removal, but it still needs that iron. Pull the foot back so that you can force the iron between the shell and the upper portion of the meat, moving the wedge to free the muscle. (The outside of the foot, which logically is called the sole, is the part that clings to the rock. The front of the abalone is where you see the respiratory holes; the other end is the heel.) Grasping the foot firmly, carefully pull it from the heel of the shell, leaving the viscera attached to the shell. Wash the meat in cold water.

To continue, trim the lacy dark portions from the edge of the foot and about ¼ inch off the sole. These trimmings can be saved (or frozen) for future use separately. Let the muscle stand until it relaxes, then, holding it firmly so that it doesn't slide, slice the meat across the grain into about ⅜-inch slices. Using light strokes, pound the slices with the smooth end of a mallet until the meat is limp and velvety, a state which has been compared to a limp pancake. Finally, you are ready to cook or freeze it. (You may be able to buy some already frozen: it is now beginning to get distribution in other parts of the country.)

Bivalves

Along our lengthy national coastline there are several varieties of clams and oysters. The Northeast has two clams, the "soft-shell," which is gently steamed or crisply batter-fried, and the "hard-shell" quahog or round clam (which may be called littlenecks, cherrystones or chowders, as well), which may be eaten raw or cooked, perhaps in New England chowders. On the West Coast the Pismo clam, which is cooked much as the eastern hard-shells are, is generally large, providing much good meat except during the mussel quarantine period, May through October, when the dark stomach must be avoided. With this exception, all of a clam is edible in varying degrees of tenderness. Some people go to great lengths to separate the clam into its various parts for various dishes.

The oyster, the rough-shelled cousin of the clam, is also edible in all his interior parts. These bivalves are in greater variety on the West Coast, primarily because there were practically no native oysters years ago. The variety ranges from the small (to 3 inches) Olympia, which is sometimes called native, to the giant Pacific, which will reach 10 inches in length, while the eastern oyster is lucky to reach 6 inches. This variety is the result of planting seed oysters from both the East Coast and Japan in response to the demand of the gold rush days.

There are two other "oysters," widely separated in habitat and probably not related. One is found clinging in a cluster to the wet roots of the Keys mangrove. The mangrove oyster is very small—the shell is no bigger than the end of your little finger—and the morsel proportionally minute. Those who know about them (and it's good to keep in mind if you have a motor breakdown in the back country) chop off the clustered root-leg and steam the oysters open over a fire, turning the limb over the heat and picking out the meat as each shell opens. The Oregon rock "oyster," on the other hand, has no shell at all. These live in rock hives which have to be broken open at low tide. These are used much like the eastern hard-shell.

Mussels, which are much more popular in Europe than here, are too often overlooked. Perhaps it's the beard which must be scrubbed off before cooking that repels people. It's really too bad because they are missing a treat. The edible mussel (the blue) has toothlike crenelations on the interior of the hinge line which the inedible horse mussel does not. The blue mussel has a somewhat pearly-white interior color bordered in deep blue purple as against the chalky, mauve-white shell lining of the horse mussel.

When it comes to opening bivalves, the oyster is most difficult and it is recommended that the amateur use heavy gloves to avoid some of the discomfort of handling the rough shell. Clams are next down the ladder, followed by mussels and scallops.

There is no reason why one bivalve may not be substituted for another, nor one crustacean for another. Also, inlanders should keep in mind that there are freshwater versions that, although they do not have the saltwater tang, are just as good to eat.

Follow the holding and flushing directions on page 18 and the cleaning and opening suggestions on page 25 for all bivalves. To steam any bivalve, for any of the following recipes, put them on a rack over shallow sea water or in 1 qt. fresh water seasoned with 1 tbsp. salt in a deep heavy kettle if you do not have a special clam steamer. Cover and bring the liquid to a boil. Start checking them after 5 minutes, removing the bivalves as they open. Mussels will start opening in a short time, while some clams may take as much as 20 minutes.

APPETIZERS

KEYS CONCH CEVICHE

1 conch, cut into narrow, short strips
1 small green pepper, diced
1 very small hot red pepper, diced

Keys Old Sour or Key lime juice
salt

Mix conch with peppers. Moisten with Keys Old Sour to taste. Salt to taste if using lime juice. Chill well.
SERVES 4 to 6.

KEYS CONCH DIP

1 cup ground conch
8 oz. whipped cream cheese
1 tbsp. milk
2 tsps. Key lime juice

½ tsp. Worcestershire sauce
1 garlic clove, crushed
2 dashes of hot-pepper sherry
salt and pepper

Mash cream cheese with the milk until smooth. Blend in the conch and remaining ingredients and mix well. Chill.
MAKES 1½ cups.

ITALIAN FISHERMAN'S CLAMS

Scrub small clams and place in a heavy kettle. Cover and place over fairly high heat. As they start to open, remove lid and sprinkle on chopped parsley and garlic to taste. Serve with the strained broth as a dip.

GREEK STUFFED CLAMS

48 clams
½ cup olive oil
1½ cups raw short-grain rice
2 medium-size onions, minced
½ cup pine nuts

½ cup tomato sauce
½ tsp. dried dillweed
½ tsp. ground allspice
⅓ cup dried currants

Open clams, saving the broth. Reserve the lower shells, and clean them. Heat oil; add rice, onions and pine nuts. Sauté, stirring, until nuts turn golden. Remove from heat. Measure clam juice and add water to make 1½ cups; pour over rice mixture. Add tomato sauce, dillweed, allspice and currants. Cover and let stand for 30 minutes. Bring to a boil, reduce heat to very low, and simmer for 12 minutes. Remove from heat and let stand for 10 minutes. Add clams and stir lightly with a fork. Let cool slightly. Spoon into the cleaned shells and chill. Can also be frozen, if well wrapped.

SERVES 8 or more.

CENTRAL AMERICAN CLAMS

12 clams, minced
1 green pepper, minced
1 onion, minced

2 tomatoes, peeled and minced
2 tsps. Worcestershire sauce

Mix all well and chill. Serve as a dip or spread on toast fingers.

SERVES 6 or more.

ITALIAN MUSSELS WITH WHITE WINE

1 lb. mussels

Put enough oil in a steamer to cover the bottom of the pan. Add 1 garlic clove, sliced. Steam the mussels until they open. Remove them from the pan. Strain the broth in the pan through a sieve lined with muslin or a double layer of cheesecloth. Add to the broth ¾ cup dry white wine, 1 or 2 garlic cloves, chopped, and a handful of chopped parsley. Cook to reduce and thicken. Remove the top shell from the mussels. Pour sauce over and chill for several hours. Another way to serve these is to place mussels on strips of fried Italian bread and spread with the sauce.

SERVES 4 to 6.

MEXICAN MUSSELS

2 to 3 lbs. mussels, steamed open
1 cup minced sweet red pepper
⅓ cup minced red onion
6 tbsps. corn oil

3 tbsps. lemon juice
1 tsp. salt
1 tsp. fresh black pepper

Blend all ingredients except mussels and spoon over mussels. Chill for several hours.

SERVES 10 to 12.

ITALIAN MUSSELS WITH OIL AND TOMATO

5 lbs. mussels
2 garlic cloves
6 to 8 peppercorns
¼ cup water
2 tbsps. white-wine vinegar

¾ cup olive oil
¼ cup tomato paste
3 whole cloves, crushed
   salt and pepper

Put mussels in a pan with garlic, peppercorns and water. Cover and steam until shells open, about 10 minutes. Blend together vinegar, oil, tomato paste, crushed whole cloves and salt and pepper to taste. Shell the mussels and combine with vinegar and oil mixture. Marinate, chilled, for several hours.

SERVES 6 to 8.

FRENCH BROILED MUSSELS

mussels on the half shell

Top mussels with minced parsley and sprinkle on some minced garlic. Top with soft bread crumbs moistened with melted butter. Dot with a little additional butter and broil until browned.

MEXICAN SCALLOPS

3½ lbs. shucked sea scallops, cut small
    Mexican or Key lime juice
2 large red onions, minced
1 (4-oz.) can of chopped peeled green chiles
3 garlic cloves, minced
2 tbsps. chopped fresh coriander or basil
⅓ cup olive oil
2 tsps. sugar
¼ tsp. Tabasco
1 tsp. salt
¼ tsp. pepper

Put scallops in a deep bowl and add enough lime juice to cover them. Cover the bowl and refrigerate for 3 hours. Drain thoroughly. Mix remaining ingredients. Add scallops and toss well. Chill.

SERVES 12 or more.

ENGLISH GRILLED OYSTERS

6 oysters per serving, on the half shell

Melt 2 tbsps. butter with 1 tsp. Worcestershire sauce. Put 1 tsp. of this on each oyster; season with salt and pepper. Put under the broiler until the edges begin to curl. Serve with lemon wedges.

OYSTERS ROCKEFELLER FROM THE GULF

36 oysters
6 tbsps. butter
6 tbsps. minced raw spinach
3 tbsps. minced onion
3 tbsps. minced parsley
3 tbsps. minced celery

5 tbsps. bread crumbs
6 drops of Tabasco
1 tbsp. Pernod or anise-flavored
   liqueur
½ tsp. salt

Shuck and drain oysters, leaving each one in the lower shell. Melt butter, and add all the remainder except oysters. Cook, stirring constantly, for 15 minutes, or until soft. Press through a food mill or sieve. Cool. Put rock salt on pie tins; arrange oysters on the half shell on top of the rock salt. Top each oyster with a spoonful of the sauce. Broil under medium heat until the sauce begins to brown. Leave on the rock salt bed to serve.

SERVES 6 or more.

HAITIAN PICKLED OYSTERS

36 oysters, minced
2 cups vinegar
12 small white onions, peeled
3 chile peppers, minced, or ¾ tsp.
   dried ground chile pepper

2 tsps. salt
6 peppercorns

Combine vinegar, onions, chiles, salt and peppercorns in a large glass jar with a tight lid. Put oysters in a bowl and pour on boiling water. Let stand for 3 minutes and drain well. Add oysters to jar. Tighten cover and turn upside down several times. Refrigerate for at least 3 days.

SERVES 6 or more.

GERMAN OYSTER ROUNDS

chilled shucked oysters

Sauté 1½-inch rounds of thin-sliced white bread in melted butter, and drain. Spread melted butter thinly on toast rounds. Place an oyster on each toast, and circle caviar, red or black, around the oysters. Chill well.

FRENCH PICKLED OYSTERS

36 oysters

Marinade:

1½ cups dry white wine
1 cup water
2 tbsps. olive oil
2 tbsps. tarragon-flavored white vinegar
1 onion, minced

1 carrot, minced
4 parsley sprigs, minced
2 garlic cloves, minced
¼ tsp. dried thyme
1 tsp. salt
¼ tsp. pepper

Shuck oysters, saving all the juices. Bring marinade ingredients to a boil and simmer for 1 hour. Strain into another pan and add the oysters and their juices; bring to a boil. Remove immediately from the heat and allow to cool in the marinade. Chill. Serve with enough marinade to moisten.

SERVES 6 or more.

ENGLISH MARINATED OYSTERS

24 oysters
2 tbsps. grated fresh horseradish
4 tbsps. lemon juice
1 tsp. Worcestershire sauce

¼ tsp. salt
¼ tsp. paprika
2 to 4 tbsps. butter

Shuck and drain oysters. Mix remaining ingredients except butter to make a marinade and pour over the oysters. Marinate for several hours. Drain. Melt butter; add oysters and cook, stirring, until edges begin to curl. Serve with reserved marinade on the side.

SERVES 4.

ENGLISH OYSTERS, SKEWERED OR BATTER-FRIED

large oysters, shucked

Wrap each oyster in a thin slice of half-cooked bacon and skewer. Bake in a 350° oven until bacon is done.

Or make a batter; mix 1 cup sifted flour, ⅛ tsp. salt and 1 tsp. baking powder, blend well. Gradually add 1½ cups milk and 1 well-beaten egg. Dip oysters into batter and quickly deep-fry. Serve on food picks or on toast.

SOUPS

WEST COAST ABALONE CREAM SOUP

2 cups abalone trimmings	¼ tsp. dried thyme
1 tbsp. butter	1 medium-size tomato, peeled,
1 tbsp. chopped green pepper	seeded and chopped
⅓ cup chopped scallions, including	½ tbsp. lemon juice
some green part	½ cup heavy cream
½ cup diced celery	¼ tsp. salt
3½ cups chicken broth	2 egg yolks, slightly beaten

Melt butter until bubbly; add green pepper, scallions and celery and sauté until just tender, about 8 minutes. Add broth, thyme and tomato. Cover and simmer for 15 minutes. Rinse abalone trimmings well, scraping off as much black film as possible. Put twice through a food chopper with a fine blade, saving juices. Whirl the soup in a blender a bit at a time, or purée through a sieve. Return soup to pan and add ground abalone and juices. Cover and simmer for 15 minutes. Strain and discard solids. Return soup to pan; add lemon juice, cream and salt. Blend about 1 cup of this mixture with egg yolks, then return to soup. Stir over low heat without boiling for 2 minutes.
SERVES 4 or 5.

NEW ENGLAND CLAM BROTH

24 hard clams, in the shell
2 cups cold water

Put clams in a deep kettle with the water and bring slowly to a boil. Cook gently, covered, for 10 to 20 minutes, until clams open. Strain the broth and serve hot. Can be topped with a spoonful of whipped cream, dusted with paprika.
SERVES 4.

For a beverage, chill the broth and add, to taste, lemon juice, Tabasco, salt and freshly ground pepper. Shake well and pour.

SEASONED CLAM BROTH

3 cups New England Clam Broth
3 tbsps. lemon juice
2 tbsps. ketchup

½ tsp. grated onion
few drops of Tabasco
salt and pepper

Mix broth with lemon juice, ketchup and onion. Add Tabasco, or more to taste, and salt and pepper to taste. Mix thoroughly and chill. Strain before serving.
SERVES 4 or 5.

CLAM BROTH MUSH

Heat 3 cups clam broth; while scalding hot, add 1 tsp. gelatin softened in 1 tsp. cold water. Stir until dissolved. Cool, then freeze to mushy stage, stirring 2 or 3 times during freezing. Serve as a chilled soup.
SERVES 3 or 4.

GULF COQUINA BROTH

Coquinas are small marine clams of the genus *Donax,* found by sieving sand at water's edge. Wash clams in cold fresh water, then place in a kettle of hot salted water (3 tbsps. salt to 1 qt. water) just to cover. When water comes to a boil remove from the heat and strain out shells. Allow meat to go through strainer, or pick out and return to broth. Precooked potato and onions can be added and heated to make a chowder. Some of the potato could be mashed and added to make a thicker stew.

NEW ENGLAND JELLIED CLAM BOUILLON

2 cups New England Clam Broth
1 envelope unflavored gelatin
2 tbsps. cold water
⅓ cup pale dry sherry

dash of cayenne
dash of grated nutmeg
salt and pepper
lemon wedges

Heat 1 cup of the clam broth. Soften gelatin in cold water. Add softened gelatin to hot clam broth, stirring until gelatin is dissolved. Stir in remaining cold clam broth, wine and seasonings. Pour into a shallow dish and chill until set, about 2 hours. Cut into small cubes and serve in chilled bowls with lemon wedges.
   SERVES 6.

FRENCH CLAM SOUP

80 littleneck clams, small as possible
 4 tbsps. butter
 1 large onion, minced
 4 shallots, minced
 1 garlic clove, minced
 1 tsp. minced fresh thyme
 1 tbsp. minced fresh tarragon

2 tbsps. flour
1 bottle dry white wine
2 cups heavy cream
2 egg yolks
 salt and pepper
 Tabasco

Scrub the clams. Heat butter and simmer the onion, shallots and garlic, stirring, until onion is wilted. Sprinkle with thyme, tarragon and flour. Add the wine, stirring constantly. Simmer for 5 minutes and add clams. Cover and cook, shaking pan occasionally, until clams open, 5 to 10 minutes. Add half of the cream to the kettle and stir in. Blend remaining cream with the egg yolks and stir into soup. Cook over low heat almost to the boiling point, but do not let boil. Season to taste with salt, pepper and Tabasco.

SERVES 8.

JAPANESE CLAM SOUP

24 clams
4 cups dashi, or 2 cups chicken broth
    and 2 cups clam juice
2 tbsps. soya sauce

2 tsps. minced parsley
1 tbsp. sake or sherry
3 tbsps. minced onion

Scrub the clams. Mix *dashi* with soya sauce, parsley and sake. Bring to a boil and add clams and onion. Cook over medium heat until clams open.

SERVES 4.

KOREAN CLAM SOUP

36 clams
½ lb. beef, cut into thin slices
2 tbsps. sesame oil
2 tbsps. ground sesame seeds

1 garlic clove, minced
3 tbsps. soya sauce
5 cups water
¼ tsp. dried ground chile pepper

Scrub the clams. Brown beef in the oil. Add sesame seeds, garlic, soya sauce, water and chile pepper. Bring to a boil and cook, covered, over low heat for 30 minutes. Add the clams and steam open with the kettle covered.

SERVES 6.

ITALIAN CLAM SOUP

40 littleneck clams, small as possible
⅓ cup olive oil
½ cup minced onion
4 garlic cloves, minced
8 flat anchovy fillets, minced
6 basil leaves
3 tbsps. minced parsley
1 tsp. dried orégano

1 tsp. crushed fennel seeds
1 tsp. ground saffron
1 (6-oz.) can tomato paste
½ cup chopped peeled plum tomato
½ cup dry white wine
2 cups water
   salt and pepper

Scrub the clams. Heat oil and add onion and garlic. Cook, stirring, until onion is wilted. Add anchovies and herbs. Cook, stirring, for 5 minutes. Add tomato paste, chopped tomato, wine and water; stir well to blend. Simmer, covered, for 5 minutes. Add clams. Cover, and cook, shaking kettle occasionally, until clams open, 5 to 10 minutes. Season to taste.
   SERVES 4.

NEW ENGLAND CLAM CHOWDER

36 chowder clams
2 oz. salt pork, diced
1½ cups sliced onions
6 cups diced raw potatoes
½ tbsp. salt

¾ tsp. white pepper
2 cups light cream, scalded
4 cups milk, scalded
2 tbsps. butter

Shuck the clams and reserve the juice. Mince or grind the hard part of the clams; coarsely chop the soft parts. Render salt pork until golden. Remove pork and reserve the bits. Drain off all but ⅓ cup of the fat. Add the onions and sauté for 5 minutes, not allowing them to brown. Add potatoes, salt, pepper, and clam liquor with enough water to make 6 cups. Bring to a boil, reduce heat, cover, and simmer for 15 minutes, or until potatoes are tender. Add clams, cream and milk./Reheat without boiling. Swirl in butter. Top servings with reserved salt pork bits.
   SERVES 12.

MANHATTAN CLAM CHOWDER

24 hard-shelled clams
2 oz. salt pork, diced
½ cup chopped onion
½ cup chopped green pepper
¼ cup chopped celery
½ cup thinly sliced leeks
½ cup diced carrot

3 cups diced potatoes
6 cups water
1 bay leaf, crumbled
  salt and pepper
1 cup canned tomatoes
½ tbsp. dried thyme
¼ cup chopped parsley

Shuck the clams and reserve the juice. Mince or grind hard part of the clams; chop the soft part coarsely. Render salt pork until golden. Pour off all but 2 tbsps. of the fat. Add onion, green pepper, garlic, celery and leeks and sauté until golden. Add carrot, potatoes, water, bay leaf, and salt and pepper to taste. Add hard part of clams, with clam juice, and simmer, covered, over low heat for 30 minutes. Add soft part of the clams, tomatoes and thyme. Simmer for 10 minutes. Sprinkle with parsley.

Serves 8 to 10.

IRISH COCKLE OR CLAM SOUP

8 cockles or clams
1 onion, chopped
2 celery ribs, chopped
3 tbsps. butter
2 cups milk

3 tbsps. cornstarch
  salt and pepper
  small pat of butter
  minced parsley

Cook onion and celery in 3 tbsps. butter, covered, for about 10 minutes. Add clams and boiling water to almost cover. Cook, covered, until clams open. Remove clams from shells, transfer them to a tureen, and keep warm. Cook strained broth over high heat until reduced to about 2 cups. Stir in milk and bring to the boiling point. Make a smooth paste of the cornstarch with a bit of cold milk and stir into the soup. Cook over low heat, stirring frequently, for about 10 minutes. Season to taste, and add to clams in the tureen. Melt butter pat on top and sprinkle with parsley.

Serves 6.

BAHAMA CONCH SOUP

4 conch, scalded
4 potatoes, peeled
2 qts. water
¼ lb. salt pork, diced

1 large onion, chopped
1 sweet pepper, chopped
2 cups peeled and chopped tomatoes
1 tbsp. flour

Grind conch and potatoes in a food chopper with a coarse blade. Add the water and boil. In another pan try out salt pork; add onion and pepper and cook until softened. Add tomatoes and sprinkle on the flour. When well blended, add to conch and cook for about 1 hour, until conch is done and the soup is thickened. Top each serving with pat of butter.

SERVES 8 to 10.

CARIBBEAN CONCH CHOWDER

8 large conch
¼ lb. salt pork, diced
3 lbs. white potatoes, peeled
2 medium-size onions, chopped
4 garlic cloves
1 large green pepper, chopped
1 (20-oz.) can tomatoes
1 (6-oz.) can tomato paste

10 bay leaves
2 tbsps. barbecue sauce
1 tsp. poultry seasoning
1 tbsp. dried orégano
2 qts. hot water
1 tbsp. white vinegar
salt and pepper

Grind the conch through a food grinder with a coarse blade. Try out salt pork; add potatoes, onions, garlic and green pepper and cook to soften. Add tomatoes, tomato paste and seasonings. Cook slowly until well blended. Cook conch in hot water with the vinegar. When liquid starts to boil add the other ingredients. Cook slowly, covered, for at least 1 hour. (If potatoes are small and will cook too quickly, add after chowder has cooked for a while.)

SERVES 10 to 12.

KEYS CONCH CHOWDER

6 conch
6 qts. water
½ cup Key lime juice
3 tbsps. salt
2 cups chopped green peppers
1 cup chopped onions
2 cups chopped celery

2 cups chopped parsley
6 garlic cloves, minced
½ tsp. crushed red pepper
½ tsp. dried thyme
1 cup olive oil
1½ cups raw rice

Dice conch and combine with the water, lime juice and salt. Bring to a boil, cover, reduce heat, and simmer for 30 minutes. Sauté green peppers, onions, celery, 1 cup parsley, the garlic, red pepper and thyme in the oil until tender. Add to conch. Simmer for 1 hour. Add rice and simmer for 30 minutes more. Add remaining 1 cup parsley.

MAKES 8 quarts.

KEYS CONCH SOUP

1 lb. conch steak
2 tbsps. salt
1 cup raw barley

¼ lb. salt pork, diced
2 large onions, chopped
1 sweet pepper, chopped

Pound conch steak, salt heavily, and let stand for 15 minutes. Cook barley in water according to directions. Drain and rinse conch and put through a food chopper with a coarse blade. Try out the salt pork. Add onions and pepper and cook until barely softened but not browned. Add the conch; stir to coat well. Add the barley and barley cooking water. Cover and cook, adding water as necessary, until conch is done.

SERVES 4 to 6.

MUSSEL BROTH

1½ lbs. small mussels
1 cup water
1 large onion, chopped

1 garlic clove, crushed
2 bay leaves

Put all into a kettle; cover and steam until mussels open. Strain liquid through a fine cloth twice. Reserve mussels for another use. Serve broth hot; reheat if necessary.

SERVES 6.

IRISH MUSSEL SOUP

3 lbs. mussels
1 onion, chopped
1 parsley sprig, chopped
½ cup cider
4 tbsps. butter
2 leeks, minced

1 celery rib, minced
½ cup flour
4 cups milk, scalded
½ tsp. grated nutmeg
  salt and pepper
2 tbsps. cream

Put mussels in a kettle with chopped onion and parsley and cider. Cover and put over moderate heat. Cook, shaking frequently, until mussels are open. Remove from heat; remove meat from mussels and reserve. Strain broth well and reserve. Melt butter and sauté leeks and celery without browning for 3 minutes. Blend in flour without browning. Stir in scalded milk, nutmeg, and salt and pepper to taste. Simmer for 20 minutes. Put through a sieve; add cream, mussel broth and mussels. Reheat to serving temperature.

SERVES 6.

ITALIAN MUSSEL SOUP

3 lbs. mussels
  olive oil
1 onion, thinly sliced
1 tbsp. chopped celery
3 garlic cloves, slivered
2 tsps. fresh marjoram, thyme or basil

2 tsps. pepper
2 lbs. plum tomatoes, sliced
½ cup dry white wine
  grated lemon rind
  chopped parsley

Cover the bottom of a heavy 4-qt. kettle with a skin of oil. Warm the oil, add the onion, and cook until golden. Add celery, garlic, fresh herbs and pepper. Cook for 2 minutes and add tomatoes. Stew for 3 or 4 minutes and add wine. Simmer for 2 minutes. Cover, reduce heat, and cook to a pulp.

Add about 1 cup hot water to make a thick sauce and simmer for a few minutes more./Reheat, if necessary, and add mussels; let them cook fairly fast until they open, about 10 minutes. Garnish with grated lemon rind and chopped parsley before serving.

SERVES 4 to 6.

MEDITERRANEAN MUSSEL SOUP

8 lbs. mussels
1⅓ cups dry white wine
2 cups minced onions
¾ cup minced parsley
¼ cup olive oil
1 (1-lb.-13-oz. or 2-lb.) can Italian
    tomatoes

2 large garlic cloves, mashed
2 tsps. sugar
2 tsps. anchovy paste
2 tsps. chopped fresh basil

Steam mussels with wine. Remove mussels, strain and reserve broth. Remove meat from shells and reserve. Sauté onions and ½ cup parsley in oil until onions are translucent. Strain tomatoes, reserving juice, and crush. Add enough water to juice to equal 4 tomato cans of liquid. Add tomatoes, water, ¼ cup parsley, garlic, sugar, anchovy paste and basil. Bring to a boil, cover, reduce heat, and simmer for 30 minutes. Add reserved mussels and their broth and simmer for 5 minutes longer. Freezes well.

SERVES 16 to 18.

CANADIAN PURÉED OYSTER SOUP

1 pint drained oysters
2 tbps. minced shallots
¼ cup melted butter
1 qt. chicken bouillon

1 cup light cream
4 egg yolks, beaten
2 tbsps. chopped parsley
2 tbsps. chopped chives

Purée oysters in a blender or food chopper. Sauté shallots in butter until softened. Add bouillon. Mix the cream with the yolks; add a bit of the hot bouillon to blend; add to remaining mixture and stir until thickened. Add puréed oysters, parsley and chives and heat without boiling.

SERVES 6.

ITALIAN OYSTER STEW

1 qt. oysters, shucked and drained
3 strips of bacon
½ medium-size onion, sliced
2 (6-oz.) cans tomato paste

1 cup water
1 garlic clove, minced
  salt and pepper
1½ tbsps. butter

Fry the bacon; remove from pan, drain, crumble, and reserve. Brown the onion in the bacon fat. Add tomato paste and cook for 15 minutes. Add the oysters and water. Let come to a boil. Add garlic, salt and pepper to taste, and the butter; serve.

SERVES 2 or 3.

NEW ENGLAND OYSTER BISQUE

1 cup shucked oysters, with liquor
3 cups milk
1 onion slice
2 celery ribs, diced
1 parsley sprig, minced

1 bay leaf
¼ cup crumbled pilot crackers
3 tbsps. butter
2 tsps. salt
  paprika

Scald milk with the onion, celery, parsley and bay leaf for 15 minutes. Strain. Heat the oysters in their own liquor until the edges begin to curl. Chop oysters well and add with liquor to milk with cracker crumbs, butter and salt. Dust with paprika.

SERVES 4.

NEW ENGLAND OYSTER STEW

6 oysters
4 tbsps. butter
¾ cup scalded milk

salt or celery salt and pepper
paprika

Shuck oysters, reserving the liquor. Heat half of the butter, add oysters, and heat until the edges begin to curl. Add oyster liquor and bring just to the boiling point. Pour into hot scalded milk, season to taste, and melt remaining butter on top. Serve dusted with paprika.

SERVES 1.

NEW YORK OYSTER BAR STEW

28 oysters
6 tbsps. butter
2 tsps. Worcestershire sauce
1 tsp. paprika

½ tsp. celery salt
1 cup milk
1 cup light cream

Shuck oysters, reserving the liquor; there should be about 1 cup of the liquor. Melt 4 tbsps. butter. Blend in Worcestershire sauce, paprika and celery salt. Add oysters and juice and bring barely to a simmer. Add milk and cream, stir briskly once or twice, and bring almost to a boil. Pour into bowls, and top each with ½ tbsp. pat of butter.

SERVES 4.

HOT FRENCH SCALLOP SOUP

1 lb. bay or sea scallops
2 cups dry white wine
2 tbsps. chopped shallots
4 parsley sprigs
3 tbsps. butter

¼ tsp. cayenne pepper
6 mushrooms, chopped
  salt and pepper
1 cup heavy cream
3 egg yolks, lightly beaten

If using sea scallops, cut them into small pieces. Combine scallops, wine, shallots, parsley, butter, cayenne, mushrooms, and salt and pepper to taste. Bring to a boil and simmer for 5 minutes. Strain and reserve both the scallops and broth. (Scallops can be chilled and used in another dish later.) Return liquid to a simmer. Combine cream and egg yolks. Add a bit of hot liquid to the yolks, then add eggs to hot liquid, stirring rapidly. Do not boil, but cook slowly until soup is thickened: best done over hot, not boiling, water, in a double boiler.

SERVES 4 to 6.

COLD FRENCH SCALLOP SOUP

1½ lbs. bay or sea scallops
2 cups Chablis wine
½ cup chopped onion
½ cup chopped celery
2 tsps. whole peppercorns
½ tsp. salt

½ tsp. ground thyme
2 tbsps. olive oil
2 tbsps. flour
2 cups heavy cream
2 tbsps. chopped parsley

If using sea scallops, cut them into small pieces. Combine scallops, wine, onion, celery, peppercorns, salt and thyme. Bring to a boil, reduce heat, and simmer for 5 minutes. In a separate saucepan, combine the oil and flour well. Strain scallop broth and add to oil mixture, stirring well. Bring to a boil, then simmer for 10 minutes, stirring frequently. Dice strained scallops finely. Remove broth from heat; add scallops. Allow to cool and chill thoroughly. Add cream and stir well before serving. Garnish with chopped parsley.

SERVES 6.

IRISH SCALLOP CHOWDER

½ lb. sea scallops, diced
3 slices of bacon or 1 oz. salt pork, diced
2 onions, chopped
4 large potatoes, diced
6 cups fish stock or clam broth

3 tomatoes, peeled and chopped
1 tsp. salt
fresh pepper
3 soda crackers, crushed
1 cup heavy cream

Fry bacon almost crisp. Add onions and cook until they soften. Add potatoes and stock and cook for 15 minutes. Add tomatoes and season with salt and pepper to taste. Simmer for 10 minutes more, covered. Add scallops, soda crackers and cream. Simmer for a few minutes to heat, being careful not to boil.

SERVES 6.

ENTRÉES

CALIFORNIA ABALONE STEAKS

Dip into flour, then into lightly beaten egg, then into cracker meal. Pan-fry quickly in butter; overcooking toughens abalone.

WEST COAST ABALONE POT ROAST

---

1 whole abalone (¾ to 1 lb.), pounded
   seasoned flour
2 to 3 tbsps. olive oil

1 garlic clove, mashed
1 cup dry red wine
½ cup water

Flour the abalone and quickly brown on all sides in hot oil. Add garlic, wine and water. Cover and simmer slowly for 40 minutes. Slice across grain thinly to serve.

SERVES 3 or 4.

WESTERN HANGTOWN FRY

Attributed to a miner who hit gold in the west. Oysters and eggs were the most expensive things available, so that's what he ordered.

8 to 10 medium-size oysters, drained
   salt and pepper
   flour
5 eggs, lightly beaten
1 cup dry bread crumbs

butter
3 tbsps. milk
4 strips of bacon, half-cooked and
   diced
paprika

Dust oysters with salt and pepper and roll in flour. Roll in beaten eggs, then in bread crumbs, and brown on one side in ⅛ inch of butter. While browning, beat remaining egg liquid with milk and diced bacon. Turn oysters and pour on egg batter. Cook as you would an omelet. Sprinkle with paprika.

SERVES 2.

PHILADELPHIA OYSTER FRY

24 oysters
1½ cups mayonnaise

2 cups rolled cracker crumbs
fat for deep-frying

Shuck oysters, drain and dry them. Dip oysters into mayonnaise, then into crumbs; again into mayonnaise and crumbs. Deep-fry in fat heated to 375°; drain. Handle as little as possible, and gently then.
SERVES 2 to 4.

NEW ORLEANS "LA MÉDIATRICE"
(morning-after hangover cure)

A sandwich of French bread which has been lightly fried in hot butter and drained, filled with broiled or fried oysters.

NEW ENGLAND FRIED OYSTERS

shucked oysters

Drain oysters and pat dry. Season with salt and pepper. Dip into flour, then into cracker crumbs, then into egg beaten with a bit of water, then into crumbs again. Deep-fry.

SPANISH PANNED OYSTERS

1 pt. shucked oysters, drained
¼ cup butter
2 tbsps. dry white wine
1 tbsp. lemon juice

1 tsp. hot-pepper sherry
½ tsp. salt
1 cup hot cooked rice

Sauté oysters in butter for 5 minutes. Remove oysters and add wine and seasonings to pan; heat. Return oysters briefly and heat. Pour over hot rice.

SERVES 2.

NEW ENGLAND OVEN-FRIED OYSTERS

12 oysters, shucked
 1 cup flour
 1 tsp. salt
 ¼ tsp. pepper

 1 egg, lightly beaten
 fine crumbs
 olive oil

Roll oysters in flour mixed with salt and pepper. Dip into beaten egg and roll in crumbs. Sprinkle oysters with olive oil. Bake on a cookie sheet or in a shallow dish at 400° for about 15 minutes, or until brown.

SERVES 1 or 2.

CHINESE GINGERED OYSTERS

1½ cups shucked oysters, drained
10 scallions
 ⅛ tsp. Chinese five spices
 ½ tbsp. cornstarch

 4 tsps. soya sauce
 3 tbsps. sake or sherry
 2 tbsps. sesame oil
 4 thin slices of fresh gingerroot

Separate white parts of scallions from green tops. Cut white parts into halves. Keep only 3 inches of the green tops and cut them into halves. Mix oysters with five spices, 1 tsp. cornstarch and 1 tsp. soya sauce. Let stand for 10 minutes. Blend remaining cornstarch and soya and the sake. Heat oil over highest heat and add gingerroot and white part of scallions. Cook, stirring, for barely 30 seconds. Remove scallions from pan. Reduce heat and add oysters, spreading them out in the pan. Cook over medium heat, turning once, until oysters are slightly firmed, about 2 minutes. Remove oysters. Brown the pan drippings, then blend in cornstarch mixture. Cook, stirring, until thickened. Blend in scallions and green tops and oysters, and heat until simmering.

SERVES 2 or 3.

HAWAIIAN OYSTER FRITTERS

1½ cups chopped oysters
4 egg yolks, beaten
3 tbsps. minced onion
¼ cup sifted flour
¼ cup ground almonds

½ tsp. salt
¼ tsp. white pepper
4 egg whites, beaten stiff but not dry
fat for deep-frying

Blend all but egg whites and fat; fold egg whites into mixture carefully. Drop by tablespoon into deep fat heated to 370° and fry to golden brown. Drain and serve with a dip or sauce.
    SERVES 6 to 8.

EARLY AMERICAN OYSTER AND SWEETBREAD PIE

1 pint oysters

Shuck oysters and reserve the juices. Prepare 1 pair of sweetbreads for frying and cut into cubes. Mix sweetbreads and oysters into a well-seasoned thin white sauce and put in a 9-inch pie dish or 1-qt. casserole. Top with a flaky pastry crust; cut vents in the top. Brush top of pastry with cream. Bake at 350° for 40 minutes.
    SERVES 4 to 6.

CEYLONESE CURRIED OYSTERS

12 large oysters, shucked
4 shallots, minced
1 garlic clove, minced
½ medium-size green pepper,
    minced
3 tbsps. butter
1 tbsp. curry powder

1-inch cinnamon stick
1 small bay leaf
2 cloves without heads
1 cup coconut milk
    dash salt
1 cup hot cooked rice
    juice of 1 lemon

Brown shallots, garlic and green pepper in butter. Add curry powder, cinnamon stick, bay leaf and cloves. When well blended, stir in the coconut milk and salt. Cook for 3 minutes, until thickened slightly. Add oysters and cook gently for 3 minutes. Remove oysters and place on hot rice. Stir lemon juice into curry sauce, and pour over oysters on rice.

SERVES 2.

KEYS CONCH FRITTERS

1 cup finely ground raw conch
¾ cup flour
½ tbsp. salt
½ tbsp. baking powder
3 eggs, lightly beaten

2 tbsps. melted butter
1 medium-size onion, finely ground
½ tsp. dried thyme
fat for deep-frying
Key lime wedges

Sift together the flour, salt and baking powder. Add eggs and melted butter and beat mixture well. Stir conch, onion and thyme into mixture thoroughly. Drop by scànt teaspoons into deep fat heated to 390° and brown on both sides, turning once. Drain and serve with lime wedges.

SERVES 6.

KEYS CONCH AND AVOCADO SALAD

2 conch, ground or minced
1 medium-size onion, minced
½ green pepper, minced
¼ tsp. salt
½ tsp. curry powder
black pepper

1 tbsp. vinegar
juice of 3 Key limes
½ cup olive oil
Keys Old Sour
2 avocados

Mix conch with onion and green pepper. Sprinkle with salt, curry powder and black pepper to taste; add vinegar, lime juice, oil, and Old Sour to taste, mixing well but gently. Chill overnight and mound in avocado halves.

SERVES 4.

CARIBBEAN FRIED CONCH

1 conch, sliced
1 cup cracker meal
2 eggs, slightly beaten

salt and pepper
fat for deep-frying

Dip slices into cracker meal, then into eggs, then into meal again. Season well and deep-fry in fat heated to 390°.
SERVES 2.

KEYS CONCH STEAK

Conch steaks

Dip into batter and deep-fry in fat or oil heated to 390°.

BAHAMA STEWED CONCH

6 conch, cut into bite-size pieces
1 small onion, chopped
3 tbsps. lard

2 tbsps. flour
2 cups water
1 large potato, peeled and cubed

Fry the onion in the lard. Add the flour, stirring, and when brown add the water, conch and potato. Cook slowly, covered, until potato is done; 20 to 30 minutes.
SERVES 4.

ANTIGUAN CONCH SALAD

2 conch, diced small
3 tomatoes, seeded and diced
1 medium-size onion, chopped
4 celery ribs, diced
1 tsp. minced parsley

⅓ cup lime juice
2 tbsps. olive oil
dash of Worcestershire sauce
dash of Tabasco
salt and pepper

Mix all together with seasoning to taste and chill for at least 1 hour.
SERVES 2 to 4.

TURKISH FRIED MUSSELS

1 qt. shucked mussels, patted dry
1 envelope of dry yeast
4 tbsps. warm water
2 tbsps. shortening
⅔ cup flour
2 egg yolks

2 tsps. salt
⅓ cup warm water
2 egg whites, beaten stiff but not dry
flour
shortening for frying

Dissolve yeast in 4 tbsps. warm water. Cut shortening into flour. Make a well in the center and add the egg yolks, salt and dissolved yeast. Gradually stir in ⅓ cup warm water until thoroughly blended. Cover bowl of batter with a damp cloth and put in a warm place to rise for about 1 hour. Fold stiff egg whites into batter just before dipping in the mussels. Before dipping the mussels, dust them lightly with flour. Coat mussels well with batter. Fry them in about ½ inch of hot shortening until golden on both sides. Drain and keep warm.

Usually served with walnut sauce. Remove crusts from 3 slices of white bread; soak in water and squeeze dry. Put bread in a blender with 1 garlic clove, chopped, ½ cup walnut meats, ¼ tsp. salt, 2 tbsps. lemon juice, 2 tbsps. water and 1 tbsp. olive oil; blend until smooth. Sprinkle sauce with chopped fresh mint.

SERVES 4 to 6.

SPANISH MUSSELS

4 lbs. mussels, steamed open
2 large garlic cloves, minced
½ cup olive oil
2 tsps. flour

1 tbsp. dry white wine
1 cup mussel broth
2 tsps. minced parsley

Cook garlic in oil without browning until soft. Stir in flour, wine and mussel broth. Add parsley and cook, covered, for 3 minutes. Pour sauce over mussels in bowls.

SERVES 4.

NEW ENGLAND BAKED MUSSELS

Shuck mussels and put into a buttered baking dish. Season with salt and pepper; sprinkle on minced onion. Cover with thin slices of bacon and sprinkle with Parmesan cheese. Bake at 350° for 15 minutes. (Can be done on the half shell or not.)

FRENCH GLAZED MUSSELS

4 lbs. mussels	2 cups light cream
4 shallots, chopped	1 cup thick white sauce
salt and pepper	2 tbsps. butter
3 cups dry white wine	6 tbsps. whipped cream

Steam mussels with shallots, salt and pepper and wine. Remove upper shells and arrange mussels in lower shells in a single layer in an ovenproof dish. Cook wine mixture over low heat for 20 minutes. Blend in light cream and white sauce. Add butter, a bit at a time, stirring constantly. Boil for 4 or 5 minutes. Remove sauce from heat and stir in whipped cream. Pour sauce over mussels. Broil about 8 inches from the source of heat for 2 or 3 minutes, or until well browned.

SERVES 4.

MUSSELS NORMANDY STYLE

36 small mussels	6 tbsps. butter
1 cup applejack	1 piece of carrot
3 shallots, diced	1 cup heavy cream
1 bay leaf	salt and white pepper

Put mussels in a deep pan; add applejack, shallots, bay leaf, 2 tbsps. butter and the carrot. Cover and steam until shells open, about 5 minutes. Remove mussels and set aside in shells in a warm dish. Strain the sauce; stir in 4 tbsps. butter and the cream and add salt and pepper to taste. Warm sauce and pour over mussels.

SERVES 2 to 4.

MEDITERRANEAN FISHERMAN'S MUSSELS

3 lbs. mussels
1 cup dry white wine
1 tsp. minced shallots

1 tsp. minced parsley
1 tbsp. butter
cayenne pepper

Steam mussels with wine, shallots and parsley. Drain; reserve mussel liquor and reduce it to ¾ cup. Remove top shell of mussels. Add butter and cayenne to taste to broth, and pour over mussels.

SERVES 3 or 4.

GREEK FRIED MUSSELS

Shuck mussels, roll in flour, and fry in hot olive oil. Serve very hot, with a strong garlic-flavored sauce.

BELGIAN STEAMED MUSSELS

36 mussels
1½ cups white wine
½ cup water
2 tbsps. chopped parsley
2 tbsps. prepared mustard

1 tbsp. sugar
1 tbsp. celery seeds
1 tbsp. dried dillweed
1 garlic clove, chopped
3 tbsps. butter

Mix everything except mussels in a kettle. Steam mussels over the mixture. Serve with the strained broth.

SERVES 6.

BASQUE-STYLE MUSSELS

1 lb. mussels

Steam mussels with white wine, parsley sprigs and a bay leaf. Seed and dice 3 firm tomatoes. Cook tomatoes slowly in 3 tbsps. butter with 3 tbsps. diced stale French bread and a little salt and pepper until tomatoes are well softened. Add the opened mussels and enough of the strained broth to bring the sauce to rather thick consistency. Simmer briefly and serve.

SERVES 2 or 3.

GREEK STUFFED MUSSELS

36 large mussels
2 large onions, minced
¼ cup olive oil
3 garlic cloves, minced
1 cup raw rice
½ cup pine nuts
⅓ cup dried currants

⅓ cup chopped parsley
salt and pepper
3 cups fish or vegetable stock or water
juice of 1 lemon
chopped fresh mint
lemon wedges

Open mussels but leave them in lower shells; keep top shells. Sauté onions in oil until transparent. Add garlic and cook for 2 minutes. Add rice, pine nuts, currants, parsley, and salt and pepper to taste. Add 2 cups stock, cover, and cook gently until liquid is absorbed. Top mussels with rice mixture. Sprinkle with lemon juice. Close shells and tie each mussel together tightly. Arrange in layers in a pan; pour on stock to cover. Cover and simmer for 30 to 35 minutes. Drain and cool. Untie, remove top shells, and sprinkle with mint. Serve with lemon wedges.

SERVES 6.

IRISH SCALLOPS

2 cups bay scallops, shucked
2 tbsps. butter
1 tbsp. Spanish brandy, warmed
1 tbsp. lemon juice

½ tsp. salt
⅛ tsp. black pepper
   dash of cayenne
¼ cup light cream

Sauté scallops in butter for 5 minutes. Add brandy and ignite. Sprinkle with lemon juice, salt, black pepper and cayenne. Add cream, and heat but do not boil.
SERVES 4.

FRENCH SCALLOPS IN RED WINE WITH ALMONDS

2 lbs. bay scallops, shucked
2 cups red wine, approximately
1 tsp. salt
½ tsp. dried thyme
7 tbsps. minced, fresh parsley

4 shallots, minced
4 garlic cloves, minced
12 tbsps. butter
6 tbsps. chopped almonds

Poach scallops in red wine to cover with salt, thyme, 1 tbsp. parsley, 1 tsp. shallot and 1 minced garlic clove for about 1 minute. Remove scallops as soon as done and arrange in individual baking shells. Cream butter with rest of garlic, shallots and parsley. Top each dish with butter mix; sprinkle with chopped almonds. Put under broiler just long enough to brown top well.
SERVES 4 to 6.

FRENCH SCALLOPS WITH HERBS

1 lb. scallops, shucked
   lemon juice
   pepper
   about ½ cup flour
   olive oil

2 tbsps. minced shallots
1 garlic clove, mashed
2 tbsps. butter
2 tbsps. minced parsley

Cut scallops into ½-inch pieces. Dry them, then place on wax paper. Sprinkle with lemon juice and pepper. Dredge with flour, shaking excess off in a sieve just before adding scallops to sauté pan. In a skillet heat a very thin film of oil almost to smoking. Add scallops and stir gently for 4 to 5 minutes, until lightly browned. Add shallots and garlic and cook for a moment; then add butter and parsley. Serve as soon as butter is melted.

SERVES 2 or 3.

FRENCH SCALLOPS IN CREAM SAUCE

1 lb. scallops, shucked
2 cups sliced mushrooms
¾ cup dry vermouth
2 tbsps. minced shallots

½ tsp. salt
dash of white pepper
½ bay leaf

Cut scallops into ½-inch-thick slices. Put scallops and mushrooms in vermouth with shallots and seasoning. Add water, if needed, to barely cover. Poach for 5 minutes. Remove scallops and mushrooms and reduce liquid to 1 cup.

3 tbsps. butter
4 tbsps. flour
  about ¾ cup milk
2 egg yolks

½ cup heavy cream
3 tbsps. grated Swiss cheese
1 tbsp. melted butter
lemon slices

Melt butter; stir in flour and cook slowly for 2 minutes without browning. Remove from heat and beat in reduced scallop liquid. Return to fairly high heat and cook, heating, until thickened. Thin with milk. Blend yolks with half of the cream; beat in the hot sauce very slowly. Return to moderately high heat and stir until sauce comes to a boil. Thin out as necessary with more milk or cream. Fold two thirds of the sauce into the scallops and mushrooms, and spoon into buttered individual baking dishes. Spoon on remaining sauce, and sprinkle with cheese and melted butter. Refrigerate. Reheat to bubbling in a moderately hot oven and brown under a moderately hot broiler. Serve with lemon slices.

SERVES 2 or 3.

CHINESE SCALLOPS AND EGGS

¾ lb. shucked bay scallops, or sea
    scallops cut into quarters
4 tbsps. sesame oil
¾ cup chopped onion

1 tbsp. soya sauce
6 scallions, thinly sliced
4 eggs, lightly beaten

Heat the oil and in it soften the onion. Add the scallops and cook for 5 minutes. Add soya sauce and scallions to beaten eggs; pour over the scallops and cook over low heat until set.

    SERVES 4.

PORTUGUESE CLAMS

48 hard-shelled clams
6 tbsps. olive oil
2 garlic cloves, minced
2 or 3 large onions, minced
1 tsp. paprika
¼ tsp. crushed red chile pepper
½ tsp. fresh ground black pepper
2 bay leaves, crumbled

1 tbsp. tomato paste
3 tomatoes, peeled, seeded and
    chopped
¾ cup dry white wine
½ lb. Portuguese or Spanish sausage
½ lb. lean ham, minced
4 tbsps. chopped fresh coriander

Scrub the clams. Poach sausage in water to cover for 10 minutes. Skin the sausage and crumble meat coarsely. Heat oil in a heavy deep pan; sauté garlic, onions, paprika and chile pepper until onions are soft and golden but not browned, about 5 minutes. Mix in the black pepper, bay leaves, tomato paste, tomatoes, wine, sausage and ham. Bring to a boil, reduce heat, and simmer for 20 minutes. If too thin (it will be thinned by the clam juices later) reduce over high heat until thick. Put clams on top of the sauce, cover, and steam until clams open, about 10 minutes. Put opened clams in deep bowls; sprinkle with coriander and pour sauce over them. (There's a special Portuguese dish for this, a *cataplana,* which looks like a hinged paella pan.)

    SERVES 4 to 6.

NEW ENGLAND DEEP-DISH QUAHOG PIE

1 qt. shucked quahogs
8 small white onions
8 small new potatoes, halved
1 small carrot, sliced
1 small white turnip, cut into eighths
½ tsp. salt

⅛ tsp. pepper
1 bay leaf
2 cups thin white sauce, approximately
flaky pastry for 1-crust pie

Grind the quahogs and reserve the juices. Mix clams and juices (plus water if needed to make 2 cups) with vegetables, and season to taste. Add bay leaf and white sauce. Put all into a buttered 2-qt. deep baking dish. Cover with crust of flaky pie pastry, and make vents in the top. Bake at 350° for 45 minutes. Don't let the filling get too thick. If it thickens too much, heated additional clam juice or broth (bottled) can be added through pastry vents.

SERVES 6.

NEW ENGLAND FRIED CLAMS

Use only small clams; don't be tempted to use large ones and cut them up. Roll clams in cornmeal; remove excess cornmeal by rolling in a sieve. Deep-fry in fat heated to 350° for 1½ minutes. Drain and salt well.

NEW ENGLAND DEVILED CLAMS

1 pint shucked clams, chopped and drained
½ cup clam juice
1 tbsp. chopped onion
1 tbsp. chopped green pepper
¼ cup chopped celery

4 tbsps. butter
2 hard-cooked eggs, diced
¾ cup fine crumbs
1 tsp. salt
⅛ tsp. pepper

Cook clams in juice for 5 minutes; cool. Sauté onion, pepper and celery in 2 tbsps. butter for 5 minutes to soften, but do not brown. Add to clams with eggs, crumbs and seasonings. Put in 6 buttered ramekins and dot with rest of the butter. Don't freeze, but you can refrigerate the ramekins. Bake at 400° for 20 minutes.

SERVES 6.

NEW ENGLAND CLAM FRITTERS

2 cups shucked clams, chopped and drained
2 cups sifted flour
2 tsps. baking powder
2 eggs, beaten
½ cup milk
½ cup clam broth
¼ tsp. salt
⅛ tsp. pepper
fat for deep-frying

Combine flour, baking powder, eggs, milk and clam broth, and stir smooth. Add clams and seasonings. Drop by small spoonfuls into deep fat heated to 375° and fry for a few minutes, until golden. Don't overcrowd fat.

SERVES 6.

JAPANESE BROILED CLAMS

24 shucked clams
½ cup soya sauce
½ cup sake or sherry
4 tbsps. condensed black-bean soup
3 tbsps. sugar
2 tbsps. oil

Combine all but the clams and bring to a boil. Dip the clams into the hot liquid to coat thoroughly and arrange them on a greased broiler rack. Broil for 2 minutes each side. Can also be skewered and broiled, of course. Serve remaining sauce as a dip. Also good as hors d'oeuvres.

SERVES 4 to 6.

ITALIAN BAKED CLAMS

24 cherrystones, on the half shell
1 cup fine dry bread crumbs
1 garlic clove, minced
2 tbsps. grated Romano cheese
1 tbsp. dried orégano

1 tbsp. chopped parsley
1 tsp. pepper
⅓ cup olive oil
¾ cup white wine, warmed

Combine crumbs, garlic, grated cheese, orégano, parsley and pepper; sprinkle evenly over the clams. Drizzle on the oil. Place clams in a pan with the warmed white wine. Bake in 400° oven, basting occasionally, for 15 minutes, or until browned. Serve with pan juices and lemon wedges.

Serves 4 to 6.

Crustaceans

Crawfish, crayfish, crawdads, spiny lobster, rock lobster or lobster . . . it seems there are almost as many names to call the main ingredient as there are recipes to prepare them. They all, however, can, with only a bit of adjustment, be used in place of one another, except, naturally, for those recipes calling for the whole true lobster to be served. Yet even these preparations can be applied to the other crustaceans, all of which share the common characteristic of being exoskeletal. The only true lobster has 2 large, hard-shelled forward claws.

The true lobster can be killed by being put head first into boiling water until cooked, or it can be killed before cooking, which is particularly recommended for broiled lobster. Whether the lobster is alive or boiled, the same parts are discarded. If the lobster is alive, hold it just behind the head on a heavy board (be sure the claws are pegged!). Using a heavy, long knife, put the point deep into the cross just behind the head. This kills the lobster. Then the lobster can be cut clear through the tail in one sweep; it's easiest to do by hitting the back of the knife with a mallet, cutting through the whole of the top shell. Turn the lobster over and turn back the two halves. Remove the head and the stomach (the sand sac just behind the head) and the intestinal vein (it appears stringlike) that runs the length all the way through the tail. If you don't want two separate halves, you can cut away the under-shield of the lobster with heavy shears (I use pruning shears) and remove the head, stomach and intestinal vein. Whichever way you finish, be sure to save the liver and coral, preferably in the shell to serve with the rest of the meat. The claws can be twisted off to save room on a broiler rack.

Crabs, which are related to the lobster, also really should be cleaned before cooking, although not many do it. Most cooks seem to prefer to boil the crabs, let them cool, then clean and pick out the meat. Of course, some dishes require the eater to do the cleaning. On the other hand, precleaning a crab is not difficult. Lay the crab on its back and grab it from the rear; it helps to hold the last leg or two on each side. Use a heavy knife or cleaver to split it completely through the top shell and along its full length in one quick motion. (After you get the cleaver in position and holding the crab, you can let go of the legs and hit the top of the cleaver with a mallet.) Twist off the legs and claws if desired. Scrub the crab and pry off the top shell (a knife sometimes helps with the larger ones). Remove the gills and the spongy material in the body. Save the soft crab butter (tomalley). Wash again and cut again, if necessary, as with the large Dungeness crabs of the West Coast. The pieces can now be steamed or boiled. The crab is done when the flesh turns opaque.

Soft-shell crab requires much less prior cleaning. Kill the crab by plunging a sharp knife point between the eyes. Carefully lift the pointed ends of the top shell and scrape off the spongy white matter between the shell and body on each side. Turn the crab over and with the knife remove the apron (the piece that comes to a sharp point just about the middle) and wash. Cook immediately.

Smaller, hard-shelled crabs are generally boiled or steamed, uncleaned, and the diner attends to the cleaning. Stone crab claws are steamed and generally eaten cold. Both are usually served with drawn butter for a dip.

The true lobster shares its exoskeletal form with both salt and freshwater shrimps and crawfishes. (While some people differentiate the freshwater varieties by spelling it crayfish, the differences are so minute and technical aside from the salinity of the water that I and many others prefer to use the one word "crawfish" for all of them.) In some freshwater species the resemblance between shrimp and crawfishes is so close that one is frequently misnamed for the other.

There is less confusion between the saltwater crawfishes and shrimp, although big shrimp, which some incorrectly call scampi or prawns, can look mighty like small crawfish. With both the shrimp and crawfish, fresh and saltwater, it is the tail meat that is the portion used. The cleaning of the saltwater crawfish is detailed on page 19 since it is usually done close to the traps from which they are taken.

Shrimp are tastiest when shelled and cleaned after cooking whenever possible. Raw or cooked, however, the head snaps off easily and the fine legs and thin shell peel off without effort. All that remains to be done is to remove the fine black line of the intestinal vein. While there is a gadget for this, the point of a paring knife is sufficient. This can be done without removing the shell; simply slit the shell down the back.

There are literally hundreds of species and subspecies of both fresh and saltwater shrimp and crawfishes on the North American continent alone. Shrimp can range from the size of the end of your little finger to the legitimately called prawn, a particular species of shrimp, large enough to require only a few per serving. In the same way, crawfishes in their variety may be as little as 1 inch in length to a generous 16 inches.

Freshwater crawfish are only found in good, clean, slow-running fresh water. They are so susceptible to adverse conditions, as a matter of fact, that in some areas they are used to indicate the purity of water supplies. In many places they are completely protected by law. Where they can be taken legally they should be rinsed, cooked in a white-wine-based court bouillon and eaten on the spot, for they do not keep well.

The white-wine-based court bouillon is best for cooking all freshwater shellfish. Marine shellfish are cooked, by purists who have a handy supply, in fresh sea water. Lacking natural salt water, substitute tap water in which 1 tablespoon of salt has been dissolved per quart. All shellfish is fully cooked when the flesh turns opaque. Some cooks assume that the shells, if left on, must turn bright red or that the outer flesh of shelled shellfish must at least become pinkish. Unfortunately not all varieties within the various species follow this pattern. The best test is the opacity of the flesh; overcooking to try to reach a certain color will undoubtedly lead to toughness. Cooking times must of necessity be approximate: all these shellfish molt, and a "newer" shell is thinner, to say nothing of the variables depending on the size. Small shrimp may take only 2 minutes; large, 10 minutes; small, hard-shell crabs 20 to 25 minutes; a 1-lb. lobster around 7 minutes; a 2-lber, about 10 minutes.

APPETIZERS

SPICED BOIL

This can be used for all crustaceans, preferably still in the shell, for either a spiced cold appetizer or a highly flavored hot dish. The broth can be frozen in small batches, then melted for doing the shellfish, but do *not* freeze the broth after cooking shellfish in it.

1 tbsp. salt	⅛ tsp. cayenne
4 garlic cloves, sliced	3 peppercorns, whole
4 allspice, whole	3 cloves, whole
1 cup chopped celery ribs and leaves	1 cup chopped onions
3 bay leaves, roughly crumbled	¼ tsp. thyme
3 sprigs parsley, minced	1 tsp. Worcestershire sauce
3 slices lemon	6 cups water

Bring all to a boil. Cover and simmer for 25 minutes. Strain. Thaw if necessary. Reheat to boiling, add shellfish and bring again to a boil. Lower heat and loosely cover pot; cook until shellfish are done. Allow shellfish to cool slowly in the liquid if to be served cold or drain shellfish from broth to serve hot.

MAKES about 2 qts.

BAHAMA CRAWFISH CEVICHE

Raw crawfish

Shell crawfish and chop into bite-size pieces. Mix about ½ cup Key lime juice, about 1 tsp. soya sauce, about 1 tsp. Worcestershire sauce, about 2 tbsps. olive oil, and salt and pepper to taste. Marinate crawfish in the mixture for several hours, chilled.

POLYNESIAN LOBSTER RUMAKI

Raw rock lobster, lobster tail or large crawfish

Shell crustaceans and cut into ½-inch medallions. Mix equal parts of sherry and soya sauce for marinade. Prepare sliced water chestnuts and thin slices of bacon. Marinate the lobster slices in marinade for several hours, chilled. Drain well; combine each slice with a slice of water chestnut and wrap in a piece of bacon; skewer to hold together. Bake at 400° until the bacon is crisp.

BRAZILIAN SHRIMP

largest shrimp you can find

Split shells down the back to remove vein, but leave shells on. Heat ¼ inch of olive oil in a skillet, to about half-cover the shrimp. Cook shrimp until done. Drain, sprinkle with plenty of salt, and serve in the shells.

CHINESE SHRIMP TOAST

1¼ lbs. cleaned shrimp	1 tsp. pepper
16 thin slices of slightly stale white bread	1 tsp. minced onion
	2 egg whites, lightly beaten
⅓ cup larding pork	sesame seeds
1 tsp. salt	sesame oil for pan-frying

Dry bread slices in a very slow oven for 15 minutes. Mince shrimp with salt pork. Stir in seasonings, onion and 1 beaten egg white; mix well. Brush bread slices with 1 beaten egg white and spread evenly with the shrimp paste. Cover paste with sesame seeds; press them in with the flat side of a knife. Fry slices, shrimp side down, in shallow sesame oil for 3 minutes, or until golden. Turn and fry on the other side for 2 minutes longer. Drain on paper towels and serve hot.

MAKES 16.

ECUADOREAN SHRIMP CEVICHE

2 lbs. shrimp, cleaned
1½ cups orange juice
½ cup lemon juice
1 large tomato, peeled, seeded and chopped

1 large onion, minced
1 fresh hot or green pepper, minced
salt and pepper

Cook shrimp in boiling salted water for 3 to 4 minutes. Drain. Mix remaining ingredients and toss with shrimp. Let stand for 1 hour.
SERVES 6.

GERMAN SHRIMP IN BEER

3 lbs. raw shrimp, cleaned
12 oz. flat beer
1½ cups water

½ cup white vinegar
6 juniper berries
1 tbsp. crushed dried red peppers

Bring all but shrimp to a boil. Let stand for 1 hour. Bring back to a boil; add 12 shrimp, bring to boil, and remove shrimp; repeat. Continue until all shrimp are cooked. Chill well.
SERVES 8 to 10.

MEXICAN PICKLED SHRIMP

2 lbs. shrimp, cleaned
¾ cup olive oil
2 onions, chopped
3 garlic cloves, minced
2 onions, thinly sliced
½ cup white vinegar

½ tbsp. salt
½ tsp. black pepper
¼ tsp. dry mustard
¼ tsp. dried ground chile pepper, or 2 pickled chile peppers, cut into strips

Heat ¼ cup oil and sauté chopped onions and garlic for 10 minutes, stirring frequently. Add shrimp and sauté until done, about 7 minutes, stirring occasionally. Cool shrimp in the pan for 15 minutes. Combine sliced onions, ½ cup oil, vinegar, salt, black pepper, mustard and chiles. Drain shrimp and add to oil-vinegar mix, stirring gently to coat thoroughly. Marinate for 24 hours, basting several times.

SERVES 6 or more.

MEXICAN BARBECUED SHRIMP

large shrimp

Shell shrimp, but leave tails on for a handle. Dip shrimp into barbecue sauce; drain. Grill over coals or in a broiler 4 inches from the source of heat, turning once, for about 2 or 3 minutes per side. Do *not* let shrimp stand in barbecue sauce.

SCANDINAVIAN DILLED SHRIMP

1½ lbs. raw shrimp, cleaned
4 tbsps. lemon juice
¾ tsp. salt

3 tbsps. oil
1 tbsp. chopped fresh dill, or 1½ tsps. dried dillweed

Sprinkle shrimp with lemon juice and salt and let stand for 30 minutes. Heat oil and add the shrimp. Cook them opaque, about 7 minutes, and add dill. Keep warm over hot water; serve with food picks.

SERVES 6 or more.

SPANISH BROILED SHRIMP

large shrimp in the shell

Slit shrimp to remove veins. Brush with olive oil and broil for 7 minutes, or until done, turning once or twice.

SPANISH SHRIMP WITH GARLIC

1½ lbs. small raw shrimp
¾ cup olive oil
2 or 3 whole garlic cloves

1 tbsp. chopped parsley
½ tsp. salt

Shell shrimp but leave tails on for a handle. Mix remaining ingredients well. Stir in the shrimp and let stand for at least 1 hour. Turn into a casserole and bake at 450° for 5 to 7 minutes, or until shrimp turn opaque. Discard garlic cloves and serve shrimp hot with food picks. Can also be arranged in individual serving shells for table service.

SERVES 6.

SOUPS

SCOTCH CRAB SOUP

1 cup cleaned crab meat, diced
¼ cup raw rice
1 tbsp. butter
2 cups milk

1 anchovy fillet, minced
1½ cups hot chicken bouillon
½ cup light cream
salt and pepper

Bring rice, butter and milk to a boil; cover and simmer for 20 minutes, or until rice is quite soft. Add crab meat and anchovy to soup. Force through a food mill or whirl in a blender until smooth. Return to stove and add bouillon and blend well. Heat to boiling and simmer for a few minutes. Stir in cream, season to taste, and serve.

SERVES 4.

TIDEWATER SHE-CRAB SOUP

1 lb. white crab meat, including coral, from female crab
2 cups milk
4 blades of whole mace
2 pieces of lemon peel

4 tbsps. butter
2 cups cream
¼ cup cracker crumbs
salt and pepper
2 tsps. sherry

Put milk in top of a double boiler with mace and lemon peel; simmer for a few minutes. Add crab meat, butter and cream and cook for 15 minutes. Thicken with cracker crumbs; season with salt and pepper and allow to stand on back of stove for a few minutes to develop the flavor. Just before serving, add sherry. (A similar soup can be made with shrimp, which should be ground.)
SERVES 6.

POLISH CRAWFISH SOUP

20 large or 30 small crawfish
1 bunch of fresh dill
2 to 3 tbsps. butter
6 cups clear fish stock or chicken bouillon

½ cup dairy sour cream
1 tbsp. flour
1 tbsp. chopped fresh dill

Stuffing:
1 tbsp. butter
2 hard-cooked egg yolks
2 or 3 tbsps. bread crumbs

1 tsp. minced fresh dill
salt and pepper

Add the bunch of dill to a large pot of salted boiling water; add crawfish and cook until barely done. Drain, reserving cooking liquid. Clean the crawfish, saving 8 smallest shells for stuffed garnish. Pound the remaining shells, small claws and interior fat well in a mortar. Sauté this in butter in a heavy skillet for 30 minutes. Combine with reserved cooking liquid and simmer, skimming butter into a separate cup as it rises to the surface. After all the fat has been removed, reduce liquid to 1 cup. Strain and combine with stock.

Add sour cream blended with flour and allow to bubble up once. Add the cleaned crawfish, the skimmed butter and the chopped dill.

Meanwhile, scrub reserved shells and make the stuffing. Cream butter with egg yolks; add the crumbs and minced dill and mix well; season to taste. Divide among the reserved shells. Add them to the soup for a final minute before serving to heat. Float a stuffed shell on each serving.

SERVES 8.

JAPANESE LOBSTER AND MUSHROOM SOUP

½ lb. raw lobster meat
1 tsp. salt
12 dried mushrooms, softened in water
5½ cups dashi

2 tsps. soya sauce
2-inch section of peeled cucumber, sliced very thin
6 small, thin strips of lemon rind

Cut lobster into small dice and sprinkle with salt. Pat the salted flesh into 12 oval shapes and steam over water until cooked. Boil mushrooms briefly in ½ cup *dashi* with 1 tsp. soya sauce. Heat remaining *dashi* and soya sauce to serving temperature. Put 2 shapes of meat, 2 mushrooms and a few slices of cucumber in each serving bowl; pour on the heated *dashi*. Top each with a strip of lemon rind.

SERVES 6.

JAPANESE MINCED LOBSTER SOUP

½ lb. raw lobster meat, minced
1 tsp. miso
5 oz. miso

4 cups dashi
½ lb. tofu, cut into ½-inch dice
ground ginger

Mix lobster flesh well with 1 tsp. *miso*. Bring 5 oz. *miso* and the *dashi* to a boil and add lobster and *tofu*. When lobster is opaque, pour into bowls with a small dash of ground ginger.

SERVES 6.

CHINESE HOT-SOUR SHRIMP SOUP

½ lb. shrimp
1 tbsp. soya sauce
1 tbsp. cornstarch
½ tsp. salt
4 cups chicken broth

2 eggs, beaten
1½ tbsps. vinegar
black pepper
watercress sprigs

Clean shrimp and cut them lengthwise into halves. Add soya sauce, cornstarch and salt to 1 cup of broth. Heat 3 cups of broth, when boiling, add the cornstarch mixture. Stir for a few seconds, reduce heat, and slowly pour in the beaten eggs, stirring constantly. Add the vinegar, pepper to taste and shrimp. Cook slowly until shrimp are opaque. Garnish with watercress when serving.

SERVES 4 to 6.

ORIENTAL SHRIMP-SHELL SOUP

shells from 5 lbs. raw shrimp
1 cup ground raw shrimp
¼ cup peanut oil
3 tbsps. soya sauce
½ cup sherry or mirin
⅓ cup chopped onion
1 garlic clove

1 small piece of fresh gingerroot
6 cups clear fish or vegetable stock
2 tbsps. minced water chestnuts
2 tbsps. minced scallions
2 tbsps. cornstarch
1 egg
6 lemon slices

Cook shells in oil until they turn a pinkish-brown. Add soya sauce, sherry, onion, garlic and ginger. Pour in the stock and simmer slowly for 30 minutes. Strain through a double layer of cheesecloth, cool, and skim. Mix ground shrimp, water chestnuts, scallions, cornstarch and raw egg together and form into 24 walnut-size balls. Reheat the soup, add the shrimp balls, and poach until they are done, about 10 minutes. Serve 4 balls in each bowl of broth with a slice of lemon.

SERVES 6.

GUIANAN SHRIMP SOUP

12 shrimp, cleaned
2 lbs. raw spinach, stemmed
1 onion, chopped
½ lb. smoked ham, sliced
2 qts. water

12 pieces of okra, stemmed
12 shallots, chopped
½ tsp. pepper
⅛ tsp. dried thyme

Combine spinach, onion, ham and water and cook over medium heat for 20 minutes. Add the okra, stirring, and the shrimp, shallots, pepper and thyme. Cook for 20 minutes. Adjust seasoning to taste. Remove the ham, dice it, and return it to the soup.

SERVES 6.

PERUVIAN SHRIMP SOUP

24 shrimp, cleaned
2 tbsps. olive oil
2 onions, chopped
2 garlic cloves, chopped
3 tbsps. tomato sauce
6 cups boiling water
½ cup raw green peas
½ cup raw corn kernels

5 raw potatoes, peeled and diced
2 tsps. salt
¼ tsp. dried ground chile pepper
¼ tsp. dried marjoram
¼ lb. cream cheese
4 eggs
6 small pieces of fish, fried (optional)

Heat the oil; sauté the onions and garlic for 10 minutes, not allowing them to brown. Add tomato sauce, boiling water, peas, corn, potatoes, salt, chile pepper and marjoram; cook for 20 minutes. Mash the cheese and milk to a smooth paste and add to the soup. Add the shrimp and cook until just opaque. Beat the eggs and gradually add 2 cups of the hot soup, stirring constantly. Return egg mixture to the soup, stirring well. Reheat but do not let boil. If desired, put a piece of fried fish in each bowl before adding soup.

SERVES 6.

PORTUGUESE SHRIMP SOUP

1 lb. shrimp in shells
1 large onion, sliced
1 carrot, sliced
2 tomatoes, chopped
2 tbsps. olive oil
¼ cup white wine

1 tbsp. port wine
1 qt. water
½ cup raw rice
1 tsp. salt
¼ tsp. pepper
1 tbsp. butter

Heat onion, carrot and tomatoes in oil. Stir in the wines and add the shrimp. Poach until shrimp begin to turn opaque. Pour in the water and bring to a boil. Remove the shrimp and clean them. Add rice, salt and pepper to kettle. Reserve a few shrimp for garnish and pound the rest in a mortar or blender. Add to the soup and cook until rice is tender. Force the soup through a sieve. Before serving (reheat if necessary) add the butter.

SERVES 4.

ZAMBOANGAN CORN AND SHRIMP SOUP

½ lb. shrimp, shelled and diced
¾ cup thinly sliced onions
2 garlic cloves, minced
2 tbsps. oil
2 cups clam broth
2 cups water

½ tsp. freshly ground black pepper
1½ cups cooked or canned corn
  kernels
½ cup shredded watercress or
  spinach

Sauté onions and garlic in oil until soft but not colored. Add shrimp and sauté until barely opaque. Stir in clam broth, water, pepper and corn. Bring to a boil, reduce heat, cover, and cook slowly for 10 minutes. Add the watercress or spinach and cook, covered, for 2 minutes longer.

SERVES 4 to 6.

FRENCH SHELLFISH BISQUE, CONSOMMÉ-BASED

8 lbs. live lobsters, preferably small ones
   or 4 to 5 lbs. crawfish
   or 5 to 6 lbs. small shrimp
   or 4 to 5 lbs. large shrimp
   or 3 lbs. crabs
¾ cup butter
½ cup chopped onion
½ cup chopped carrot
2 shallots, minced
2 parsley sprigs

1 thyme sprig
1 bay leaf
½ cup brandy
1½ cups dry white wine
1 tsp. salt
   black pepper
   dash of cayenne
14 cups consommé
1½ cups raw rice
½ cup heavy cream

All shellfish should be in their shells. Kill the lobsters or crabs as described on pages 250–251. Melt ¼ cup butter in a kettle. Add onion, carrot, shallots, parsley, thyme and bay leaf. Cook until vegetables are lightly browned. Add the shellfish. Cook over high heat until they turn opaque. Warm the brandy, ignite it, and pour flaming over the shellfish. Extinguish the flames with the white wine. Add salt, black pepper and cayenne to taste. Cook briskly until the pan is almost dry. Add 2 cups consommé and simmer for 10 minutes. Remove shellfish; separate meat from shells. Save enough shellfish meat to garnish servings. Put rest of meat and the vegetables and pan juices into a blender container and whirl at high speed until smooth, adding more consommé if necessary. Strain into the top of a double boiler.

Boil rice in 9 cups of consommé in a separate pan for 30 to 40 minutes. Whirl rice and consommé (rice will not have absorbed all the liquid in cooking) in the blender until smooth and add to purée. Add about 3 cups more consommé, or as much as is needed to bring soup to the desired consistency. Season to taste. Heat, keeping surface of soup covered with a film of melted butter to prevent a skin forming. Just before serving, stir in ½ cup soft butter and the cream. Garnish with finely diced reserved shellfish.

SERVES 12.

FRENCH SHELLFISH BISQUE, TOMATO-BASED

8 lbs. live lobsters, preferably small ones
  or 4 to 5 lbs. crawfish
  or 5 to 6 lbs. small shrimp
  or 4 to 5 lbs. large shrimp
  or 3 lbs. crabs
2 tbsps. oil
3 tbsps. butter
1 cup minced celery
1 cup minced onion
1 cup minced carrot
2 cups cored and quartered tomatoes

3 garlic cloves, minced
1 thyme sprig
1 bay leaf
1 cup dry white wine
4 cups chicken stock
1 cup raw rice
3 tbsps. Cognac
1 (6-oz.) can tomato paste
  salt and pepper
  Tabasco
2 cups heavy cream

All shellfish should be in their shells. Kill the lobsters or crabs as described on pages 250–251. Heat oil and butter; add vegetables, herbs, wine, stock and rice. Bring to a boil; add Cognac and tomato paste. Cover and cook for a total of 45 minutes, adding the shellfish at the end of the cooking time only long enough to cook them. Remove shellfish and take meat from shells; reserve a few pieces and dice finely for garnish; chop the rest. Put chopped meat and the stew mixture through a food mill (not a blender), pushing as much liquid out as can be extracted. Put the extracted liquid, a little at a time, into a blender and blend smooth. Put into the top of a double boiler and season to taste with salt, pepper and Tabasco. If the lobster has a coral, put that and the liver through a sieve and add. Add the cream and bring barely to a boil. Serve hot, or chill and serve cold.
  SERVES 12.

ENTRÉES

SAUTÉED SOFT-SHELL CRABS

1 to 3 soft-shelled crabs, cleaned as on page 251

Wash and pat dry. Sauté carefully in butter until golden brown.
  SERVES 1.

DEEP-FRIED SOFT-SHELLED CRABS

1 to 3 soft-shelled crabs, cleaned as on page 251

Wash and pat dry. Sprinkle with salt and pepper, dip into 1 egg beaten with 1 tbsp. unflavored oil and then roll in fine bread crumbs, plain or flavored. Drop into deep fat heated to 370°. These are so light they will turn by themselves in the hot fat; when they have turned 2 or 3 times, they should be golden brown. Remove and drain on paper towel. Serve hot.

SERVES 1.

MEXICAN CRABS

2 lbs. fresh crab meat	10 almonds, blanched and chopped
1 tbsp. minced onion	1½ tbsps. drained capers
3 tbsps. olive oil	2 hard-cooked eggs, chopped
1 can tomatoes	fine dry bread crumbs
1 red pimiento, chopped	melted butter
10 pitted green olives, chopped	1 tsp. paprika or red chile powder

Fry the onion in the oil until transparent. Add tomatoes and cook for 5 minutes. Add pimiento, olives, almonds, capers and crab meat. Cook gently for 15 minutes to blend flavors. Thicken, if necessary, with fine crumbs. Remove from heat and add chopped eggs. Fill individual baking shells, top with crumbs, and drizzle on melted butter. Bake at 375° until crumbs brown. Sprinkle with paprika.

SERVES 6 to 8.

GULF DEVILED CRABS

1 lb. cooked or canned crab meat	1 cup milk
3 tbsps. butter	1 tbsp. lemon juice
2 tbsps. chopped onion	1 tbsp. barbecue sauce
2 tbsps. flour	1 egg, beaten
1 tsp. dry mustard	1 tbsp. chopped parsley
½ tsp. salt	½ cup soft bread crumbs
½ tsp. dried sage	2 tbsps. melted butter
⅛ tsp. cayenne	

Melt the butter and sauté the onion in it. Blend the flour and seasonings. Gradually add milk, stirring constantly, to make a creamy sauce. Add lemon juice and barbecue sauce. Blend a little hot sauce into egg; stir egg into sauce; mix well. Add crab meat and parsley. Put into 6 individual ramekins. Top with bread crumbs mixed with melted butter. Bake at 375° for 15 minutes, or until lightly browned.

SERVES 6.

AUSTRIAN CRAWFISH

2 or 3 crawfish per serving

Poach crawfish in white-wine court bouillon to cover until done. Remove crawfish and reduce bouillon to 1 cup by boiling. Thicken reduced bouillon to mayonnaise consistency with butter. Season with paprika and pour over crawfish; sprinkle with parsley.

BAHAMA GRILL-ROASTED CRAWFISH

Marinate crawfish in cooking oil with Worcestershire sauce and soya sauce to taste for a few hours. Grill shell side down on a hibachi; turn to brown the top lightly.

FRENCH CRAWFISH IN CREAM

24 crawfish
    or tails and claws of 3 (1¼-lb.)
      lobsters in shells
7 tbsps. butter
½ tsp. and a pinch of white pepper
4 tbsps. Cognac
2 tbsps. chopped parsley

1 tbsp. chopped shallots
12 oz. dry white Burgundy wine
2 tbsps. tomato purée
5 tbsps. heavy cream
¼ tsp. salt
⅛ tsp. minced fresh tarragon
    butter

If you are using lobsters, cut tails into 4 pieces, remove claws and crack shells well. Melt 6 tbsps. butter; add shellfish and ½ tsp. white pepper. Cook until done (5 minutes for crawfish, 10 for lobster), stirring a few times. Heat 3 tbsps. Cognac, ignite it, and pour over the shellfish; let it burn itself out. Stir in parsley, shallots, white wine, tomato purée and 4 tbsps. heavy cream. Cover and simmer for 10 minutes for crawfish, 15 for lobster. Remove shellfish to a warm platter. Reduce sauce by one quarter. Add remaining 1 tbsp. butter, the salt, pinch of white pepper, tarragon, remaining 1 tbsp. Cognac and 1 tbsp. heavy cream. Dot top of sauce with butter; pour over shellfish. Serve with rice.

    SERVES 4 to 6.

KEYS CRAWFISH BURGERS

2 lbs. chopped raw crawfish meat
¼ cup diced onion
¼ cup diced green pepper
4 tbsps. flour

1 tsp. pepper
1 egg, lightly beaten
    fat for deep-frying

Mix all except the egg and fat thoroughly. Shape into small patties; dip into beaten egg and fry in deep fat heated to 370° until golden brown.

    SERVES 4.

DANISH LOBSTER TAILS

6 (½-lb.) crawfish in shells
4 tbsps. butter
1 tbsp. salad oil
1 carrot, minced
1 onion, minced
2 garlic cloves, minced
½ tsp. salt
⅓ cup brandy

4 tbsps. tomato paste
⅓ cup clam juice
1½ cups dry white wine
½ tsp. dried tarragon
½ lb. mushrooms, sliced
1 tbsp. lemon juice
1 cup hollandaise sauce (p. 355)

Heat 2 tbsps. butter and 1 tbsp. oil. Add crawfish meat side down, the carrot and onion and sauté over high heat for 2 minutes. Add garlic and salt. Warm the brandy, ignite it, and pour over the tails. After flames die add tomato paste, clam juice, wine and tarragon. Cover and simmer for 5 or 6 minutes. Remove crawfish and let cool. Loosen meat from shells and chill. Simmer sauce for 10 minutes longer, then purée in blender or force through a strainer. Sauté mushrooms in 2 tbsps. butter with the lemon juice. Stir into tomato purée. Chill. To serve, put crawfish on a baking pan and heat in a 350° oven for 10 minutes. Spread over them a thick layer of room-temperature hollandaise sauce. Put under broiler for 1 minute, or until sauce browns. Reheat tomato and mushroom sauce and serve separately.
SERVES 6.

JAPANESE FRIED LOBSTER TAILS

3 crawfish, shelled
1 cup fish stock
¼ cup sake or sherry
¼ cup soya sauce
1 tsp. ground ginger

1 cup sifted flour
4 eggs, beaten
¼ cup water
    fat for deep-frying
¼ cup grated daikon or turnip

Boil stock, sake or sherry, soya sauce and ginger. Cool. Combine flour, eggs and water and mix well to make a batter. Slash the meat; dip into the batter. Fry in deep fat heated to 350° until well browned. Remove and drain. Put cooled sauce into 6 individual bowls, add grated daikon or turnip, and serve as a dip for the shellfish.
SERVES 6.

BROILED LOBSTER

1 (1-lb.) lobster *or*   melted butter
1 crawfish tail

Kill, split and clean the lobster as detailed on page 250 or remove the bottom shell from the crawfish as on page 19. Brush the flesh side of the meat well with melted butter and put 4 inches under the broiler flame for a few minutes (up to 5 minutes for the lobster) until the flesh begins to turn opaque. Turn and brush the shell liberally with melted butter and return to broiler shell side up and continue to cook until finished, possibly 10 to 15 minutes for the lobster. Serve with drawn butter sauce.

SERVES 1.

FRENCH LOBSTER WITH CREAM AND CHEESE

3 (2-lb.) lobsters, split   2 cups heavy cream
¼ cup olive oil   3 tbsps. flour
   salt and fresh pepper   1 cup milk
¾ cup butter   ½ cup grated Parmesan cheese
¼ cup prepared mustard

Brush cut sides of lobsters with oil; sprinkle with salt and pepper. Broil under medium heat for 5 minutes. Remove from broiler and dot with 6 tbsps. butter. Bake in a 400° oven for 10 minutes. Carefully remove meat from shells (reserve coral) and slice. Brush inside of each shell lightly with mustard. Simmer cream over low heat for 30 minutes, stirring occasionally. Melt 4 tbsps. butter; stir in flour and ½ tsp. salt. Add milk slowly, stirring, and cook until sauce thickens, stirring constantly. Mix in cream and lobster coral. Return sliced lobster meat to shells and cover with sauce. Sprinkle with grated cheese and dot with remaining 2 tbsps. butter./Bake at 400° for 10 minutes (25 to 30 minutes if refrigerated).

SERVES 6.

CHINESE FRIED LOBSTER

½ lb. raw lobster meat, sliced thin
oil
½ lb. bean sprouts
¼ lb. bamboo shoots, sliced thin
½ cup sliced onions

¼ cup dried mushrooms
cornstarch
soya sauce
salt and pepper

Soak dried mushrooms in warm water for 15 minutes. Drain, and slice the caps. Cook lobster slices in a bit of oil in a skillet for about 1 minute. Add vegetables and cook for 1 minute. Mix a scant teaspoon of cornstarch with a little cold water and stir into mixture. Add a few drops of soya sauce and cook for a few minutes longer until sauce is thick and clear. Season to taste. SERVES 6.

CHINESE LOBSTER WITH PORK

2 (1-lb.) lobsters
3 tbsps. cooking oil
1 garlic clove, mashed
½ lb. pork, minced
¼ cup soya sauce
2 cups chicken broth

1 tsp. sugar
2 tbsps. cornstarch
¼ cup water
¼ cup chopped scallions, including tops
1 egg, lightly beaten

Crack the lobsters, clean them, and cut into 2-inch pieces. Heat oil, add garlic and pork, and sauté until pork loses its pink color. Stir in soya sauce, chicken broth and sugar, and bring to a boil. Add lobster, cover, and cook for 10 minutes. Mix cornstarch and cold water until smooth. Add to the lobster and cook, stirring, until sauce is thickened and clear. Stir in the scallions. Pour in the lightly beaten egg and stir just until egg is set. SERVES 4.

FRENCH LOBSTER WITH AMÉRICAINE SAUCE

2 (2-lb.) lobsters
½ cup olive oil
½ cup butter
¼ cup chopped onion
1 tbsp. chopped shallots
1 garlic clove, crushed
⅓ cup Cognac, warmed
1 cup dry white Burgundy wine

4 tbsps. tomato paste
salt and pepper
½ cup chopped parsley
1 bay leaf
1 tbsp. dried tarragon
pinch of dried thyme
pinch of dried chervil
1 tbsp. butter

Cut lobsters into small pieces and clean; save all the juices. Heat oil and butter; add lobster pieces and cook until barely opaque. Add onion, shallots and garlic. Pour on Cognac and ignite. When flames die out, add white wine and tomato paste. Sprinkle with salt and pepper to taste. Cover and cook for 20 minutes. Remove lobster and keep hot. Pound lobster liquid and intestines into a paste with parsley, bay leaf, tarragon, thyme, chervil and butter; add to sauce. Boil for 5 minutes. Pour sauce over lobster and serve hot.
    SERVES 4.

FRENCH LOBSTER THERMIDOR

3 (1½-lb.) lobsters
butter
salt and pepper
2 tbsps. olive oil
2 tbsps. butter
3 shallots, chopped

½ cup dry white wine
2 cups Mornay sauce
1 tsp. dry mustard
1 tsp. minced parsley
1 tbsp. whipped cream
grated Parmesan cheese

Split lobsters and clean them. Remove and crack claws. Dot the lobsters with butter and season with salt and pepper. Put oil in a large flat baking dish and add lobsters and cracked claws. Bake them at 400° for 10 to 15 minutes. Melt 2 tbsps. butter and add shallots and wine. Cook until reduced to one quarter. Add Mornay sauce, dry mustard and parsley. Cook briskly, stirring with a whisk. Check seasoning. Remove meat from body, reserving shells. Dice meat and mix with two thirds of the sauce. Brush a bit of sauce into the shells, fill with lobster mixture, and spread tops with remaining sauce mixed with whipped cream. Sprinkle with grated cheese/and put under broiler until browned. (If refrigerated, heat to bubbling in 350° oven, then brown.)

SERVES 6.

ITALIAN LOBSTER

---

6 (1-lb.) lobsters, split
¾ cup olive oil
3 cups tomato sauce
6 tbsps. minced parsley

3 tbsps. minced garlic
1 tsp. salt
¾ tsp. dried orégano
fresh pepper

Sauté lobsters, cut side down, in oil for 5 minutes. Arrange cut side up in a large roasting pan. Spoon mixture of sauce and seasonings on top. Add ¼ inch of water to the pan, cover tightly, and cook over low heat for 30 minutes.

SERVES 6.

RUSSIAN LOBSTER IN DILL

---

1 (3-lb.) lobster, cut into pieces and cleaned
1 onion, sliced
½ lemon, sliced
1 tbsp. salt
1 tbsp. whole peppercorns
1 tbsp. dill seeds

4 sprigs of fresh dill
2 parsley sprigs
3 tbsps. butter
2 tbsps. flour
1 cup dairy sour cream
¼ cup Madeira wine
¼ cup chopped fresh dill

Put lobster in water just to cover. Add onion, lemon, salt, whole peppercorns, dill seed, sprigs of fresh dill and parsley sprigs. Bring to a boil, lower heat and simmer, covered, until lobster is done. Remove lobster. Strain liquid and reserve 1 cup. Remove meat from shells and cut into even dice. Melt butter and stir in flour. Remove pan from heat and stir in reserved liquid. Return pan to low heat and cook, stirring, until smooth. Blend in sour cream, wine and chopped fresh dill. Add the lobster meat and reheat thoroughly. Sprinkle with paprika.

SERVES 6.

SPANISH LOBSTERS WITH CHICKEN

2 (2-lb.) lobsters
2 (2-lb.) fryer chickens
1 (6-inch) Spanish sausage
3 tbsps. olive oil
4 tbsps. butter
⅛ lb. very lean pork, ground
1 carrot, minced
1 celery rib, minced
1 small onion, minced
1 garlic clove, minced
2 large tomatoes, peeled, seeded and chopped
1 cup chicken stock

½ cup fish stock
½ cup tomato purée
½ cup dry white wine
1 parsley sprig
1 thyme sprig
1 bay leaf
¼ tsp. paprika
⅛ tsp. ground saffron
   salt and pepper
½ cup ground toasted blanched almonds
⅓ cup Spanish brandy, warmed

Remove claws from lobsters and separate tails from bodies. Reserve head and legs for sauce. Cut chickens into serving pieces. Cut sausage into ½-inch slices. Heat olive oil and 3 tbsps. butter in a large skillet. Cook ground pork until thoroughly cooked and transfer to a large casserole. Sauté sausage slices and chicken pieces until chicken is well browned, then cover the skillet and cook until chicken is tender. Transfer both meats to the casserole.

Melt remaining 1 tbsp. butter and in it lightly brown the carrot, celery, onion and garlic. Crush the lobster head and legs in a mortar and add to browned vegetables with tomatoes, chicken and fish stocks, tomato purée, white wine, herbs and seasonings. Simmer, covered, for 30 minutes. Strain through a fine sieve and put into another pan. Add almonds. Reserve sauce and keep warm. Crack lobster claws, cut tails into 4 pieces, and split bodies. Remove and reserve tomalley. Add lobster meat pieces to chicken casserole and cook, covered, for 5 minutes. Skim off fat. Ignite warmed brandy and pour over casserole. Add tomalley to reserved sauce; pour into casserole and cook for 5 minutes, stirring once or twice to distribute sauce evenly.

SERVES 6 to 8.

NEW ENGLAND CLAM-STUFFED LOBSTER

1 (1½- to 2-lb.) lobster, split and cleaned
½ cup minced clams
4 tbsps. butter
2 tbsps. minced parsley

1 tbsp. lemon juice
¼ cup clam broth
1 cup tiny bread cubes
grated Parmesan cheese
butter

Remove liver and coral from lobster and chop for stuffing. Melt butter. Put lobster meat side up on a broiler rack and brush with half of the butter. Broil 3 inches from the source of heat for 10 minutes. Combine remaining melted butter, parsley, lemon juice, clams, clam broth, bread cubes and chopped liver and coral. Toss lightly and spoon into the lobster cavity. Sprinkle with cheese and dot with butter. Return to broiler for 5 to 10 minutes, or until crumbs are lightly browned and lobster meat is white.
SERVES 1.

CHINESE SHRIMP BALLS

1 lb. cleaned shrimp, minced
½ lb. fat pork, minced
1 tsp. sake or sherry
1 tsp. salt
⅛ tsp. pepper

½ tsp. scraped fresh gingerroot
3 tbsps. cornstarch
bread crumbs
oil for deep-frying

Mix shrimp, pork, sake, salt, pepper, gingerroot and cornstarch. Form lightly into 1-inch balls and coat with crumbs. Heat deep oil to 300°. Fry balls, well separated, for 5 minutes and drain. When all are fried, increase heat to 375° and fry again until golden. Drain.
SERVES 4.

HAWAIIAN SHRIMP

1 lb. cleaned shrimp
2 tbsps. sesame oil
2 scallions, cut into 2-inch lengths
2 tsps. sugar

dash salt
1 tbsp. soya sauce
2 tsps. toasted sesame seeds

Heat oil over high heat. Add shrimp, scallions, sugar, salt and soya sauce. Cook, stirring constantly, until shrimp are done. Sprinkle with sesame seeds.

SERVES 2 to 3.

ITALIAN SHRIMP IN WINE

2 lbs. shelled large shrimp
½ cup flour
½ cup olive oil
½ cup dry white wine
¼ cup warm water
1 tsp. salt

½ tsp. pepper
1 tbsp. chopped parsley
1 scallion, chopped
2 tsps. lemon juice
   dash of cayenne

Roll shrimp in flour. Heat oil and brown shrimp. Drain and save the oil. Add wine to shrimp and cook over low heat until wine is absorbed. Combine reserved oil, the warm water, salt, pepper and tomato paste, and cook over low heat for 5 minutes. Pour over the shrimp, add parsley and scallion, and cook for 5 minutes longer. Add lemon juice and serve topped with cayenne.

SERVES 6.

SPANISH PAELLA

2½ lbs. large shrimp
12 mussels in shells
12 small clams in shells
 1 Spanish chorizo (sweet, spiced
     sausage)
 1 (2½-lb.) frying chicken or rabbit
½ cup olive oil
 1 large onion, chopped
 1 garlic clove, minced
 2 cups raw short-grain rice
 1 large tomato, peeled and chopped
 1 (10-oz.) package frozen peas,
     thawed

 1 (10-oz.) package frozen Italian
     green beans or artichoke
     hearts, thawed
 3 to 4 cups dry white wine
2½ tsps. salt
½ tsp. ground saffron
 1 tsp. paprika
   pimiento strips
   olives
   lemon wedges

Shell and devein the shrimp. Scrub mussels and clams. Poach the sausage and slice it. Disjoint the chicken or rabbit. Sauté the chicken in the oil until golden brown. Remove and reserve. Sauté shrimp in remaining oil, stirring frequently, until opaque. Remove and reserve. Steam clams and mussels in a little water until they open. Drain clams and mussels, reserving juices, but leave them in the shells. In remaining oil, sauté onion and garlic until pale gold. Add rice and cook, stirring constantly, until grains are coated with oil. Put rice in a shallow 12- to 14-inch paella pan or flame-proof casserole or skillet. As evenly as possible arrange the shrimp, chicken pieces, tomato and other vegetables over the rice. Measure clam-mussel broth and add enough dry white wine to make 4½ cups. Bring to a boil. Stir in and dissolve the salt, saffron and paprika. Heat the paella pan and pour the hot broth over the rice. Cook over moderately high heat for 10 minutes. Reduce heat to medium and cook for 15 minutes longer, or until the rice is tender and the liquid is absorbed. (Or bake at 350° for 25 to 30 minutes.) Arrange clams and mussels, still in shells, on top. Garnish with warm pimiento strips, olives, lemon wedges. [Note: If you can't get the short-grained rice (Spanish, Italian or converted), use any other regular rice, but cook it in the broth separately, then mix just before serving. Unless it's short-grained, it gets gummy cooking under the other pieces.]

SERVES 6.

PAELLA SALAD

---

18 jumbo shrimp	2 tbsps. chopped pimiento
6 lobster tails	2 oz. anchovy fillets, drained and
1 cup raw long-grain rice	chopped
2¼ cups boiling water	1 tbsp. capers
½ tsp. salt	3 tbsps. lemon juice
⅛ tsp. ground saffron	½ tsp. dry mustard
⅓ cup and ½ cup olive oil	tomato sections
3 tbsps. tarragon-flavored white vinegar	pitted ripe olives
2 scallions, chopped	pimiento-stuffed green olives

Cook shrimp, shell and devein. Cook lobster tails and split them. Cook rice in the water with salt and saffron until it is barely tender and the water is absorbed. Make a dressing with ⅓ cup oil, the vinegar, scallions, pimiento, anchovies and capers. Mix into the hot rice. Cool and chill for at least 4 hours.

Loosen lobster meat in shell, and put in a shallow pan with shrimp. Make a marinade with ½ cup olive oil, the lemon juice and mustard. Pour over shellfish and chill for several hours, turning occasionally. To serve, mound rice and surround with lobster and shrimp. Decorate with tomato sections and olives.

SERVES 6.

CHAPTER EIGHT

The Unusual

Fish and shellfish are the foods we most normally think of as coming from the water, and it's undeniably true that these are the most available. Yet there are other food sources there which, at least in this country, are more often ignored.

Roe is undoubtedly the most familiar here, with shad roe a delicacy on menus, but other roes are also good eating and can be handled in the same way. Caviar, of course, is the most expensive form of roe. Commercially, sturgeon roe is used for the prime product and the U.S. was a major exporter of it many years ago. Red caviar is a product of the salmon, while Icelandic lumpfish (lumpsucker), paddlefish and whitefish roes are similarly processed and artificially colored black to make a less expensive version of caviar available on the market shelf. Red mullet roe is cured for the Greek caviar, *tarama*. But there is no reason not to make your own less expensive "caviar" of any available *edible* roe. It's really simple.

NOTE: NOT ALL ROES ARE EDIBLE. According to the National Oceanographic Institute, the roes of pufferfishes and freshwater gars contain poisonous eggs and should not be eaten. Also, fishes that might have ingested a toxic substance should be avoided. As noted earlier in the Introduction, some fishes of our southeastern salt waters do this and the internal parts will particularly accumulate the toxins.

Male fishes, incidentally, are sometimes found with a soft, creamy white substance, the milt; in edible species this can be cooked as the female roe is, but it is not used for caviar.

Roes

APPETIZERS

CAVIAR

To make your own "caviar," remove the roe in its unbroken membrane (the whole piece is called a skein) immediately upon killing the fish. Do *not* wash it, as that softens the eggs, but keep it cold until you can treat it. Do this as quickly as possible.

Do not mix varieties; if you are working with prime sources, such as sturgeon or salmon, do not mix the skeins from several of them; the eggs vary in size and taste. More mature roes will have larger, more easily handled eggs.

With your fingers, gently pop the eggs individually out of the skein into a measuring cup. For each 1 to 2 cups eggs, stir ½ cup fine pure salt into 2 cups cold water. (The amount of salt depends on your own preferences.) Pour in the eggs and swirl briefly and gently. Let stand for about 30 minutes to firm up and absorb some of the salt. Pick out any remaining membrane (which has turned white). Drain through a strainer and immerse the strainer, with the eggs, in a large bowl of cold water, swirling gently to rinse. Drain. Pick out any remaining membrane. Store in cooled, thoroughly cleaned containers with tight lids. Caviar can be eaten within a few hours, but is best aged for at least a month. Will keep for several months refrigerated.

CAVIAR À LA FRANÇAIS

Chill caviar and serve in small croustades of oven-toasted white bread; or spoon into the hollow of small cream puffs; or put into hollowed-out cherry tomatoes and top with finely sieved hard-cooked egg white; or put into the yolk cavity of the smallest hard-cooked eggs available and top with sieved hard-cooked yolk; or season with a few drops of lemon juice and onion juice, seal between 2 small rounds of puff paste, and deep-fry in oil heated to 375° until lightly browned.

DELAWARE RUMAKI

1 pair fresh shad roe (about ¾ lb.)	1 tsp. minced shallots
1 qt. water	12 bacon strips, halved
juice of 1 lemon	additional lemon juice
salt and pepper	

Bring water to a boil and add lemon juice. Add shad roe and simmer gently for 4 minutes. Remove roe and cool with cold tap water. Cut into ½-inch cubes. Sprinkle with salt, pepper and shallots and wrap each cube well with ½ bacon slice. Put in a pan with bacon ends folded under and broil until bacon is moderately browned. Pour off excess fat and put into a 400° oven for 4 or 5 minutes. Put a foodpick in each cube and sprinkle lightly with lemon juice.
    MAKES ABOUT 24.

GREEK TARAMASALATA DIP

8 oz. prepared tarama
4 slices of white bread
½ cup lemon juice

½ cup minced onion
2 cups olive oil or salad oil, or a mixture

Remove crusts from bread. Dip bread into water and squeeze to remove excess moisture. Put bread, *tarama,* lemon juice and onion in a blender and whirl until smooth. Gradually pour in the oil; whirl until thick and creamy. Chill, covered.

MAKES 4 cups.

GREEK TARAMA SPREAD

8 oz. prepared tarama or salmon roe
6 thin slices of toast
1 tbsp. minced onion

⅓ cup olive oil
juice of 2 small lemons
ripe olives

Remove crusts from toast. Soak toast in water and squeeze dry. Mix toast, *tarama* and onion well but gently. Stir in, alternately, the olive oil and lemon juice. Chill slightly. Serve on a lettuce leaf or crusty bread, and garnish with ripe olives.

SERVES 8 to 12.

GREEK TARAMA PATTIES

1 part tarama
minced scallions

chopped parsley
4 parts freshly mashed potatoes

Blend *tarama* and potatoes with as much scallion and parsley as you like; do this thoroughly but gently; form into small patties. Dip into flour and fry in deep fat; or brush with melted butter and broil, turning and oiling once. Serve hot or cold.

SOUPS

AUSTRIAN CARP ROE SOUP

6 oz. carp roe
3 cups chopped celery
3 cups chopped onions
3 cups chopped carrots
5 tbsps. butter
3 tbsps. flour

6 cups chicken stock or bouillon
1½ cups water
1 tbsp. lemon juice
⅓ cup red wine
¾ tsp. salt
6 tbsps. sour cream

Slowly brown the chopped celery, onions and carrots in 2 tbsps. butter. In another pan slowly brown the flour in 3 tbsps. butter. Add browned vegetables and stock. Simmer for 40 minutes. Purée in a blender. Simmer roe in 1½ cups water with the lemon juice for 20 minutes. Drain and chop fine. Add to heated stock with wine and salt. Serve topped with sour cream.

SERVES 6.

ENTRÉES

To cook roe, dry pairs gently, being careful not to break the covering membrane. Pat dry with paper towels. Do not separate the set until after cooking or leave unseparated. Test for doneness by making a slit in the thickest part; the eggs should be opaque.

AMERICAN BUTTER-BROILED ROE

Arrange 1 pair shad roe (¾ lb.) in a well-buttered broiling pan, or on a metal steak plate. Melt 3 tbsps. butter and stir in 1½ tbsps. lemon juice; brush roe with this. Broil about 4 inches from the source of heat for about 5 minutes on each side, brushing several times with the melted butter. Any butter remaining can have 1 tsp. each of minced chives and parsley added; pour this over the roe, if desired.

SERVES 2.

AMERICAN SAUTÉED ROE

1 pair shad roe (about ¾ lb.)

Dust roe lightly with 2 tbsps. flour seasoned with ¼ tsp. each of salt and pepper. Heat 2 tbsps. butter in a small frying pan over medium heat and sauté roe gently on both sides until done.

Or brown 2 bacon slices. Remove them from the pan and drain them while cooking the roe in the bacon fat. Top with bacon for serving.

SERVES 2.

CONNECTICUT MARINATED ROE

2 pairs shad roe

Marinade:
6 tbsps. olive oil

1 tbsp. chopped parsley
3 tbsps. lemon juice
1 small onion, thinly sliced
salt and pepper

Make the marinade. Marinate roes in it for 1 to 2 hours, basting or turning over frequently but gently. Drain roes and arrange in a shallow pan. Broil about 4 inches from the source of heat, basting often and turning only once, until nicely browned.

SERVES 4.

FRENCH BAKED ROE

1 pair shad roe (about ¾ lb.)
¾ cup heavy cream
¼ tsp. each of minced fresh marjoram and chervil
½ tsp. salt

dash of pepper
1 onion slice, ¼ inch thick
1 bay leaf
2 parsley sprigs

Arrange roe in a small baking dish (7½ by 5½ inches) which has been generously buttered. Combine cream, marjoram, chervil, salt and pepper, and pour over the roe. Top with onion slice, bay leaf and parsley. Cover and bake at 350° for 30 to 40 minutes, or until the roe tests done. Remove onion, bay leaf and parsley, and serve.

SERVES 2.

FRENCH ROE EN PAPILLOTE

1 small pair shad roe

Coat roe on both sides with melted butter. Butter a square of cooking parchment or foil. Lay roe in center of square; sprinkle generously with lemon juice and chopped parsley and season with a little salt. Wrap roe tightly in paper or foil and cook in 400° oven for about 12 minutes.

SERVES 1.

FRENCH ROE MOUSSE

3 small pairs shad roe	3 cups heavy cream
3 egg whites	salt and pepper

Cut pairs apart and remove as much membrane as possible. Purée the roe in a blender, a little at a time, and transfer to a large bowl. Stir in egg whites, cream, and salt and pepper to taste. Beat with an electric beater for about 10 minutes. Pour into a well-buttered 9-inch ring mold. Chill for at least 30 minutes. Stand the mold in a pan of hot water and bake at 350° for about 1¼ hours, or until a knife inserted in it comes out dry. Run knife around the sides and center tube and invert onto a warm platter. Garnish and serve with your choice of sauce, lemon-flavored preferably.

SERVES 6.

GREEK-STYLE DEEP-FRIED ROE

Dip pairs of roe into seasoned flour or cracker meal. Fry in deep olive oil heated to about 375°.

NEW ENGLAND ROE CROQUETTES

1½ lb. haddock roe
3 tbsps. butter
⅓ cup flour
1¼ cups milk, scalded
    salt and pepper
1 tbsp. grated onion

1 tsp. minced parsley
½ tsp. Worcestershire sauce
1 egg, beaten
    dry bread crumbs
    shortening for deep-frying

Make a thick white sauce with butter, flour and scalded milk; season to taste. Add onion, parsley and Worcestershire sauce. Cook roe in salted water until done; drain. Break up the roe well and add to sauce. Spread on a platter, cool. When cold, form into croquettes. Dip into beaten egg, then into crumbs. Deep-fry in shortening heated to 375° until browned.

SERVES 6 to 8.

NORWEGIAN ROE

1 small pair cod roe (about ¾ lb.)

Simmer roe gently in salted water until done. Serve sprinkled with vinegar (about 1 tbsp., depending on size of roe) and black pepper.

SERVES 2.

POLISH ROE PATTIES

½ lb. roe
2 cups vegetable stock
½ medium-size onion, minced
3 tbsps. butter

1 tbsp. flour
⅓ cup sour cream
    salt and pepper
2 tbsps. bread crumbs

Simmer roe in vegetable stock for 10 minutes. Reserve the stock, and dice the roe. Simmer onion in 1 tbsp. butter until transparent. Blend in the flour and add 2 or 3 tbsps. of the reserved vegetable stock; blend until smooth. Add sour cream and season to taste. Add the diced roe and mix gently. Put the mixture into 2 or 3 baked patty shells, or scallop shells. Brown the bread crumbs in remaining butter and sprinkle over roe mix. Bake at 400° for 10 minutes.

SERVES 2 or 3.

ENGLISH ROE SALAD

---

1 lb. roe

Simmer roe in water with lemon juice, 2 whole cloves and 1 bay leaf until tender, about 5 minutes. Chill in cooking water. Drain and break into bite-size pieces. Marinate in a good, well-seasoned French dressing for at least 1 hour. Serve on lettuce.

SERVES 4.

RUSSIAN CAVIAR OMELET

---

2 tbsps. black or red caviar
3-egg omelet mixture
2 tbsps. sour cream
2 hard-cooked eggs, sieved
2 tbsps. chopped parsley

1 tbsp. chopped onion
1 to 2 tbsps. melted butter
1 or 2 tsps. lemon juice
  lemon slices

Cook the omelet. Remove to warm platter. Spread with caviar and top with sour cream. Do not fold. Blend remainder and spoon on. Garnish with lemon slices.

SERVES 1 or 2.

FRENCH CAVIAR EGGS

---

3 tbsps. caviar
8 eggs
2 tbsps. milk
  juice of ½ lemon

few drops of Tabasco
4 tbsps. butter
  sour cream

Beat the eggs well; stir in the caviar and milk gently, then the lemon juice and Tabasco. Melt butter in the top of a double boiler over hot but not boiling water. When melted, pour in the egg mixture. Cook the eggs, stirring gently with a whisk, until creamy and barely set. Serve on toast with sour cream on the side.

SERVES 4 to 6.

Seaweed

Seaweed is seldom thought of as a food source, yet it is high in iodine and can be useful in cooking. Various red seaweeds of North America, Asia and Europe are eaten semidried, when it's quite chewy, out of the hand; or they are dried, roasted and used to thicken puddings, gravies and stews in many parts of the world. The seaweed that makes the dulse of New England, which is now sold in cellophane packages in many markets, is *Rhodymenia palmata; Porphyra,* which is available on our West Coast, is known as laver in Britain and *nori* in Japan. The Japanese also use *hombu* (tangle), *wakame* (lobe-leafed undaria) and *hijili* (spindle-shaped bladder leaf). The Irish use a fine, ferny seaweed (white, pink or pale tan), which is dried and sold in bunches for their moss blancmange dessert.

To prepare, thoroughly rinse seaweed that has been taken from low tide-water; use living seaweed, not the stuff found already washed up. Lay weed on paper towels to dry for about 3 hours. Roast a few pieces at a time by holding with tongs over either a gas or electric stove element until pieces turn color and crumble easily.

PACIFIC SEAWEED SOUP

3 (2 by 5) strips of dried and roasted seaweed

1 tbsp. sesame oil

1 small onion, thinly sliced

1 cup thawed frozen snow peas

¼-inch slice of fresh gingerroot, minced

1 tbsp. soya sauce

2 cups well-flavored fish stock, heated

Heat the oil and sauté the onion until translucent. Stir in remaining ingredients and bring to a boil. Reduce heat and simmer for 5 minutes, covered.
SERVES 4 to 6.

IRISH SEAWEED PUDDING

Clean a couple of handfuls of dried seaweed. Let stand in cold water to expand. Drain and add to 1 qt. milk in the top of a double boiler. Cook over hot, not boiling, water until the milk coats a metal spoon. Remove from heat and strain. Rub the seaweed lightly through a sieve into the milk. Add 1 tsp. vanilla extract. Pour into a buttered mold and chill until firm. Serve with cream and sugar.

HOT DULSE LEMONADE
(New England treatment for coughs and colds)

Mix the juice of 1 lemon and 1 tbsp. sugar in a tall glass. In water boil a handful of dried dulse. Strain out dulse and fill glass with the water. Drink while hot.

Skate

Skate, if thought of at all by most Americans, brings to mind not much more than fake scallops. Again, we are not taking full advantage of what the seas offer. Skate wings, the pectoral fins, are the part usually used, although the liver is considered a delicacy. The sand skate or sand rock (a small dotted skate) and the buckled skate can be found in some markets. To prepare a skate for cooking (and the wings should always be precooked for tenderizing), cut the wings off the body (coffer) and simmer in a hot court bouillon for 10 to 20 minutes. (If you want the liver, carefully slit the middle of the body skin and remove it.) A wing a yard across will weigh about 2 lbs. and provide about 2 cups meat. Immediately after tenderizing, skin the wing and cut it into pieces of the desired size.

ENTRÉES

FRENCH SKATE MEUNIÈRE

3½ to 4 lbs. prepared skate
    seasoned flour
⅓ cup hot butter

fresh pepper
minced parsley
2 tbsps. chopped capers

Cut skate into 6 serving pieces and pat dry. Roll pieces in seasoned flour and sauté rapidly in hot butter. Remove from butter and season highly with freshly ground pepper; sprinkle with parsley and capers. Serve with hot butter from skillet poured over.
    SERVES 6.

FRENCH SKATE ST. ÉTIENNE

2 lbs. prepared skate
½ lemon
½ cup water
1½ cups dry red wine
    few peppercorns
1 bay leaf
¼ cup olive oil
2 tbsps. flour
½ tsp. salt

dash pepper
2 oz. unsweetened chocolate,
    grated
½ cup fresh tomato pulp
1 garlic clove, bruised
36 small white onions
6 tbsps. butter
2 tbsps. chopped parsley

Rub the skate with the lemon half. Put skate in a buttered baking dish with the water, wine, peppercorns and bay leaf. Cover with a buttered piece of wax paper and poach in a 350° oven for 20 minutes. Heat the oil in a pan and stir in the flour and salt and pepper. Strain the skate stock and stir into the *roux*. Add chocolate, tomato pulp and garlic. Heat, stirring, to a boil. Check seasoning and correct as needed. Boil onions in water to cover until tender. Drain and let them dry. Heat the butter, add the onions, and shake over moderate heat until golden brown all over. Arrange skate pieces on a heated platter and pour on the sauce. Drain onions well, mix with the parsley, and pile around the sauced skate.

SERVES 4.

INDIAN CURRIED SKATE

2 cups shredded prepared skate	1 to 1½ tbsps. curry powder
1 apple, peeled and diced	2 tbsps. flour
2 tbsps. minced onion	1 cup fish stock
1 tsp. minced parsley	1 tbsp. lemon juice
2 medium-size tomatoes, diced	salt
3 tbsps. butter	½ cup dry white wine

Sauté the apple, onion, parsley and tomatoes in the butter. When softened, add the curry powder and flour and blend well. Add the stock and bring to a boil. Add skate and simmer for 5 minutes. Add the lemon juice and wine, and heat enough to reduce the alcohol in the wine. Salt to taste. Serve on steamed rice with curry accompaniments.

SERVES 4.

ITALIAN-STYLE SKATE

1½ lbs. prepared skate wings	1 cup grated sharp cheese
1 qt. rich Italian tomato sauce	½ cup dry bread crumbs

Put some of the sauce in the bottom of a baking dish, add the pieces of skate, and cover with sauce. Top with cheese, then with crumbs. Bake at 425° for 15 minutes.

SERVES 4 to 6.

Squids and Inkfish

Squid is apt to be a bait for most fishermen, but it and its cousins, the octopus and the inkfish or cuttlefish, are all edible and popular with many. The smaller of the species are the more tender. Some people recommend simmering these until they are tenderized, but overcooking toughens them. The ink, incidentally, is used to make a sauce in Latin countries.

To prepare, kill the squid or octopus by stabbing into the brain through the eye. (In the Pacific Island area, I understand, the proper way is to bite out the eyes!) Under running water, rub and pull off the speckled membrane, exposing the pure white meat. Pull the transparent sword out from the hood and discard. Gently pull the body from the hood, stripping off and discarding the material that easily separates from the body; save the ink sac if desired. Squeeze out and discard the contents of the hood and rinse it out. Pop out the beak from between the legs. Wash well. The hood or mantle can now be stuffed, or sliced into rings or strips. The body, if small, can be cooked whole with the legs attached. The body and tentacles can also be sliced into ¼- to ½-inch rings and cooked.

Rings and small squid are crisp and delicious deep-fried in salad oil heated to 375°. First sprinkle them with garlic salt and coat with equal parts of flour and fine dry bread crumbs.

APPETIZERS

GREEK FRIED KALAMARIA

Clean large squid and cut into rings or small strips. Fry in olive oil 1 inch deep for 15 minutes, until well browned. Baby squid (finger-sized) can be cleaned and left whole and fried the same way in butter for an appetizer. Serve with lemon and oil sauce.

ITALIAN PRESERVED INKFISH

6-inch-long inkfish, cut into rings

Drop into boiling vinegar and cook for a few minutes. Strain and let cool. When cold put into sterilized pint jars and cover with olive oil. To each jar, add 1 tbsp. fresh orégano or thyme or marjoram. Cover and let stand for at least 6 weeks. Serve on an antipasto tray or as an hors d'oeuvre.

ENTRÉES

LEVANTINE SIMMERED SQUID

2 lbs. cleaned squid
1 small onion, chopped
2 garlic cloves, minced
¼ cup olive oil
2 tbsps. minced parsley

salt
pepper
⅓ cup chicken stock
juice of ½ lemon

Cut squid into thin strips and simmer in salted water until tender. Drain, and rinse in cold water. Sauté the onion and garlic in oil until pale gold. Stir in the squid, parsley, salt and pepper. Add chicken stock and simmer for about 5 minutes. Stir in lemon juice and cook for 2 minutes longer.
SERVES 6.

ITALIAN OCTOPUS SALAD

Clean several 1½-lb. octopi and boil in salted water until tender but still firm; don't overcook. Allow them to cool in the cooking liquid. Drain and cut into 1-inch lengths. Put into a dish with enough oil and vinegar (3 parts oil to 1 of vinegar) to coat when tossed. Add 5 to 7 garlic cloves, slivered, a generous ½ cup chopped parsley, and salt and pepper to taste. Cover and refrigerate at least overnight. Remove from refrigerator about 15 minutes before serving.
SERVES 6.

ITALIAN STEWED INKFISH

1 lb. prepared inkfish
olive oil
2 large onions, sliced
2 or 3 tomatoes, peeled and seeded
good pinch each of marjoram and
thyme

3 garlic cloves, mashed
½ cup red wine
1 scant tbsp. tomato paste
salt
lemon juice

Cut the inkfish body into ¼-inch rings; cut the tentacles into narrow strips. Heat barely enough olive oil to cover the bottom of a skillet. Add the onion rings and cook until barely golden. Add the inkfish and cook for 2 minutes. Add the tomatoes, marjoram, thyme and garlic, and cook for 2 minutes longer. Add the wine and allow the sauce to reduce somewhat. Add tomato paste. Add enough hot water to come just to the top of the ingredients. Cover and cook very slowly for 1½ hours. Season to taste with salt and lemon juice.

SERVES 4 to 6.

ITALIAN STUFFED SQUID

6 squid
¼ cup fresh bread crumbs
2 tbsps. minced parsley
1½ tbsps. grated Romano cheese
2 tsps. minced garlic
1 egg, lightly beaten

¼ cup olive oil
salt and pepper
4 whole garlic cloves
½ cup peeled, chopped tomatoes
¼ cup dry white wine

Clean the squid for stuffing. Chop tender parts of the tentacles. To the chopped tentacles, add the crumbs, parsley, cheese, 1½ tsps. of the minced garlic, the egg and about 1 tbsp. olive oil. Blend well; add salt and pepper to taste. Spoon equal amounts loosely into each squid body; sew up the openings. Add remaining oil to a skillet just big enough to hold the stuffed squid in a single layer. Heat oil and cook the 4 whole garlic cloves, stirring, until golden brown. Discard garlic cloves. Arrange the squid in the oil and brown all sides lightly. Add tomatoes, remaining minced garlic, wine, and salt and pepper to taste. Cover tightly and cook for 20 to 30 minutes. Remove threads from squid. Serve either whole or sliced, topped with the sauce.

SERVES 3 or 4.

NEW ENGLAND BOILED SQUID

Young, tender squid, about 8 inches long. Clean. Boil squid hard in salted water (¼ cup salt to each gallon of fresh water) for 15 to 20 minutes. Cut the underside of the body and scoop out the intestines. Discard intestines and the center cartilage. These are usually eaten hot, without sauce or seasonings.

NEW ENGLAND FRIED SQUID

Cut prepared squid into 1-inch squares and dip into seasoned flour. Shallow fry in shortening until golden brown.

Turtles

Aquatic turtles, those that spend most of their lives in water, whether salt, brackish or fresh, present a cleaning problem, after the really major one of killing them. My own personal solution, when I manage to catch up with a snapper in the local pond, is securely to lasso a hind leg and hoist the turtle up over a sturdy tree limb. I then get a shotgun and as neatly as possible I blow its head off. An accurately swung axe, of course, presupposes a chopping block.

Turtles are prehistoric holdovers and seem impossible to kill. Even after the head is off, and the body has been hanging to bleed literally for hours, the heart, when thrown into the sink, may still pulse. Even though the creature is medically dead, the extremely strong muscles continue contracting and releasing for hours, hampering dressing operations considerably. The larger, stronger saltwater turtles, of course, offer proportionately increased problems.

When the turtle has been thoroughly bled, get out a good heavy, very sharp knife, a hatchet and pair of heavy pliers. Using the hatchet remove the feet just behind the last claw. Turn the turtle onto its shell and attack from the underside. Some people recommend pinning the shell to a firm plank with a couple of spikes, but this does destroy the shell for further use. Separate the skin from the upper and lower shells where they join. With the pliers, grip the skin and pull, inverting it over the feet and neck at the front and over the feet and tail at the rear. It will be necessary to cut the membrane that binds the muscles to the skin as you go along.

When the skin is removed, separate the upper (carapace) and lower (plastron) shells at their union on the sides; look closely for the faint crack where they come together. Trim any meat that clings to the plastron as you lift it up. Sever the cartilaginous connections between the leg-tail assembly and the roof of the carapace. Carefully, to keep the yield clean, cut the unit free from the viscera. Repeat the same procedure to free the front legs and neck from the shell and viscera.

At this point, if you have a turtle of sufficient size (at least a 20-pound snapper, and it makes little sense to go through all this for anything smaller), edible flesh remaining in the shell is the tenderloin section along the backbone clinging to the carapace. To get this out, the riblike struts that shoot out at right angles to joint the roof of the shell must be cut with a heavy knife or nippers. After these have been cut, the meat can be filleted from the shell. Legs, tail and neck can be cut into sections at the joints. Wash well and soak all the meat in salty water for about an hour. Slice large pieces of meat into thin steaks and tenderize them with a mallet or the side of a heavy plate. All turtle meat requires long, slow cooking.

(The carapace, if it has not been nailed down, can be scrubbed with a stiff brush and thoroughly dried. Rubbing the top, after the drying, with a good quality wax gives it a nice shine, or it can be lacquered.)

YELLOW TURTLE EGGS

It is illegal to take turtle eggs after they have been laid, but there is talk that once the green turtle stock is replenished, it might be possible to make excess eggs available from commercial turtle kraals. Sometimes today eggs are found in turtles when they are taken. This is the way turtle eggs were cooked in the early days along the Keys:

1 lb. eggs	3 tbsps. butter
pinch of salt	dash of pepper

Remove the membrane from the eggs very carefully. Put eggs into a colander and wash carefully. Season with salt and pepper and allow to stand for 10 minutes. Melt butter to simmering; reduce heat to low and wait; the eggs will burst if the butter is too hot. Handling the eggs carefully, slide them into the pan and cook slowly for 20 minutes. Remove and serve as an unfolded omelet with grits and American cheese.

SERVES 4.

SOUPS

COLONIAL VIRGINIA TURTLE SOUP

Put all but the tender parts and the eggs of a turtle in a pot of water with 2 onions, chopped, some parsley, thyme, cloves and allspice, and salt and pepper to taste. Allow to simmer for several hours. About 1 hour before dinner, flour and fry the tender meat pieces in butter until done. Add these and the eggs to the soup pot. About 30 minutes before serving thicken the soup to taste with equal parts of flour and butter, browned. Just before serving, stir in a wineglass of claret or Madeira.

CREOLE TURTLE SOUP

4 cups diced turtle meat
4 tbsps. butter
2 tsps. dry mustard
1 fresh thyme sprig, chopped
1 qt. milk

dash of Tabasco
salt and freshly ground black
    pepper
½ cup sherry

Brown and cook the turtle meat in half of the butter, stirring in the mustard and thyme. Add milk and remaining butter, and season to taste. Heat to just under boiling. Simmer until tender. Add sherry just before serving.

SERVES 4.

ENGLISH TURTLE CONSOMMÉ

turtle meat

Cut equal amounts of stewing beef and stewing chicken into chunks; add some chopped soup vegetables. Cover meats, turtle, and vegetables with at least 2 inches of water. Add herbs (basil, marjoram, savory, thyme) and spices (whole coriander berries and peppercorns). Bring to a boil, reduce heat, and simmer, covered, for some hours, until the turtle is tender. Strain, reserving stock. Pick over and dice turtle meat (save for future use, or it can be added to the consommé just before serving). Reheat stock and add Madeira or sherry wine in the proportion of 1⅛ cups to each quart of stock.

KEYS GREEN TURTLE SOUP

2 lbs. green turtle meat
3 qts. water
2 tbsps. butter
2 large onions, minced
1 tbsp. minced parsley
  good pinch of dried thyme
1 bay leaf
6 whole cloves
6 whole allspice berries

1-inch cube of ham, minced
2 garlic cloves, mashed
2 tbsps. flour
  salt and pepper
  dash of cayenne
1 Key lime, finely chopped
1 wineglass of dry sherry
2 hard-cooked eggs, sieved

Parboil the turtle in the water for 10 minutes. Drain, saving the cooking liquid. Bone meat and cut into 1-inch pieces. Melt butter and brown the onions lightly. Roughly crush the herbs and spices and add to the onions with turtle, ham and garlic. Stir constantly until brown. Add the flour blended smooth with a bit of turtle cooking liquid. Season with salt and pepper and add remaining liquid. Simmer for 1 hour, stirring frequently. Check seasoning and correct if needed. Add cayenne and Key lime and cook until lime is tender. Just before serving add the sherry and garnish with sieved eggs.

SERVES 6.

LADY CURZON SOUP

This dish, which is attributed to the wife of a British official on duty in India, is virtually unknown in both India and the United Kingdom. It is well known in its variations in Austria, Holland and Switzerland, but rarely found in France. It is based on clear turtle consommé and properly served in demitasse cups.

Basic Lady Curzon Soup
To 1 cup clear turtle soup add ½ tsp. curry powder, or more to taste; dissolve. Stir in 2 tbsps. heavy cream and reheat without letting soup boil. Float 1 tsp. of warm cream over each serving.

Variations:
I. Cook ½ tsp. curry over low heat, stirring, until lightly browned. Warm and ignite 1 tbsp. Cognac and pour flaming over curry powder. Extinguish flame with 1 tbsp. Madeira. Blend in 1 cup clear turtle soup and heat. Stir in ¼ cup cream and reheat without boiling. Float 1 tsp. warm cream on each serving.
II. Follow variation I, but instead of just ¼ cup cream, thoroughly combine 1 egg yolk with ¼ cup cream and stir carefully into heated soup, stirring over low heat until thickened slightly.
III. Follow variation II, and brown the surface of each serving under a broiler.

Other clear turtle soup combinations include boula-boula and mermaid soup.

BOULA-BOULA

Combine equal parts of green turtle consommé and cream of pea soup. Top with a garnish of whipped cream and place under the broiler to gild.

MERMAID SOUP

Combine equal parts of clear turtle soup (which can have diced meat in it) and green pea soup. Flavor to taste with Madeira wine.

BLACK TURTLE SOUP

Combine equal parts of clear green turtle soup and black bean soup. To each portion add 1 tbsp. Marsala wine and 2 tsps. brandy. Top with 1 paper-thin slice of lemon sprinkled with sieved hard-cooked egg white.

MEXICAN TURTLE SOUP

1½ lbs. turtle breast meat	8 garlic cloves
1 lb. turtle flipper and body meat	½ cup oil
3 qts. water	4 tbsps. red-wine vinegar
1½ lbs. tomatoes	1 tbsp. dried orégano
1 cup fresh green peas	½ tsp. ground ginger
2 cups red wine	½ tsp. salt
12 small green chiles, sliced	⅛ tsp. pepper

Cut breast meat into bite-size pieces, and dice the flipper and body meat. Put turtle meat into the water and bring to a boil. When it boils, add remaining ingredients and simmer covered until the meat is tender, a matter of hours. Correct seasoning if needed.

SERVES 8 to 10.

ENTRÉES

CARIBBEAN RED TURTLE

4 thin medium-size turtle steaks, pounded	flour seasoned with salt and pepper
1 garlic clove	2 cups dairy sour cream
butter	2 tbsps. sherry
	paprika

Brown the garlic clove in enough butter to cover the bottom of a heavy skillet; remove garlic. Dredge steaks with seasoned flour and brown on both sides in the butter. Pour on the sour cream and sherry. Add enough paprika to make the sauce a rosy pink. Bake at 300° until tender, about 45 minutes. Mushrooms can also be added. Serve on rice.

SERVES 4.

CREOLE TURTLE

Soak 1 lb. cleaned turtle meat, cut into bite-size pieces, overnight in vinegar to which has been added 1 large onion, sliced, and 1 garlic clove, chopped. Drain meat and cook in boiling salted water until tender, about 1 hour. When tender, drain and pat dry. Fry in fat until brown. Add 1 onion, minced, and 3 garlic cloves, minced. When onion and garlic are tender, add 1 cup canned tomato sauce and cook for 15 minutes more.

SERVES 2.

GULF STEAMED TURTLE

2 lbs. prepared turtle steaks
salt and pepper
4 medium-size onions, sliced
¼ lb. turtle fat
1 (20-oz.) can tomatoes
4 celery ribs, chopped

3 tbsps. chopped parsley
½ cup water
flour
1 tbsp. lard
1 tbsp. Worcestershire sauce
2 tbsps. chili sauce

Season meat with salt and pepper, cover with onions, and let stand refrigerated for 2 hours. Put turtle fat, tomatoes, celery and parsley into a stewpot and let simmer down. When cooked, add the water. Dredge the meat with flour and fry very slowly in lard. Add meat and onions to stewpot and let steam down very slowly. Add Worcestershire sauce and chili sauce after first hour of cooking. Should take 3 hours of very slow cooking.

SERVES 4.

GULF TURTLE STEW

2 lbs. turtle meat
2 tbsps. fat
4 cups boiling water
1 tbsp. lemon juice
1 tsp. Worcestershire sauce
1 garlic clove
1 medium-size onion, sliced
1 or 2 bay leaves

1 tbsp. salt
1 tbsp. sugar
½ tsp. pepper
½ tsp. paprika
dash of ground allspice
6 carrots, halved
1 lb. small white onions

Cut turtle meat into ½-inch dice and brown on all sides thoroughly in hot fat. Add water, lemon juice, Worcestershire sauce, garlic, sliced onion, bay leaves and seasonings. Cover and simmer for 2 hours. Add carrots and whole onions. (Cubed raw potatoes can also be added.) Cover and cook for 30 minutes more, or until vegetables are tender. If desired, remove meat and vegetables, thicken liquid, and combine everything to serve.

SERVES 6 to 8.

HAITIAN GREEN TURTLE PIE

5 lbs. prepared turtle steaks
3 lbs. turtle calopy (flippers and underbelly)
½ cup minced celery
2 tbsps. minced parsley
½ tsp. dried thyme
3 eggs
    salt and pepper
    Worcestershire sauce
    flour
    butter
2 lbs. potatoes, peeled and sliced
1½ lbs. small onions, peeled
1 lb. carrots, cut into chunks
5 or 6 tbsps. beurre manié
    sherry
    flaky pastry topping

Simmer meat in water to cover, flavored with celery, parsley and thyme, until tender. Remove steaks, reserving broth and calopy. Put steaks through the medium blade of a food chopper. Mix the ground meat and eggs with salt, pepper and Worcestershire sauce to taste; blend well. Form into small balls. Roll these in flour and sauté in butter until golden. Add potatoes, onions and carrots to the pot of broth and calopy, and simmer until vegetables are tender. Strain, discarding calopy and saving the vegetables. Thicken the broth with *beurre manié*. Season to taste with salt and pepper and flavor with sherry. Arrange meatballs and vegetables in alternate layers in a deep baking dish and cover with the sauce. Seal the top with flaky pastry and bake at 375° until crust is golden.

SERVES 10 to 15.

KEYS BREADED TURTLE STEAKS

1 lb. prepared thin turtle steaks
  salt and pepper
  juice of 1 Key lime
  cracker meal

2 eggs, beaten
¼ cup cream
1 garlic clove
  fat for pan-frying

Season steaks with salt and pepper and squeeze on the lime juice. Let stand for about 15 minutes. Roll in cracker meal, then dip into eggs beaten with the cream, then again roll in cracker meal. Brown the garlic in a moderate amount of fat. Remove garlic, and fry the turtle steaks in the same fat. Cook slowly until tender.

Serves 2 to 4.

KEYS TURTLE STEAKS WITH SOUR CREAM

1½ lbs. thin turtle steaks, pounded
  flour
6 tbsps. butter
  salt and pepper

1 tbsp. paprika
½ cup white wine
1 cup dairy sour cream

Dust steaks with flour and sauté in butter over high heat until well browned on both sides. Season with salt and pepper to taste and sprinkle with paprika. (Can be served at this point.) To continue, pour on the wine and simmer the steaks, covered, for about 1 hour. Transfer meat to a heated platter. Add sour cream to pan juices and heat but do not boil. Pour over steaks and sprinkle with more paprika and minced parsley.

Serves 6.

COOKED AND LEFTOVER TURTLE

SOUTHERN TURTLE MEAT LOAF

3 cups ground cooked turtle meat
1 onion, chopped
2 slices of bread, crumbled

2 eggs
2 celery ribs, chopped

Make a meat loaf in the conventional manner with the above ingredients. Make a mixture of brown sugar, ketchup and prepared mustard to taste, and spread over top of meat loaf. Bake at 350° for 30 to 45 minutes.

SERVES 4 to 6.

GULF TURTLE À LA KING

2 cups chopped cooked turtle
6 hard-cooked eggs, separated
2 tbsps. butter
2 cups light cream

½ tbsp. salt
dash of white pepper
dash of grated nutmeg
dash of ground allspice

Sieve egg yolks and whites separately. Cream egg yolks with butter. Scald cream in the top of a double boiler. Add seasonings and beat in the yolk-butter. Add the turtle meat and heat. Garnish with sieved egg whites before serving on toast, in patty shells, or with rice.

SERVES 4.

CHAPTER NINE

Seafood Combinations

Some of the most famous recipes for seafood, and undoubtedly the most intricate, combine varieties from either fresh or salt water or both, and it is this mixing of textures and flavors that have made these dishes world renowned. Many are hearty dishes that serve as both soup and main dish. Some, in the original recipes, call for species that are not available in our waters; if you use substitutes from the same categories, there is no reason why your personal version should not be equally successful. Do *not* use precooked seafood except in the salads and other recipes given at the end of the chapter.

STEWS, CHOWDERS AND SOUPS

BOUILLABAISSE

Bouillabaisse is an outstanding example of a combined seafood dish. The traditional ingredients in the *bouillabaisse Marseillaise,* which is perhaps the best known, cannot be found anywhere else, not even elsewhere in France. Yet versions are made in practically every French coastal (and even interior) town. The recipe which follows (the Marseilles version) lists the original seafood and the suggested U.S. substitutions.

Always use the freshest possible fish; leave the smaller ones whole and cut the larger fish into slices. Also, always combine at least 5 varieties of fish from the following list, half firm, half soft.

baudroie (goosefish)
congre (conger eel)
dorade (dory, John dory)
felian (none in U.S. waters; substitute small eel)
galinette (none available here; use grouper)
grondin (flying fish)
langouste (spiny or rock lobster)
merlan (kingfish)
rascasse (none available here; use sea bass, hog snapper)
rougier (none here; use eel)
sard (none here; use cod or haddock)
turbot (use flounder if true turbot is not available)

Among the more familiar U.S. varieties that go well in this dish are sea robin, scup, mullet, halibut, sea bass, red snapper, hake, yellow perch and tautog. In fact, any edible fish can be used. Around Marseilles you won't find a variety of shellfish in bouillabaisse. The *most* you might find would be split spiny or rock lobster and/or crab, and that only in *some* of the restaurants. In other parts of France, however, you may well find a variety of bivalves included.

Bouillabaisse always has olive oil, saffron and tomatoes plus the seasonings. The proportions to 2 pounds of fish (and it makes little sense to do all this with anything less) are:

1 onion, sliced	2 tbsps. olive oil
1 tomato, peeled and pressed	1 leek, white part only, chopped
1 bay leaf	2 garlic cloves, crushed
generous pinch of ground saffron	1 tbsp. chopped parsley
generous pinch of ground summer	pinch of dried fennel
savory	pinch of dried thyme

Put the vegetables, oil and herbs in the bottom of a deep, fireproof casserole. Put the shellfish (if you use it) on top, then layer with the firm-fleshed fish. Add just enough stock (or water or white wine or both) to cover. Season with salt and freshly ground pepper. Cover and bring to a rapid boil. Boil for about 8 minutes. Add the soft-fleshed fish in a layer and cook briskly for another 7 minutes. Remove from the heat. Arrange pieces of seafood in a deep serving bowl. Strain the broth over slices of fresh white bread in individual soup bowls. Sprinkle the fish with chopped fresh parsley, and serve with the broth. Fish and broth, of course, can be served all together, if you prefer.

COTRIADE FROM BRITTANY

1 eel, skinned	1 tsp. dried chervil
1½ lbs. haddock or cod	1 tsp. dried tarragon
1 to 1½ lbs. sea bass	1 tsp. dried thyme
6 large potatoes, peeled and quartered	1 tsp. salt
	¼ tsp. pepper
1 large onion, chopped	3 cups white wine
3 tbsps. butter	garlic toast
2 tbsps. chopped mint	chopped parsley
1 tsp. dried marjoram	

Cut eel into 1-inch pieces, and haddock and sea bass into bite-size pieces. Cook potatoes in lightly salted water until tender but not mushy. Brown the onion in butter. Add to drained cooked potatoes with herbs, eel, fish, salt, pepper and wine. Simmer for 20 minutes, or until fish is tender. Pour into a heated tureen lined with garlic toast; garnish with parsley.

SERVES 6.

POCHOUSE (BURGUNDY FRESHWATER FISH STEW)

2½ to 3 lbs. assorted freshwater fish
    including eel
4 cups white-wine court bouillon
2 slices of salt pork
1½ tbsps. butter
8 small white onions

powdered sugar
3 tbsps. beurre manié
½ cup heavy cream
¼ cup Cognac
garlic-fried toast

Cut fish including eel into serving pieces. Make the court bouillon with Burgundy wine (this stew is a specialty of Burgundy) and strain it. Cut salt pork into bits and try out in ½ tbsp. butter. Cook onions in a small amount of water until just tender, then drain and brown in 1 tbsp. butter. As they brown sprinkle them with a little powdered sugar to glaze. Add fish to court bouillon and cook until just tender, about 15 minutes. Remove fish to a hot dish and keep hot. Strain broth and reduce over high heat to about 1½ cups. Add bits of *beurre manié* to broth, stirring constantly, and cook until thickened. When thickened and smooth, add bits of salt pork, browned onions and heavy cream. Stir and blend well. Heat Cognac, pour over fish, and ignite it. Pour sauce over fish and serve with garlic-fried toast.

SERVES 4.

GULF BOUILLABAISSE

 3 lbs. assorted firm-fleshed fish
16 medium-size oysters
 1 cup fresh small shrimp
 1 cup fresh crab meat
 2 large garlic cloves, mashed
 4 whole cloves, crushed
 6 allspice berries, crushed
 1 tsp. coarse salt
 ½ tsp. cracked pepper
 2 tbsps. butter
 2 tbsps. oil
 2 large onions, minced
 2 small carrots, thinly sliced

 3 garlic cloves, minced
 1½ cups chopped, peeled and seeded tomatoes
 ⅛ tsp. ground saffron
    generous pinch of dried crushed red pepper
 8 cups fish stock
 1 small lemon, seeded and thinly sliced
    salt
    Tabasco
 ¼ cup dry sherry

Cut fish into 1½-inch slices or chunks. Shuck oysters and reserve the juices. Blend together the mashed garlic, crushed cloves and allspice, coarse salt and cracked pepper; rub fish well with it. Wrap tightly in a plastic bag and refrigerate for 1½ to 2 hours. Melt butter with oil and sauté onions, carrots and minced garlic until just brown. Arrange fish over sautéed vegetables. Add tomatoes, saffron, crushed red pepper and stock. Cover and simmer for 20 minutes. Add shrimp, carb meat, oysters and their liquor, lemon, and salt and Tabasco to taste. Cover and simmer for 7 minutes; add sherry and simmer for 3 minutes more.
Serves 8.

CIOPPINO

There's a lot of debate as to whether this dish originated with the Italians or Portuguese, but in any case it is probably most familiar on our West Coast. Regardless of its origin, it's well worth the effort to make it.

24 to 36 clams or mussels in shells
2 Dungeness crabs, or 1 lb. hard-
  shell crabs, preferably live
3 lbs. sea bass or striper filleted
1 lb. cleaned raw shrimp
¼ lb. dried mushrooms
½ cup olive oil
1 large onion, chopped
2 garlic cloves, chopped
1 green pepper, chopped
4 tomatoes, peeled and chopped
4 tbsps. Italian tomato paste
2 cups red wine
1 cup water
  salt and pepper
1 tsp. dried basil, or 2 tbsps. minced
  fresh basil
3 tbsps. chopped parsley

Cut fish or fillets into serving pieces. Soak dried mushrooms in water for 15 minutes and drain. Heat oil and cook onion, garlic, green pepper and mushrooms for 3 minutes. Add tomatoes and cook for 4 minutes more. Add tomato paste, wine and water. Season to taste and simmer for 20 minutes. Correct seasoning and add the basil. Cover and cool if desired. Clean and crack crabs and put in the bottom of a large Dutch oven or kettle. Add mussels in shells, pieces of fish, and shrimp on top. Pour on hot sauce, cover, and simmer until clams open, about 20 to 30 minutes. Serve in large bowls and sprinkle with parsley.

SERVES 6.

CREOLE GUMBO

2 lbs. shrimp, shelled and deveined
6 fresh crabs, cleaned
1 pint freshly shucked oysters
1 lb. firm fish fillets, cut into bite-
  size pieces
2 tbsps. bacon drippings
3 tbsps. flour
2 qts. rich chicken stock
3 slices of bacon, diced
1 (1-lb.) can tomatoes
2 large onions, minced
2 garlic cloves, mashed
1 small green pepper, minced
3 cups chopped okra
1 tsp. salt
1 tsp. black pepper
¼ tsp. cayenne
¼ tsp. Worcestershire sauce
4 bay leaves
¼ tsp. Tabasco
  salt
½ tsp. filé powder
3 to 4 cups hot, cooked rice

Heat bacon drippings in a heavy pan. Stir in flour and cook until lightly browned. Gradually stir in stock. Set aside. Sauté bacon in a Dutch oven until crisp. Remove bacon, drain, and reserve. Drain tomatoes and reserve the juice. Add onions, garlic, green pepper, okra and drained tomatoes to Dutch oven. Cover and cook, stirring occasionally, until onions are soft. Stir stock mixture into vegetables. Add reserved tomato liquid and all seasonings. Bring to a boil; simmer covered for 2 hours. About 30 minutes before serving, add seafood and salt if necessary. Cook slowly until seafood is done. For each serving mold ½ cup cooked rice in a custard cup, and turn it out into a deep soup bowl. Sprinkle ⅛ tsp. filé powder in each bowl and ladle on the gumbo, dividing seafood among the bowls. (Filé will become stringy if heated in the kettle.) Top each serving with crumbled reserved bacon.

SERVES 6 to 8.

SPANISH SEAFOOD STEW

---

6 squid, cleaned and dried	1 garlic clove, minced
12 shrimp in shells	2 large tomatoes (1 lb.), peeled,
12 mussels in shells	seeded and chopped
1 lb. red snapper fillets	1 tbsp. flour
12 clams, scrubbed	½ cup chicken stock or bouillon
1 (1½ lb.) lobster	½ cup dry white wine
¼ cup olive oil	¼ tsp. sweet paprika
1 small onion, minced	salt and pepper

Cut snapper fillets into 1-inch pieces. Crack lobster claws and cut the tail, shell and all, into pieces. Heat olive oil, add squid, and cook covered for a few minutes. Remove and cut into ½-inch-thick slices; set aside. In the remaining oil, brown the onion and garlic lightly. Add tomatoes and cook until reduced almost to a paste. Blend in the flour and gradually add stock and wine, stirring constantly to make a smooth thick sauce. Season with paprika and salt and pepper to taste. Steam mussels in the shells in a small amount of water until they open. Strain mussel broth and add to sauce. Add fish, shellfish and squid to sauce. Cover dish and bake at 375° for about 15 minutes, stirring from time to time, until the clams open and fish is tender. Serve with shellfish still in their shells.

SERVES 6.

ITALIAN SEAFOOD STEW

½ lb. squid, cut into ½-inch pieces
1½ lbs. lobster, cut into 6 pieces
½ lb. bay scallops or quartered sea scallops
½ lb. halibut fillet, cut into bite-size pieces
½ lb. haddock fillet, cut into bite-size pieces
¼ cup olive oil

½ cup chopped onions
1 tsp. minced garlic
1 tsp. dried sage
½ cup dry white wine
1 cup water
1 tbsp. tomato paste
¼ tsp. salt
1 bay leaf

Combine oil, onions, garlic and sage and cook over medium heat for 5 minutes without browning. Add wine, water, tomato paste, salt and bay leaf. Bring to a boil, stirring constantly. Reduce heat and simmer for 10 minutes. Add squid, and simmer covered for 10 minutes longer. Add lobster, baste thoroughly, and cover pot. Simmer for 10 minutes, turning the lobster after 5 minutes. Add the scallops, halibut and haddock, immersing each in the broth. Cover and simmer for 8 to 10 minutes, or until fish is opaque.

SERVES 6 to 8.

BRAZILIAN FISH STEW

1 (4-lb.) red snapper, cut into 1-inch slices
2 lbs. cleaned small shrimp
6 medium-size ripe tomatoes, peeled and chopped
2 scallions with tops, sliced

¼ cup chopped parsley
2 bay leaves
1 tsp. ground coriander
2 tsps. salt
¼ tsp. pepper
Tabasco

Put snapper slices in a pan with tomatoes, scallions, parsley, bay leaves, coriander, salt and pepper; let stand in the refrigerator for several hours. Add water just to cover the fish, and bring to a boil. Reduce heat and simmer until fish is done, about 20 minutes. Carefully remove fish to a hot platter. Discard bay leaves. Add shrimp to the mixture; add Tabasco and salt and pepper to taste. Simmer until shrimp are done, about 3 minutes. Serve sauce over fish in deep bowls.

SERVES 8.

FRENCH SEAFOOD STEW

2 lbs. mussels
1 lb. flounder fillets
1½ cups white-wine court bouillon
   olive oil
1 cup white wine

salt and pepper
1 onion, minced
4 slices of bread, fried in garlic-
   flavored oil

Steam mussels in court bouillon until they open. Remove meat; strain broth and reserve 1 cup. Sauté fillets in a little olive oil until barely opaque. Pour ½ cup white wine and ¼ cup reserved broth over fish; season to taste and cook, turning once, until fish flakes. Drain liquid from pan and reserve it. Soften onion in a little olive oil, but don't brown it. Add ½ cup more white wine, ½ cup of the reserved mussel liquid and ¾ cup reserved fish liquid; cook over high heat until reduced by one quarter. Put fillets on bread slices and spoon mussels around the bread. Pour on the broth. (Can be topped with 2 tbsps. heated tomato sauce.)

SERVES 4.

BURRIDA (GENOVESE FISH STEW)

3 lbs. assorted fish (sea bass, sea
   robin, eel, sand shark, mackerel,
   sole, mullet)
1 lb. shrimp or 12 oysters or 12
   mussels or 1 lb. squid or octopus
1 small onion, chopped
½ cup and 1 tbsp. olive oil
½ carrot, chopped
1 small celery rib, chopped

1 tbsp. minced fresh basil
1 lb. tomatoes, peeled and chopped
6 dried Italian mushrooms, soaked
   15 minutes and drained
½ cup dry white wine
2 or 3 anchovy fillets, chopped
6 pieces of bread, fried in oil
1 garlic clove, mashed
1 tbsp. chopped parsley

Sauté onion in ½ cup oil in a deep kettle until barely colored. Add carrot, celery and basil. After 5 minutes add the tomatoes and mushrooms. Simmer for 5 minutes. Arrange fish in the kettle and simmer gently to blend flavors for a few minutes. Add wine and allow it to evaporate. Add anchovies and enough boiling water to barely cover the fish. Cook fish until just tender, about 10 minutes. Add shrimp during the last 5 minutes, if using them. If using mussels or oysters, steam them barely long enough to open, open and reserve juices, and add at the last minute before serving. If using squid or octopus, simmer for 30 minutes before adding to fish in kettle. Arrange pieces of oil-fried bread in deep bowls. Sauté garlic and parsley in additional oil. Pour stew over bread pieces, and pour garlic and parsley on top.

SERVES 6.

VIETNAMESE SEAFOOD CHOWDER

---

1 lb. snook fillets
9 mussels, shucked
9 large shrimp, cleaned
⅔ cup minced onion
3 scallions with tops, sliced
1 large garlic clove, minced
4 tbsps. peanut oil
3 star anise pods
1 small bay leaf
1 small green chile pepper, minced

2 tsps. grated orange rind
¼ tsp. ground saffron
¼ cup dry vermouth or sherry
2 qts. water
2 tbsps. soya sauce
2 tbsps. cornstarch
1 (20-oz.) can pineapple tidbits, drained
3 cups hot cooked rice

Cut snook into bite-size pieces. Sauté the onion, scallions and garlic in oil for 5 minutes. Add anise pods, bay leaf, chile pepper, grated rind, saffron, vermouth and water. Bring to a boil. Add seafood and reduce heat. Cook, covered, for 10 minutes. Mix soya sauce and cornstarch to a paste; stir into the seafood and cook, stirring, until sauce is clear and slightly thickened. Add pineapple and cook for 3 minutes longer. Remove and discard anise pods and bay leaf. Divide rice among 6 bowls, and ladle on the soup and seafood.

SERVES 6.

SPANISH SEAFOOD CHOWDER

1½ lbs. assorted small fish (butter-fish, smelts, crappies, fresh sardines)
1½ lbs. assorted large fish (hake, cod, halibut, pollock, sablefish)
coarse salt
3 tbsps. olive oil
3 garlic cloves, lightly crushed
1 large onion, minced
2 qts. boiling water
1 large bay leaf
6 peppercorns
salt
⅔ cup fresh white bread crumbs
½ cup strained sour-orange juice, or ¼ cup each of orange and lemon juice
¼ cup Spanish brandy

Cut large fish into 2-inch slices or chunks. Salt fish lightly with coarse salt and refrigerate in a glass dish for 1½ hours. Drain. Heat oil and sauté the garlic until nut-brown, but be careful not to burn it. Remove and discard garlic. Add onion and sauté until it just begins to color. Add water, bay leaf and peppercorns, and cook at a rolling boil for 15 minutes. Reduce heat, add fish, cover, and simmer for 15 minutes. Strain the broth, and skin the fish if desired. Check for salt. Mash the crumbs in sour-orange juice. Stir crumb-juice mixture and brandy into sauce./Add fish and reheat to just under boiling.
    SERVES 6.

NASSAU FISH CHOWDER

3 lbs. assorted firm and coarse fish, cut into 2-inch cubes
1 tsp. salt
3 tbsps. lemon juice
¼ lb. salt pork, diced
3 onions, chopped
1 (20-oz.) can tomatoes, drained
4 potatoes, peeled and cubed
12 pilot crackers, coarsely broken
½ tsp. dried thyme
2 bay leaves
2 parsley sprigs
1 tsp. peppercorns, whole
4 cups boiling water
2 tbsps. Worcestershire sauce
¼ cup sherry

Sprinkle the fish with salt and lemon juice. Fry the pork pieces brown and discard. Sauté onions in the pork fat for 10 minutes, stirring occasionally. Add tomatoes and cook over low heat for 25 minutes. In a Dutch oven arrange layers of tomato mix, fish, potatoes and crackers. Add thyme, bay leaves, parsley and peppercorns. Pour on the boiling water. Cover and cook over medium heat for 40 minutes. Add the Worcestershire sauce and sherry and cook for 20 minutes longer.

SERVES 6.

JAMAICAN FISH CHOWDER

2 lbs. firm fish fillets	½ tsp. dried basil
1 lb. cleaned shrimp	1 bay leaf
2 small crawfish	3 peppercorns
2 qts. fish stock	pinch of ground saffron
¾ cup sliced onions	½ tsp. salt
1 tbsp. minced garlic	1 (1-lb.) can solid-pack tomatoes
½ cup olive oil	1 cup dry white wine
¼ cup chopped parsley	1 tsp. grated lemon rind

Poach fish in stock. Partially cook crawfish in stock. Keep both warm. Sauté onions and garlic in oil until soft but not browned. Add herbs, spices, salt and tomatoes and simmer over low heat for 20 minutes. Add seafood, wine and enough of the reserved strained stock to cover fish by about 1 inch. Simmer until shrimp and crawfish are done. Sprinkle with grated lemon rind.

SERVES 6 to 8.

ITALIAN SEAFOOD CHOWDER

½ lb. halibut, cut into bite-size pieces	⅛ tsp. crushed red peppr
1 lb. sea bass, cut up	⅛ tsp. dried sage
½ lb. scallops (4 sea scallops)	1¼ tsps. salt
1 live lobster, cut up in shell	2 tbsps. tomato paste
½ cup olive oil	4 cups clam juice
2 garlic cloves, minced	¾ cup dry white wine
1 tsp. minced fresh parsley	

Heat the oil and sauté garlic and parsley for 1 minute. Add the lobster, red pepper and sage. Cover and cook over low heat for 5 minutes. Stir in salt, tomato paste, clam juice, wine, fish and scallops and cook over low heat for 20 minutes. Adjust seasoning as needed.

SERVES 4.

BAHAMA SEAFOOD CHOWDER

2 lbs. assorted fillets (red snapper, mullet, jack, bluefish)
2 lbs. (shelled weight) conch, crab, coquina, mussels, clams, squid
juice of 1 large sour orange or 2 large limes
2 dried hot red peppers
¼ lb. fat salt pork, coarsely ground
6 yellow onions, diced
1 large green pepper, diced
3 small garlic cloves, mashed
4 cups diced peeled potatoes
3 qts. water
½ tbsp. dried thyme
1 small bay leaf
pinch of grated mace
5 or 6 drops of Angostura bitters
2 cups light cream
salt
⅓ cup minced fresh coriander

Cut fillets into 1½-inch pieces and shellfish into bite-size pieces. Put both in a large nonmetallic bowl and add orange juice and pepper pods. Mix gently but thoroughly and let stand at room temperature for 1 hour. Toss occasionally. Try out salt pork in a large soup kettle until golden. Remove solid parts and reserve. Leave fat in kettle. Sauté onions, green pepper and garlic in fat until soft without browning. Add potatoes, water, thyme, bay leaf, mace and bitters. Bring to a boil, then cover and simmer for 40 minutes. Add drained seafood and simmer for 20 minutes. (If conch or squid is used, simmer for about 15 minutes before adding rest.) Stir in light cream and salt pork pieces. Season with salt to taste and add coriander.

SERVES 8.

ZUPPA DI PESCE (ITALIAN FISH SOUP)

8 lbs. mixed haddock, trout, cod, salmon and red snapper
1 (1-lb.) lobster
½ lb. large shrimp
½ lb. squid
1 qt. water
1 celery rib with leaves
1 onion, chopped
2 tbsps. vinegar
1 tbsp. salt
½ cup olive oil
1 garlic clove, minced
1 bay leaf, crumbled
½ tsp. dried thyme
1 tsp. dried basil
2 tbsps. minced parsley
½ cup dry white wine
1½ cups chopped peeled tomatoes
pinch of saffron, or 1 thread of whole saffron
freshly ground pepper
6 slices of bread

Boil lobster and shrimp in the water with celery, onion, vinegar and 2 tsps. salt for 5 minutes. Remove; shell lobster and shrimp and return shells to broth with trimmings from fish; simmer for 20 minutes. Strain and reserve broth. Cut squid, lobster and fish into bite-size pieces. Sauté shrimp in ¼ cup oil with garlic, bay leaf, thyme, basil and parsley for 5 minutes, stirring constantly. Add fish broth, wine, tomatoes, saffron, 1 tsp. salt and a pinch of pepper. Bring to a boil, reduce heat, cover, and simmer for 10 minutes, stirring occasionally. Fry bread slices in remaining ¼ cup oil. Place bread in deep bowls, put fish and shellfish on top, and pour on broth.

SERVES 6.

VENEZUELAN FISH AND ALMOND SOUP

1 lb. sole fillets	1 cup ground blanched almonds
1 lb. shrimp, cleaned	1 tsp. salt
2 tbsps. butter	½ tsp. pepper
1 onion, chopped	1 tsp. ground saffron
¼ lb. ham, chopped	3 hard-cooked egg yolks, chopped
2 qts. stock	3 tbsps. chopped parsley
¼ cup raw rice	

Cut sole and shrimp into small pieces. Melt butter and cook the onion in it until it is soft. Add sole and shrimp with the ham and stock. Bring to a boil; reduce heat and add rice, almonds, salt, pepper and saffron. Stir and cook over low heat, covered, for 30 minutes. Add egg yolks and parsley.

SERVES 6.

PORTUGUESE FISH SOUP

3 fillets of sole or flounder	5 slices of fresh bread, trimmed
1 lb. shrimp, cleaned	6 hard-cooked egg yolks, mashed
3 tbsps. olive oil	1 cup ground almonds
6 parsley sprigs	2 tsps. salt
½ tsp. dried basil	1 tsp. pepper
6 white onions, sliced	6 slices of French bread, toasted
6 cups water	

Heat the oil and brown fillets on both sides. Remove fillets and keep warm. Combine shrimp, parsley, basil, onions and water, and cook over medium heat for 10 minutes. Add the fillets, fresh bread slices and egg yolks; cook over medium heat for 15 minutes. Force all through a sieve, or blend, and return to pan. Add almonds, salt and pepper, and cook over low heat, stirring, until hot but not boiling. Put slices of toast in bowls and ladle soup over them.

SERVES 6.

PERUVIAN SEAFOOD SOUP

1 lb. sea bass, cut into 1-inch slices	1 small bay leaf, crumbled
12 shrimp, shelled with tails left on	4 cups boiling water
12 scallops	1½ cups canned kernel corn
1 tbsp. minced onion	½ cup fresh peas
½ tbsp. dried red chile pepper, crushed	2 cups diced peeled potatoes
1 large garlic clove, minced	2 tbsps. raw rice
1 large tomato, cut into chunks	¼ cup cottage cheese
2 tbsps. tomato sauce	2 (14-oz.) cans evaporated milk
½ tsp. dried marjoram	4 eggs
	6 pimiento-stuffed olives, sliced

Put onion, chile pepper, garlic, tomato, tomato sauce, marjoram and bay leaf in a soup kettle. Cook for 3 or 4 minutes. Add water, corn, peas, potatoes and rice and cook until potatoes are nearly tender. Add sea bass, shrimps and scallops, and cook for 12 minutes. Stir in cottage cheese. Add evaporated milk and bring soup to just under boiling. Poach the eggs and put one in each of 4 deep bowls. Ladle in the soup and sprinkle with sliced olives.

SERVES 4.

NIGERIAN SEA SOUP

½ lb. shrimp, shelled and ground
1½ lbs. red snapper, cut into 4 pieces
16 small crawfish or large shrimp in shells
1 onion, sliced
¼ cup chopped tomato
¼ cup tomato paste

¼ cup palm or corn oil
½ tsp. Tabasco
½ tbsp. salt
4 cups water
⅔ cup melon seeds, or ½ cup cornmeal
2 cups raw spinach, tough stems removed

Add ground shrimp, onion, tomato, tomato paste, oil, Tabasco and salt to 4 cups water; simmer for 5 minutes. Add melon seeds or cornmeal and simmer for 15 minutes. Add red snapper and crawfish and simmer for 8 to 10 minutes. Add spinach and cook for 2 minutes longer.

SERVES 4.

LONG ISLAND SEA SOUP

½ lb. bay scallops or quartered sea scallops
12 raw shrimp
1 lb. cod, preferably tail section
3 small lobsters
12 small littleneck clams
⅓ cup olive oil
3 tbsps. minced shallots
3 garlic cloves, minced
½ cup minced parsley

1 tbsp. crushed whole saffron
3 cups tomato purée
3½ cups fish stock
1 cup dry white wine
1 tsp. crushed dry mint
1 tsp. crushed dried basil
cayenne pepper
salt and pepper
1 tbsp. Pernod or anise liqueur

Shell and devein shrimp; cut cod into 6 pieces; cut lobsters into serving pieces—split tails and crack claws; scrub the clams. Heat the oil and add shallots; cook briefly, stirring. Add garlic; cook briefly without browning. Add parsley, saffron, tomato purée, stock, wine, mint, basil, and cayenne and salt and pepper to taste. Simmer for 15 minutes. Add scallops, shrimp, cod and lobsters. Simmer again for 10 to 15 minutes. Add clams and simmer just until they open. Stir in liqueur. Serve hot with garlic toast.

SERVES 6.

GREEK LEMON FISH SOUP

24 medium-size shrimp, shelled	2 tbsps. cornstarch
2 lbs. assorted small fish fillets (halibut, tautog)	2 tbsps. water
	2 tbsps. butter
2 qts. stock	4 eggs
½ cup dry white wine	⅓ cup lemon juice
12 small new potatoes	

Bring stock and wine to a boil; add potatoes and simmer for 10 minutes. Add fish and shrimp and simmer for 5 to 10 minutes, or until shrimp turn opaque. Remove fish, shrimp and potatoes and keep them warm. Mix cornstarch with water. Bring broth to a boil, stir in butter and cornstarch paste and cook, stirring, until thickened. Beat eggs light and beat in lemon juice. Spoon a ladle full of broth over fish to moisten it. Gradually stir remaining broth into beaten eggs, then return all to the pan. Cook over very low heat, stirring, until soup is thickened to a soft custard consistency; do not boil. Serve soup with platter of fish, shrimp and potatoes, and accompany with garlic mayonnaise.

SERVES 8.

DOMINICAN FISH AND VEGETABLE SOUP

2 lbs. assorted fish	2 cups shredded cabbage
1 lobster	2 tbsps. tomato paste
2 onions, chopped	2½ cups boiling water
2 garlic cloves, minced	2 pimientos, thinly sliced
½ cup olive oil	2 tsps. salt
1 cup raw rice	½ tsp. pepper
4 potatoes, peeled and cubed	½ tsp. dried orégano
2 tomatoes, chopped	

Cut fish into bite-size pieces. Shell lobster and cut the meat into bite-size pieces. Sauté onions and garlic in oil for 5 minutes, stirring frequently. Add fish, lobster and rice and cook over high heat for 5 minutes, stirring constantly. Add potatoes, tomatoes, cabbage, tomato paste, boiling water, pimientos, salt, pepper and orégano. Stir well, cover, and cook over medium heat for 30 minutes.

SERVES 6.

ENTRÉES

AUSTRIAN SEAFOOD PACKETS

6 individual pompano fillets
12 littleneck clams in shells
12 mussels in shells
12 scallops
12 shelled fresh shrimp
½ tsp. dried thyme

½ tbsp. dried marjoram
salt and pepper
2 garlic cloves, slivered
1 tbsp. olive oil
3 tbsps. lemon juice

Prepare 6 (12-inch) squares of foil or buttered brown paper. Wash, drain, and dry fish. Put fillets diagonally across squares of foil, 1½ inches from edges. Arrange 2 clams, 2 mussels, 2 scallops and 2 shrimp on each. Sprinkle each with ¼ tsp. thyme and ¼ tsp. marjoram, a dash of salt and pepper, ⅙ of the garlic, ½ tsp. olive oil and ½ tbsp. lemon juice. Fold foil on the diagonal; fold edges twice to seal securely but leave space inside the packet for clams and mussels to open. Bake on a cookie sheet at 375° for 25 to 30 minutes, or until mollusks are opened. Slash a cross in the top of each packet and serve in the cooking juices.
SERVES 6.

FRENCH OYSTER-STUFFED INDIVIDUAL FISH

2 lbs. smelts
12 oysters
1¼ cups soft bread crumbs
white wine
1 tbsp. grated onion
2 tbsps. butter
1 tsp. lemon juice

dash of dried thyme
dash of grated nutmeg
dash of ground cloves
salt and pepper
1 egg, beaten
fine bread crumbs
melted butter

Wash fish quickly and dry well. Chop oysters and reserve oyster liquid. Soak bread crumbs in wine; gently squeeze dry and reserve the wine. Make a soft stuffing of oysters, bread crumbs, onion, butter and lemon juice; add oyster liquid if needed to soften. Season with thyme, spices, and salt and pepper to taste. Stuff and close the smelts. Brush them with beaten egg; roll in fine crumbs. Place in a buttered baking dish and bake at 350° until brown, basting frequently with equal parts melted butter and reserved wine from soaking the bread. Pour liquid over upon serving.

SERVES 4.

FRENCH FISHERMEN'S OMELET FILLING

---

3 to 4 lbs. fish (perch, carp, bream, sheepshead)
2¼ lbs. mussels
2 cups white-wine court bouillon
½ cup water
¼ lbs. mushrooms, sliced
2 tbsps. olive oil

2 tbsps. dry white wine
few drops of lemon juice
2 tbsps. butter, melted
2 tbsps. flour
salt and pepper
butter or heavy cream for glazing

Poach fish in court bouillon; strain and reserve the cooking liquid. Steam mussels in ½ cup water until they open. Remove mussels from shells and strain and reserve the broth. Mix both liquids in a saucepan. Sauté mushrooms in oil until softened. Add white wine and lemon juice. Pour pan liquid into reserved broth, and set mushrooms aside. Reduce the liquid over high heat to approximately 1 cup. Make a medium-thick white sauce with the butter, flour and reduced liquid. Cook until thick and smooth. Cut poached fish into bite-size pieces and add with mushrooms and mussels to the sauce. Season with salt and pepper and keep warm. Spread 2 to 3 tbsps. of mixture onto an individual omelet, roll up, and serve on a heated dish. Glaze top with butter or heavy cream.

MAKES filling for 12 omelets.

BRAZILIAN BAKED FISH

1½ lbs. swordfish steaks, cut ½-inch thick
1 lb. shelled fresh shrimp
3 tbsps. olive oil
1 onion, chopped
¼ cup chopped green pepper

2 garlic cloves, mashed
3 canned chiles, seeded and chopped
1 (28-oz.) can plum tomatoes
¾ tsp. salt
¼ tsp. pepper
3 tbsps. lemon juice

Heat 2 tbsps. oil; add onion, green pepper and garlic, and sauté until onion is limp. Add chiles, tomatoes (breaking them up with a fork), salt and pepper. Simmer for 20 to 25 minutes, or until thickened. Turn into a baking dish and arrange swordfish steaks on top; top with shrimp. Drizzle with 1 tbsp. oil and the lemon juice. Cover pan and bake at 400° for 30 to 35 minutes. Serve with rice.

SERVES 6.

CHINESE FIREPOT

On a large platter arrange strips of raw fillet of sole, slices of raw squid, shelled raw shrimp, raw scallops (slices of raw beef can be added), diced Chinese cabbage, slices of raw eggplant, whole scallions and presoaked Chinese mushrooms or fresh mushroom caps. Fill a firepot or chafing dish half full of consommé or clear chicken stock. Heat to a slow bubbling simmer. Provide each diner with dishes of soya sauce and chili sauce. Each person skewers his choice of foods—or uses chopsticks—and holds the food in the simmering stock until cooked through. Then the cooked food is dipped into the sauces.

ENGLISH SEAFOOD BROCHETTE

4 shrimp, shelled
2 sea scallops, halved
3 oysters, shucked

1 sole fillet, cut into quarters
salt and pepper
1 tbsp. melted butter

Thread alternate pieces on a long skewer, repeating until all are used. Sprinkle with salt and pepper and brush with melted butter. Broil for about 10 minutes, turning skewers and brushing with additional melted butter. Serve on rice with a sauce.

SERVES 1.

FILLETS STUFFED WITH SEAFOOD

Fillets of flat fish (sole, fluke, flounder)

Spread fillets with a stuffing made of seafood (see Stuffing in index). Roll lengthwise and skewer. Put the rolls into a greased baking dish and bake at 350° to 400° for 15 to 20 minutes, or until done. Serve with a compatible warm sauce.

GULF FILLETS STUFFED WITH DEVILED CRAB

2 cups flaked cooked or canned crab
    meat
8 large fish fillets
6 tbsps. butter, melted
2 tbsps. flour
1 tsp. salt
1 tbsp. prepared mustard
½ tsp. Worcestershire sauce
¼ tsp. garlic salt
4 tsps. lemon juice
    dash of black pepper
    dash of Tabasco
⅔ cup milk

Heat 3 tbsps. butter; blend in flour, salt, mustard, Worcestershire sauce, garlic salt, 1 tsp. lemon juice, black pepper and Tabasco. Gradually add milk, and cook over low heat stirring until thickened. Add crab meat and mix well. Spread on 4 fillets; top with remaining 4 fillets. Mix 3 tsps. lemon juice with remaining melted butter and brush on fish. (Fillets can be stuffed and rolled, if desired.)/Bake at 350° for 25 to 30 minutes. (If frozen, defrost before cooking.)
SERVES 8.

FILLETS STUFFED WITH SALMON

8 individual thin fillets (sole, floun-
    der or other flat fish)
1 lb. salmon steaks
    lemon-pepper seasoning
½ cup water
½ cup dry white wine
1 small onion, sliced
1 tsp. dried tarragon
2 egg yolks
¼ lb. butter, melted

Bone and skin the salmon and cut into 8 "sticks." Sprinkle fillets with lemon-pepper seasoning. Roll 1 salmon stick in each fillet from the thick end; skewer. Combine water, wine, onion and tarragon. Poach the rolls, covered, for 5 minutes, or until done. Remove rolls. Reduce liquid to ½ cup; strain. Beat egg yolks slightly in top of a double boiler over simmering water. Add one third of the melted butter. Beat in reserved liquid alternately with remaining melted butter until thick and fluffy. Spoon over fish rolls.

SERVES 8.

FILLETS STUFFED WITH SHRIMP

1½ lbs. cooked, shelled shrimp
24 small fish fillets
1½ cups fine soft bread crumbs
3 eggs, slightly beaten
¼ cup lemon juice

3 tbsps. chopped parsley
½ tsp. dried dillweed
½ tsp. salt
¾ cup chicken broth
¾ cup white wine

Mince the shrimp. Make the bread crumbs in the blender. Mix shrimp, crumbs, eggs, lemon juice, herbs and salt. Spread 1 tbsp. on each fillet; roll and skewer. Refrigerate for 1 hour./Poach in broth and wine; or bring liquid to a boil, add rolls, cover, and bake at 425° for 10 minutes. Serve with lemon sauce.

SERVES 6 to 8.

GULF FILLETS STUFFED WITH SEAFOOD

1 medium-size flounder, filleted
½ lb. shelled shrimp
½ lb. crab meat
¼ cup chopped onion
2 garlic cloves, minced

¼ cup chopped celery
¼ cup chopped green pepper
¼ lb. butter
2 slices of white bread, shredded
1 egg, lightly beaten

Sauté onion, garlic, celery and pepper in the butter until cooked down. Add shrimp and crab meat and cook down well. Add the bread and the egg and mix well. Spread on 1 fillet, top with the other. Brush with butter and

broil; or put in a baking dish set in a pan of hot water and bake in a 350°
oven until done.

SERVES 1 or 2.

FRENCH SEAFOOD-STUFFED CLAMS

12 large clams, scrubbed
1 lb. scrod
¾ cup water
1 small onion, minced
1 small green pepper, minced
3 mushrooms, minced
½ cup butter
1 cup flour

1 tsp. curry powder
3 tbsp. chili sauce
1 tsp. commercial Sauce Robert
½ tsp. Worcestershire sauce
  pinch of cayenne
  salt and pepper
1 cup Mornay Sauce

Steam clams with ¾ cup water for 6 to 10 minutes, or until open. Remove
clams from shells, reserving bottom shells. Strain broth, add scrod, and
simmer for 10 minutes. Drain scrod, reserving broth, and mince scrod and
clams. Sauté onion, green pepper and mushrooms in butter until soft but
not browned. Add flour and curry powder and cook, stirring constantly,
over very low heat for a few seconds, or until flour begins to color. Add
reserved clam broth and cook, stirring, until very thick. Add minced clams
and scrod, chili sauce, Sauce Robert, Worcestershire sauce, cayenne and
salt and pepper to taste. Fill bottom clam shells with mixture, top with
Mornay Sauce, and brown quickly under the broiler.

SERVES 6.

HUNGARIAN FISH PAPRIKA

5 lbs. assorted fish
4 onions, thinly sliced
4 parsley sprigs, chopped

1 tbsp. sweet paprika
2 tsps. hot paprika
1 tbsp. salt

Choose fish from flounder, carp, whiting, sea bass, pompano, red snapper.

Use at least 3 varieties. Leave small fish whole and cut larger specimens into steaks or 2-inch slices or chunks. Arrange alternate layers of onion slices and fish, starting with small whole fish and ending with finest steaks. Add cold water to cover; season with both kinds of paprika and salt. Bring liquid just to a boil, reduce heat, and simmer for about 1 hour, or until a thin layer of skin forms on top: don't stir or allow to come to a boil. Skim off skin, top with parsley and serve.

SERVES 6 to 8.

ITALIAN PASTA WITH SEAFOOD

18 cherrystone or littleneck clams
18 shrimp, shelled, or scallops
½ lb. flounder fillets
¾ cup olive oil
½ cup minced green pepper
¾ cup minced parsley
3 garlic cloves, minced
1 (35-oz.) can Italian plum tomatoes

2 tsps. minced fresh basil
1 tsp. dried mint
salt
cayenne
1 lb. rigatoni
3 tbsps. butter
3 tbsps. Cognac

Scrub the clams. Cut flounder into thin strips. Heat the oil; add green pepper, parsley and garlic. Put tomatoes through a food mill or sieve and add. Add basil, mint, salt and cayenne to taste. Simmer for 5 minutes. Add clams, shrimp and flounder and simmer for 10 minutes. Meanwhile, cook rigatoni in boiling salted water for 10 minutes, stirring frequently. Drain and rinse. Add to seafood mixture. Add butter and Cognac and cover. Bake at 350° for 20 minutes.

SERVES 6.

JAPANESE SEAFOOD

Platter of:
      12 shrimp, cleaned
      12 raw clams, shucked
       2 thin fillets of sole, cut into diagonal strips
          meat of 1 lobster tail, sliced
      12 bite-size pieces of porgy

Platter of:
       1 lb. tofu (bean curd) in ½-inch slices
       2 cups Japanese noodles
       6 bamboo shoots, sliced
       1 cup sliced scallions
       2 large onions, cut into ¼-inch slices

Platter of:
      12 mushroom caps, sliced through cap and stem
       2 cups washed and stemmed spinach
       2 cups shredded Chinese cabbage

Sauce of:
      ½ cup grated red or white radish, ½ cup minced scallion tops; ¼ garlic
      clove, crushed; 1 cup chicken stock; ½ cup soya sauce; 2 tbsps. lemon juice;
      2 tbsps. sake; 1 tbsp. grated fresh gingerroot. Add more sake and soya to
      make 3 cups. Chill.

Put enough chicken broth in the bottom of a firepot or chafing dish to
measure 2 inches deep. Bring to a boil; this can be done on a stove, then the
pot can be transferred to the table. Keep broth at a gentle boil. Divide sauce
into 6 individual bowls, sprinkle with sesame seeds, and offer red pepper to
taste. Put one third of vegetable and *tofu* platters in broth and top wth
one third of seafood. Simmer until vegetables are wilted and seafood opaque.
Guests help themselves, dipping pieces into cold sauce. Cook rest of platters
in same thirds, renewing broth (heated) as necessary.
      SERVES 6.

JAPANESE SEAFOOD TEMPURA

Cut the tail meat of 1 large or 2 small lobsters diagonally into ⅛-inch-thick slices. Cut 2 flounder fillets into ½-inch-diagonal strips. Discard root and green top of 2 medium-size leeks; cut leeks lengthwise into quarters and then halve quarters. Shred 1 carrot lengthwise and cut shreds into 1½-inch lengths. Trim ends from 12 green beans. Thread an assortment of seafood and vegetables on bamboo skewers. Dip into tempura batter, coating well. Heat 3-inches of peanut oil to 375° and fry skewers, a few at a time, in deep fat until barely golden. Drain.
SERVES 6.

SWEDISH PICKLED SEAFOOD

1 (2-lb.) chunk of fresh salmon	1 whole lemon, sliced and seeded
½ lb. shrimp in shells	1 bay leaf
12 whole allspice berries	1½ cups white vinegar
1 tsp. salt	6 tbsps. sugar
1 large onion, sliced	

Put salmon in a Dutch oven with water to cover. Add 6 whole allspice, the salt, 4 onion slices and the lemon. Bring to a boil, add shrimp, cover and simmer for 5 minutes. Drain and let fish cool. Separate remaining onion slices into rings. Bone fish and break along natural lines into 1½- to 2-inch chunks. Peel shrimp. Alternate chunks of fish and shrimp and onion rings in a 1½-qt. glass jar. Add bay leaf. In a pan combine the vinegar, sugar and remaining 6 whole allspice; bring to a boil. Simmer until sugar is dissolved. Pour over the fish. Cover and chill for at least 4 hours, or for up to 2 days.
SERVES 6.

NEW ENGLAND KETTLE CLAMBAKE

In a large kettle with a lid, make layers of saltwater-washed seaweed alternating with the food. Start with seaweed, then add 8 individual lobsters, more seaweed, 8 ears of corn in the husks (peel back husks, remove silk, and turn husks back again; tie if necessary), more seaweed, a layer of scrubbed clams, more seaweed. Cover and put over an outdoor fireplace or on top of an indoor stove over medium heat. Time by the heat source; it will take about 1½ hours on an open fire, less on the stove. When clams open, eat them and work down the layers, serving lobster last.

SERVES 8.

PACKET CLAMBAKE

Cut 2 pieces of cheesecloth 24 by 36 inches for each packet; also prepare 2 pieces of foil 18 by 36 inches. Dampen the cheesecloth. Put 1 (1-lb.) lobster, 1 ear of corn in the husk (prepare as in Kettle Clambake), 12 clams and some seaweed on each double piece of cheesecloth. A baking potato rubbed with butter and a peeled onion can be added, if desired. Tie cheesecloth over the food. Place the packet on a double sheet of foil. Pour 1 cup salted water over each cloth packet and fold foil over securely with drugstore folds. Leave enough room for clams to open! Put packets on a preheated barbecue, 4 inches from the coals. Cover fire with a hood or foil. Steam for 1 hour. Can also be baked in a 350° oven.

SPANISH SEAFOOD MIX

---

1 lb. salt codfish	2 bay leaves
2 cups crab meat	½ tsp. sugar
1 cup shelled shrimp	¼ tsp. cuminseeds
2 tbsps. oil	¼ tsp. dried orégano
2 garlic cloves, minced	¼ tsp. dried marjoram
2 tomatoes, sliced	freshly ground black pepper
1 large onion, thinly sliced	½ cup white wine
1 green pepper, thinly sliced	1 cup sliced mushrooms
2 tbsps. chili sauce	

Soak codfish in water overnight. Simmer in fresh water for 15 minutes. Drain, and cut into pieces. Heat oil; add garlic, tomatoes, onion, green pepper, chili sauce, bay leaves, sugar, cuminseeds, orégano, marjoram, black pepper to taste and wine. Cover and simmer for 30 minutes. Add cod and simmer, covered, for 20 minutes. Add crab meat, shrimp and mushrooms. Simmer, covered, for 10 minutes longer. Most of the liquid will be absorbed. Serve with Spanish or Mexican black beans.

SERVES 6.

SWISS SEAFOOD IN CHAMPAGNE

2 medium-size lobsters
2½ lbs. turbot fillets
1 tbsp. chopped celery
1 tbsp. chopped carrot
1 tbsp. chopped onion
7 tbsps. butter
¼ cup Cognac
2 cups dry champagne

2 tbsps. minced shallots
juice of 1 lemon
salt
1 cup fish stock
½ tsp. cornstarch
1 tbsp. milk
1¼ cups heavy cream

Split lobsters and clean them. Cut turbot fillets into serving pieces. Brown chopped celery, carrot and onion in 4 tbsps. butter. Place lobster flesh down over vegetables and cook for 2 minutes. Turn lobsters over and pour warmed Cognac over them, ignite it and shake pan until flames die. Gently heat 1 cup of champagne and pour over lobsters, steam, covered, for 5 minutes. Drain lobsters, reserving liquid. Remove meat from shells and cut into small slices; keep warm. Coat an enamelware pan with 2 tbsps. melted butter and sprinkle with shallots. Arrange fillet pieces over; sprinkle them with lemon juice and a little salt. Combine remaining champagne and the fish stock and pour over just enough to cover fillets. Cook in 350° oven for 8 to 10 minutes, or until just tender. Remove fillets and keep warm. Combine fillet liquid and reserved lobster liquid and strain. Cook over high heat until reduced to a glaze. Dissolve cornstarch in milk and combine the mixture with heavy cream. Blend thoroughly into the glaze over low heat. Cook over low heat until reduced to about ¾ cup. Stir in last 1 tbsp. butter. Add lobster slices and heat through. Pour lobster sauce over fish, and garnish.

SERVES 6.

ISRAELI GEFILTE FISH

5 lbs. pike, carp and whitefish in equal proportions
6 onions
4 tsps. salt
2 tsps. pepper
1 tsp. sugar

¼ cup matzo or cracker meal
2 eggs, beaten
½ cup cold water
6 cups boiling water
2 carrots, sliced

Fillet all the fish, reserving heads, skin and bones for stock. Grind fish fillets and 2 onions in a food chopper. Put into a wooden bowl and add 2 tsps. salt, 1 tsp. pepper, the sugar, matzo meal, eggs and cold water. Chop all very fine and blend well. Make a stock of fish scraps, 4 onions, boiling water, carrots and remaining salt and pepper; bring to an active boil. With wet hands, form the fish mixture into 2-inch balls and drop them gently into boiling stock. Reduce heat, cover, and cook over low heat for 1½ hours. Stir very gently from time to time. Correct seasonings. Strain stock into a separate container. Serve balls very cold, moistened with the stock, if you wish.

SERVES 20 or more.

PRE-COOKED SEAFOOD COMBINATIONS

BOUILLABAISSE SALAD

1 cup cooked crab meat
½ lb. cooked shrimp
1 cup cooked lobster meat
1 cup poached or steamed snook fillet

1 cup French dressing, approximately
mixed greens
2 tomatoes, sliced
6 pitted ripe olives, halved

Cut all the seafood into bite-size pieces. Toss mixed seafood with dressing. Arrange on greens and garnish with tomatoes and olives.

SERVES 6.

CARIBBEAN SEAFOOD SALAD

1 cup flaked cooked grouper
1 cup flaked cooked snapper
1 cup flaked cooked yellowtail
⅓ cup flaked cooked mackerel
1 cup diced celery
1 tbsp. chopped olives
6 tbsps. mayonnaise

2 tbsps. chili sauce
½ tsp. dry mustard
1 tsp. Worcestershire sauce
1 tsp. tarragon vinegar
4 avocados, halved
2 limes, quartered

Combine fish with celery and olives. Mix mayonnaise, chili sauce, mustard, Worcestershire sauce and tarragon vinegar. Put fish in avocado halves, top with dressing, and add a squeeze from a lime section.
SERVES 8.

ITALIAN SEAFOOD SALAD

1 part cooked and shelled mussels
1 part cooked and shelled shrimp

2 parts firm fillets, cooked and cut into bite-size pieces

Make an Italian dressing with olive oil, lemon juice, salt, pepper and parsley. Toss seafood with dressing. Arrange on mixed greens and top with fresh parsley.

ITALIAN SEAFOOD AND MUSHROOM SALAD

12 cooked shrimp
12 bay scallops

12 tiny squid

Simmer scallops and squid in salted water with a strip of lemon peel and a sliced onion for 5 minutes. Drain both and chill. Slice ½ lb. mushrooms thinly and dress with ¼ cup olive oil, juice of ½ lemon, a garlic sliver, and salt and pepper to taste. Chill overnight. Mix seafood and mushrooms with dressing together and toss lightly.
SERVES 4.

CARIBBEAN SEAFOOD CHOWDER

4 cups flaked cooked grouper
2 cups diced cooked lobster tails
1 cup cooked whole shrimp
4 cups diced potatoes
1 cup diced celery
¼ lb. salt pork, diced

1 large onion, sliced
1 garlic clove, minced
1 qt. milk, approximately
¼ tsp. dried thyme
¼ tsp. dried orégano
salt and pepper

Parboil potatoes and celery. Try out pork with onion and garlic. Combine potatoes, celery, salt pork, onion and garlic, and mash or purée. Add fish flakes and purée again. Add milk to give the desired thickness and barely simmer. Add thyme, orégano, and salt and pepper to taste. Add lobster tail meat and shrimps and heat.

SERVES 6 to 8.

CHAPTER TEN

Seafood Flavorings and Accompaniments

Since seafood is generally the most delicately flavored of any of our foods, flavorings assume a far more important role in these dishes than in those composed of meat or vegetables. Lemon, whether in the form of a wedge or slice on the serving dish or as an ingredient, is practically a tradition. Parsley, besides adding to the attractiveness of a dish when it's a bright sprig, is another familiar flavor ingredient.

Herbs and spices are important flavoring ingredients in all dishes and the selection available in the larger markets around the country can, to an unfortunate degree, confuse rather than help. All too often we get in the habit of having the same basic ones on the kitchen shelf—perhaps an assortment of six or eight on a specially built rack—and rather monotonously use them only.

Since flavoring ingredients are what "nationalize" dishes (after all, basic cooking methods are much the same the world over), the following is only a brief listing of typical choices in kitchens in various parts of the world. Remember, too, that almost every country in the world has within its borders great regional differences in cooking, just as in the United States.

In the Orient, ginger is used much more often than in the Western world, and usually in the root rather than powdered form. If you find a good source of gingerroot, it is easy to keep a supply on hand in the freezer (preferably) or the refrigerator for many months. If you freeze it, peel it carefully first and wrap well. Then, when your recipe calls for either slivered or grated ginger, the frozen root can be either thinly sliced with a very sharp knife or rubbed on a fine grater, taking off only what you need and returning the remainder to the freezer. To keep it in the refrigerator, again peel it and put the root, cut into convenient pieces, in a jar with a tight screw top and fill the jar with dry sherry.

Coconut is a familiar Oriental ingredient. The milk or the meat is used or a cream is made out of both. If you can get a fresh coconut, punch out the two "eyes" and drain and reserve the milk. Break the coconut into convenient pieces (I use a hammer) and grate the meat off. To make coconut cream, add the coconut meat to the milk and brink to a boil, reduce the heat and simmer gently a few minutes. When cooled, strain through several layers of cheesecloth. Wring the bag out firmly until all the creamy material in the grated coconut is in the milk. Chill or freeze for future use. If only canned dried coconut is available in your area, you can follow the directions on the can of unsweetened coconut to make coconut milk, then continue with another can to make the coconut cream as above, using 2½ cups meat to ¼ to ½ cup coconut milk.

In recent years more and more Oriental cooking is being done in American homes. Understandably, in large cities where there are Oriental neighborhoods and markets, finding the necessary ingredients is no problem, but others have found ways of getting the ingredients by mail, often through friends who will shop for them. If some of the ingredients listed in my Oriental recipes are completely unavailable to you, there are some reasonably adequate substitutes.

Sake, an Oriental rice-based wine, is more widely available here than ever before but for years dry sherry has been used in its place. Sherry will stand in for mirin as well. Dashi can be found in some stores canned or in a dehydrated powder. If neither of these can be obtained, nor the tangle (seaweed) soup that is suggested, use equal amounts of beef broth and clam juice. Daikon is a very particular radish which, so far as I know, can only be bought fresh. If there's no Oriental produce market handy, use a mild white turnip instead. I know of no substitute for miso, which is usually bought in a paste form that sometimes gets quite grainy, nor for tofu, bean curd. Bean curd can be bought, where available, fresh by weight or canned.

To anyone who has eaten in a good Chinese restaurant, it is obvious that their mustard differs greatly from the prepared product available here, whether a French, German or American type. Fortunately, the Chinese type is very easy to make, using dry mustard (if you can, get the Chinese dry mustard, although the usually available kind will work well). Blend the dry mustard with a bit of white vinegar to make a thick paste. Then slowly add additional vinegar to reach a somewhat thinner consistency than you want in the finished product; it thickens on standing in the refrigerator, as it should do to blend the flavors thoroughly. Some people who do not want such a sharp bite mix the dry mustard with water instead of vinegar. (Incidentally, the same dry mustard can be blended with flat beer for a good German-type mustard.) While it is not often used as an ingredient, seldom is a Chinese batter-fried dish served without mustard on the side.

Latin American cooking is noted for its use of hot peppers. But hot pepper of one variety or another is also used in other tropical zones around the globe. There are two forms which are generally available in the U.S.: the familiar dried pepper flakes in a shaker jar and the canned variety. If you are using the canned variety (or have a source of fresh hot peppers, sometimes found in Italian as well as Mexican markets), be sure to remove the seeds from the pepper before adding them to a dish; the seed is even hotter. If you can get fresh hot peppers either tie them into a string and dry them for future use or blister them in a hot oven, peel, seed, cut into convenient pieces and flash-freeze on a cookie sheet and bag for the freezer.

These hot peppers, either fresh or dried, are used to make hot pepper sherry. This is easy to make. Put 6 to 8 peppers in a 1- to 1½-cup-capacity bottle with a tight top and fill the bottle with dry sherry. The mixture will keep for months in the refrigerator. Allow it to stand for at least a week before using. It serves as a good substitute for Tabasco. The bottle can be topped off with additional sherry once or twice. Use only a drop or two of hot pepper sherry to begin with. It really is hot.

Curry seasoning, as used in India, differs in practically each Indian home, where the practice is for it to be freshly combined for each day's use and, of course, each compound varies with each household's tastes. There are several brands of curry powder available here in the U.S., and they, too, vary widely. Perhaps the best way to find your family's "hot level" is to experiment by blending these commercial mixes. If, however, you would like to start from scratch, here are two recipes for curry powders. The method for both is the same.

MILD CURRY POWDER

¼ cup coriander seeds
1 tsp. poppy seeds
4 tsps. saffron powder
    generous dash of garlic powder

1 scant tbsp. dried chile peppers
1 tsp. cumin seeds
2 tsps. salt

HOT CURRY POWDER

2 tbsps. coriander seed
2½ tsps. fenugreek
½ tsp. ground cloves
1¼ tsps. ground black pepper
1½ tbsps. turmeric

½ tsp. crushed fennel
1 tbsp. crushed cardamom
2½ tbsps. ground cumin
½ tbsp. ground ginger
½ tbsp. cayenne

Pulverize the seeds and flakes well; blend thoroughly with remaining ingredients. Other ingredients sometimes found in curries of varying strength include allspice, cassia, cinnamon, mace, dried mustard and white pepper.

Coriander, both its leaves and seeds, is frequently used in Latin America. I have seldom found coriander leaves available here—most markets seem to carry only the seeds—but this is one herb that fortunately is easy to grow in just about any part of the country. Below the border it's called cilantro; some seed packets here call it Chinese parsley. It is also used in Oriental cooking.

French recipes very frequently call for shallots, an ingredient that all too often puzzles cooks. The shallot is a cloved bulb, similar in appearance to garlic. Its flavor strikes me as a cross between garlic and a green onion. There are a few mail order sources for dried shallots flakes and just recently frozen diced shallots have started showing up in a few of the larger markets. For the gardener they are no more difficult to grow than garlic, but the problem is to get the fresh bulb from which to start new plants.

Horseradish, a sharp root crop that is most frequently used in middle Europe, is another crop that's easily grown but grating the cleaned root is a weepy problem. Blend the grated horseradish with white vinegar to the desired consistency. All in all, it is much easier to use powdered horseradish, mixing it with the vinegar a few hours before using. The powdered product keeps much longer on the shelf than the prepared product, which unfortunately starts losing its strength as soon as the bottle is opened.

Scandinavian countries—and Scotland just across the cold North Sea—both appreciate the use of dill, both the seed and the leaf (which for some reason is called "weed" on every herb jar of it I've seen). The seed form is much more frequently found here, but the weed is well worth searching for. Dill is another easily grown herb and a supply of fresh leaves during the growing season is handy for garnishes as well as flavoring.

In using any herb it is always best, if at all possible, to use the fresh version—there is no shelf-loss of flavor or strength. While the majority of these recipes call for dried herbs (after all, that's what most cooks have on hand), substituting fresh herbs will enhance the end result. Keep in mind when using fresh herbs, regardless of how finely minced, that the volume for the desired flavor strength should be increased; dried herbs have shrunk in the drying process. The rough rule of thumb that I follow is to double the amount when using fresh herbs.

There are two citrus fruits that are important flavorings in some areas. One is the Key lime, which is found only in the Florida Keys and is used for many of the local dishes. If you have visited the Keys and greatly enjoyed a house specialty, obtained the recipe and tried to duplicate it unsuccessfully elsewhere in the country, chances are that the difficulty lies in the lime juice you used. The Key lime is completely different in flavor from any variety found fresh in markets (with one exception) or any bottled juice you can buy.

I think that the reason Key limes are not available elsewhere is simply because of how and where they grow. The tree is not a big one, compared to many citrus trees, but it grows some of the biggest sharpest thorns you can imagine. Picking a supply of these limes is literally almost worth your hide. Also the Keys where they grow are all too often inundated by salt water which kills the roots. I know of several orchards that were so ruined not many years ago.

That year when Key limes weren't to be bought for love nor money (people who had their own backyard tree really guarded their supply), one of the local markets had a fruit under a sign very carefully lettered with quotes around the name "Key" limes: they were Mexican limes, which can be used interchangeably with the Keys. (This, of course, means that Mexican recipes calling for limes present the same problem as Keys recipes.) While I am nowhere near being an arborist, I have seen both the Key and Mexican lime trees growing and would be quite willing to say they are the same tree.

Keys Old Sour made from the lime juice is unique. It is made and sold only locally by a few individuals who have a supply of the fruit. The fresh juice is heavily salted and bottled. Naturally when using Old Sour add salt to the dish *only* after tasting. If you have the limes but not the Old Sour, increase the salt with a rather heavy hand.

In the Caribbean and Spain orange juice is used in a variety of dishes and, again, it differs widely from the variety to be found generally in our fruit markets. This is a sour orange, the fruit that is natural to the root stock to which the majority of our sweet orange trees are grafted. Down in Florida, back in the Everglades, many of the islands have trees of these sour oranges which the Seminole Indians use. In many Florida back yards and large orchards (and I assume in California as well) the orange trees are carefully tended to prevent the growth of suckers, yet these would produce the sour orange. When the cultivated, grafted tree is allowed to go wild thorns develop much like those on the Key and Mexican lime trees. Something tells me that the reason we can't generally buy sour oranges or Key limes is that the fruit pickers refuse to be picked apart themselves!

While I know of no way of substituting satisfactorily for the Key or Mexican lime, there is a substitute for the sour orange, and that is to use half and half regular fresh orange juice and lemon juice.

Acids are frequently used with seafood and are always an element in marinades, whether a citrus juice or a vinegar. There are many marinades throughout the book, all listed in the index under Marinades. One important point concerning acids is that they do react chemically with metal alloys. Because of this, while you may cook an acid solution in an aluminum pan without harm, marinating in such a container can have unhappy results for both the pot and the contents. *Always* marinate in glass, ceramic or plastic. The only metals that can be safely used for marinating are unchipped enamel-coated or stainless steel pans.

Scattered throughout this book are many stuffings (see Stuffings in the index) which can be used as a filling for rolled or sandwiched fillets, to fill the cavity of a baking fish or to be packed into deep slits in large shrimp or crawfish. When stuffed, brush the fish generously with melted butter and bake in a buttered or sauced baking dish in a preheated 350° to 400° oven until done.

There are 2 additional vegetable stuffings which are easy to make and delicious.

DUXELLES STUFFING

Use fresh raw mushrooms, minced. Working with 1 to 2 tbsps. at a time, wrap in a cloth towel and form into a ball; wring out as much liquid from the mushrooms as possible. When all have been wrung out, sauté in half butter and oil until the individual pieces of mushrooms separate. Season as desired after sautéing. The stuffing is best for fillets and crustaceans.

SPINACH STUFFING

2 cups chopped cooked spinach, well drained
1 tbsp. butter, melted

1 medium-size onion, minced
2 tsps. lemon juice
1 egg, beaten foamy

Mix all but egg well; blend into the beaten egg.
MAKES enough for 1½ lbs. fillets.

Many sauces given in the preceding chapters are integral to the individual recipes. There is nothing to stop you, however, from adapting them to other dishes; that's the real message of this book, after all. Keep in mind, too, that dredging materials can alter the finished dish's flavor. You can use seasoned flour, cornmeal, or fine crumbs, seasoned or not. Egg is frequently used to hold these materials to the fish; or try milk, or a seasoned light white sauce. Don't forget, either, that in sautéing or any form of frying the cooking medium makes a difference. There's butter (and a wide variety even here); flavorless oils, olive oil, or other flavored oils such as peanut and sesame; bacon grease, of course, and lard, a favorite with many excellent cooks.

There are many ways in which flavor can be enhanced in a dish. Fish should not be cooked in or over (poached or steamed) plain water; a court bouillon is a necessity here. Stock (an excellent way to get value out of the trimmings) is not difficult to make and is helpful to have on hand for sauces or for poaching.

COURT BOUILLON

This freezes well, should you wish to keep a supply on hand.

1 large onion, chopped	3 celery ribs, sliced
2 tbsps. butter, melted	2 parsley sprigs
2 qts. water	2 tsps. salt
1 cup dry white wine	6 whole black peppercorns
2 tbsps. white-wine vinegar	2 whole cloves
1 large carrot, chopped	1 bay leaf

Sauté the onion in butter until soft. Add remaining ingredients and simmer slowly for 1 hour. Remove from heat and strain. (Use half water and half dry white wine for a wine-based version.)

MAKES about 2 quarts.

BEER COURT BOUILLON (FOR SHELLFISH)

This also makes a good sauce for shellfish.

½ cup minced onion	2 cups flat beer
4 tbsps. butter	1 tbsp. sugar
2 tbsps. flour	1 bay leaf

Sauté the onion in the butter for 10 minutes. Blend in the flour and gradually stir in the beer. Add sugar and bay leaf. Cook only until liquid reaches the boiling point.

MAKES about 2 cups.

FISH STOCK

This, too, freezes well. It is best frozen in small quantities (say ½ or 1 cup) for easy use in sauces.

2 tbsps. butter
2 lbs. chopped raw fish bones, heads, skin
1 medium-size onion, minced
3 parsley sprigs

10 whole peppercorns
2 qts. water, or 1 qt. water and 1 qt. dry white wine
pinch of salt

Melt the butter in a saucepan; add the bones and trimmings, onion, parsley and peppercorns. Cover and cook gently for 15 minutes. Skim. Add the liquid and salt. Simmer gently for 25 minutes. Skim again and strain.

Makes 2 quarts.

SUBSTITUTE STOCK

Blend 6 cups bottled clam juice and 2 cups dry white wine. Simmer gently to remove alcoholic content.

In a variety of forms, butter can be of tremendous assistance to the seafood cook. Clarified butter is light and delicate; it makes an excellent sautéing medium or dressing when gently heated and poured over a broiled fillet.

CLARIFIED BUTTER

Melt ½ cup sweet butter in a saucepan very slowly without stirring, until just liquid. Skim off the foam. Carefully and gently pour off the clear fat into a container, leaving the milky residue in the pan. Cover the container tightly and refrigerate.

Makes about ⅓ cup.

Clarified butter is the best fat for a good *roux*, the mixture of some kind of starch and some kind of fat used as sauce thickening. There are three kinds of *roux,* all compounded of similar ingredients in the same proportions but cooked for different times so as to brown the starch and fat to different degrees. Blend equal amounts of clarified butter and flour. To make a brown *roux* cook the mixture in a slow oven (200°), stirring frequently, until a good light brown color is achieved. Blond *roux* is the same mix cooked in a faster oven (250°) until it becomes pale gold. White *roux* is made by cooking on top of the stove, stirring constantly, for 5 minutes. Brown or blond *roux* can of course be cooked on the stove, stirring constantly. *Roux* keeps well if tightly covered and refrigerated or frozen.

Beurre manié, which is flour and butter (usually equal amounts) blended smoothly together by working with the fingers, is also handy to have on hand in the refrigerator as a thickening agent for cooking. As is true of all dishes that contain flour, a sauce so thickened must eventually be cooked to smooth out the taste of the raw flour, and to swell the starch particles so that they can do the work of thickening.

Seasoned or compound butters are versatile; they can be used as a topping for cooked fish, or as a cooking medium, or as an ingredient in a sauce or other preparation. Margarine instead of butter can be used in these, if desired These are best used within a week or two of blending (or frozen) and they are good to have on hand. All are made the same way; blend unmelted butter and other ingredients thoroughly in a blender or with an electric mixer. For herb butters, if not using fresh herbs, crush dry herbs as finely as possible. Make these well enough ahead for the flavoring to be well blended into the butter. When used as a topping for cooked fish, such a butter is a strictly last-minute touch; it is put onto the cooked seafood for a finishing flourish.

ALMOND BUTTER

½ cup butter   2 oz. blanched almonds

Pound the almonds (or whirl in a blender) with a few drops of water (to prevent their turning to oil) to a fine paste. Blend in the butter.

MAKES ½ cup.

ANCHOVY BUTTER

½ cup butter   2 anchovy fillets, washed and dried

Mash or mince fillets and whirl in blender with butter.
   MAKES ½ cup.

BASIL BUTTER

½ cup butter   2 tbsps. minced parsley
½ cup lightly packed fresh basil 1 tbsp. lemon juice
   leaves, chopped, or 2 tbsps. ¼ cup grated Parmesan cheese
   dried basil

   MAKES ½ cup.
Note: Omit the cheese if this butter is used for frying.

FINES HERBES BUTTER

½ cup butter   ½ tsp. dried chervil
1 tbsp. minced parsley   ¼ tsp. salt
1 tbsp. chopped chives   dash of white pepper
½ tsp. dried tarragon

   MAKES ½ cup.

GARLIC BUTTER

½ cup butter   2 tbsps. minced parsley
2 or 3 garlic cloves, mashed

   MAKES ½ cup.

MAÎTRE D'HÔTEL BUTTER

½ cup butter
¼ tsp. salt
¼ tsp. dried thyme

2 tbsps. lemon juice
2 tbsps. parsley
⅛ tsp. white pepper

MAKES ½ cup.

SHALLOT BUTTER

3 shallots, peeled and minced
2 tbsps. melted butter
½ cup butter

2 tbsps. sherry
¼ tsp. salt

Sauté the shallots in 2 tbsps. melted butter until soft, about 5 minutes. Add the sherry and cook until all liquid is evaporated. Cool thoroughly. Beat with the ½ cup butter and salt until fluffy.

MAKES ⅔ cup.

BLACK BUTTER (BEURRE NOIRE)

This is a compound butter in which the butter is cooked.

½ cup butter
1 tbsp. drained capers

2 tbsps. minced parsley
1 tbsp. vinegar

Cook the butter in a saucepan until dark brown *not* black. Pour into heated sauceboat. Stir in well-drained capers and parsley. Heat the vinegar in the butter pan and stir into the sauceboat.

MAKES ½ cup.

DRAWN BUTTER

Drawn butter, which is a sauce rather than a butter, is familiar in every seafood restaurant. It's easy to make at home. It's not just melted butter!

2 tbsps. butter
2 tbsps. flour
½ tsp. salt
⅛ tsp. white pepper

1 cup hot fish stock or water
1 tsp. lemon juice
2 tbsps. butter, in small chips

Melt 2 tbsps. butter; add flour, salt and pepper, stirring until smooth. Add the hot liquid, stirring constantly. Boil gently for 5 minutes. Add lemon juice and, bit by bit, the small chips of butter. Serve as soon as all the butter is melted.

MAKES 1½ cups.

WHITE SAUCE

Undoubtedly the most useful sauce a cook can make is that old standby, white sauce. Made with fish stock as part of the liquid, it has more flavor than if made with milk only. Depending on the proportions used, the result can be a thin sauce, which will lightly coat a dish; a medium sauce, which will blend a variety of ingredients into a finished dish; or a heavy sauce, thick enough to bind ingredients together, such as one needs for croquettes.

To make these thicknesses, follow the chart. Use for all thicknesses:

1 cup liquid (scalded milk, or part milk and part fish stock, or light cream)
½ tsp. salt
⅛ tsp. white pepper
½ to ¾ tsp. herbs or spices

Then use the amount of butter and flour that is needed for the thickness desired.

Thin White Sauces		Medium White Sauce	Heavy White Sauce
butter	1 tbsp.	2 tbsps.	3 tbsps.
flour	1 tbsp.	2 tbsps.	3 tbsps.

Melt the butter slowly; sprinkle in the flour and blend thoroughly. When completely lumpfree, add seasonings (herbs and spices can be added for flavor), and gradually stir in the liquid. Cook stirring constantly for about 5 minutes, or until thickened. This can be cooked over direct heat (carefully!) or more easily in the top of a double boiler over simmering water.

MAKES 1 cup.

MUSTARD SAUCE

1 cup medium white sauce
1 tbsp. prepared mustard (or to taste)

Blend in saucepan or over hot water at least 5 minutes.

MAKES 1 cup.

HORSERADISH SAUCE

1 cup medium white sauce (or dairy
   sour cream)
¼ tsp. salt
2 tbsps. prepared horseradish

For a warm sauce, blend white sauce with horseradish and salt over low heat or in the top of a double boiler. For a cold sauce, blend sour cream with remaining ingredients and chill at least 1 hour.

MAKES 1 cup.

SHRIMP SAUCE

2 cups medium white sauce
1 tsp. Worcestershire sauce
¼ cup minced celery
2 tbsps. minced parsley
½ cup minced cooked or canned
   shrimp
¼ cup prepared mustard
¼ cup minced, pitted olives
   (optional)

Blend all in a saucepan over low heat or in the top of a double boiler for 15 minutes.

MAKES approximately 3 cups.

VELOUTÉ SAUCE

To make a basic velouté for fish, blend 1 cup of blond *roux* with 2¾ qts. of fish stock. Bring this to a boil, stirring constantly with a wooden spoon. As soon as the first bubble appears reduce the temperature to let the sauce cook very slowly for 1½ hours, skimming frequently. Strain the finished sauce through a muslin cloth and stir until completely cold. This keeps well in the refrigerator or, of course, can be frozen. A quantity kept on hand is well worth the effort. It can be used as is with just a final seasoning and warming, or as a basic ingredient in a variety of famous sauces. Some of these follow.

ALLEMANDE SAUCE

2 large egg yolks
2½ cups velouté sauce
2 cups fish stock

3 tbsps. butter
salt and pepper

Mix eggs, sauce and stock together well with a whisk in a heavy-bottomed pan. Begin cooking over fairly high heat, stirring constantly to prevent sticking. Reduce heat and let the sauce cook down carefully without boiling until it coats a spoon well. Add the butter and season to taste. Strain through a muslin cloth. Keep hot in the top of a double boiler over hot water, beating from time to time to prevent formation of a skin on top.
    MAKES 4 cups.

BERCY SAUCE

1 tbsp. chopped shallots
4 tbsps. butter
½ cup white wine

½ cup fish stock
1 cup velouté sauce
1 tbsp. chopped parsley

Soften the shallots in 1 tbsp. melted butter. Add white wine and fish stock and boil down by one half. Add velouté sauce and boil for a few moments. Remove from heat and add remaining 3 tbsps. butter and the parsley.
    MAKES 1½ cups.

CURRIED CREAM SAUCE

1 medium-size onion, minced
1 tbsp. butter
1 bay leaf
   pinch of dried thyme

1 tbsp. curry powder (see note)
¼ cup fish stock
1½ cup velouté sauce
½ cup cream

Cook onion in butter until soft but not colored. Add herbs and curry powder; mix well. Add stock and bring to a boil. Add velouté and boil for 15 minutes. Strain through a fine sieve, and stir in the cream.

MAKES 2 cups.

Note: Curry, a blend of as many as 20 spicy ingredients, is generally available in this country in either a hot or mild blend. Experiment blending these two to find just the right "hot point" for your family's tastes. Curry powder must be cooked with the dish, it can't be sprinkled on to taste after serving. Also refer to East Indian seasonings earlier in this chapter.

BÉCHAMEL SAUCE

This is another versatile French sauce that can be used alone or as an ingredient in other sauces. While it was originally a more complex sauce, today a good béchamel is simple enough to make.

1 small onion
1 leek
1 carrot
2 celery ribs
6 tbsps. butter
6 tbsps. flour
¼ tsp. salt

dash of white pepper
dash of grated nutmeg
1 parsley sprig
1 bay leaf (optional)
4 cups milk
½ cup light cream (optional)

Wash and trim the vegetables and cut them into large dice. Cook them in the butter over low heat until onion and celery look translucent; do not let them brown. Add the flour and cook, stirring, until the flour is completely mixed with the butter, then cook for a few minutes longer to make a white *roux*. Add the salt, pepper, nutmeg and herbs, and pour in the milk all at once. The mixture will look lumpy, but keep stirring over low heat until it all smooths out and becomes thick. Cook over an asbestos pad, or in the top of a double boiler, for 45 minutes to 1 hour, but stir now and then. Strain the sauce. If it has become too thick, thin with the cream, warmed, or a little more milk. Or the cream can be added to make a richer sauce at the same time you add the milk. This sauce can be frozen successfully.

MAKES 4 cups.

MORNAY SAUCE

2 cups hot béchamel sauce
3 egg yolks, lightly beaten
3 tbsps. grated Parmesan cheese

pinch of grated nutmeg
2 tsps. minced parsley

Put the egg yolks in a saucepan and pour the hot sauce into them, stirring constantly. Cook the sauce, still stirring, until it just reaches the boiling point. Stir in the cheese, nutmeg and parsley.

MAKES 2 cups.

CAPER SAUCE

1 cup béchamel sauce
½ tbsp. lemon juice

¼ cup chopped drained capers
1 tbsp. butter

Blend all in top of a double boiler over warm water and heat.

MAKES 1¼ cups.

NEWBURG SAUCE

Almost anything served in Newburg sauce pleases the palate. This is the traditional way of making it.

2 tbsps. butter
1 tbsp. flour
1 cup hot light cream

salt and cayenne
2 egg yolks, well beaten
2 tbsps. dry sherry

Heat the butter and blend in the flour without letting it color. Gradually add the hot cream, stirring, and stir constantly until thick and smooth; do not boil. Season with salt and cayenne to taste. Put egg yolks in the top of a double boiler. Pour the sauce slowly into the yolks, stirring constantly. Set the pan over hot water and cook, stirring, for 3 minutes. Flavor with sherry.
Makes 1¼ cups.

EASY HOLLANDAISE SAUCE

This is one sauce which invariably makes a hit; unfortunately such a mystique has built up around its preparation that many are reluctant to attempt it. There is an easy way, however. Not only is the method practically foolproof, but any leftover sauce can be frozen and successfully reheated. Freezing in individual ice cubes gives you just about the right amount for 1 serving. This sauce can be used cold for blending leftovers into luncheon and hors d'oeuvre spreads.

½ cup butter, soft but not melted
¼ cup lemon juice
4 tbsps. lemon juice

4 tbsps. cold water
⅛ tsp. salt
⅛ tsp. white pepper

Beat yolks lightly with a fork in the top of a double boiler. Add remaining ingredients. Cook stirring constantly over hot, not boiling, water until thickened. Don't let the bottom of the upper pot touch the water./Reheat over hot water, stirring gently from time to time with a fork. Excellent cold with cold cooked fish and shellfish.
Makes about 1¾ cups.

MAYONNAISE

This cold sauce has scared off as many cooks as hollandaise has, and for many of the same reasons. I find that this, too, is a false alarm. Even though it is certainly easy to buy in a market, making it at home offers much greater latitude in the final product. With an electric mixer it's really very easy.

Note: Mayonnaise does not freeze well, nor does any dish that contains mayonnaise.

2 large egg yolks
½ tsp. salt
⅛ tsp. white pepper
½ tsp. dry mustard

2 tsps. vinegar, lemon or lime juice, or combination
1 cup olive oil

Rinse a small mixing bowl in hot water and dry thoroughly. Beat yolks (be sure there's absolutely no white in them) with a beater at medium speed until they barely begin to thicken. Add salt, pepper, dry mustard and 1 tsp. liquid. Mix well. Start adding the oil, drop by drop, while still beating at medium speed. When a bit more than ¼ cup oil has been added, add ½ tsp. liquid, still beating, and then pour in the rest of the oil in a slow thin stream. Beat continually while stopping the oil addition from time to time to be sure that the mixture is well combined. When all the oil has been added, add remaining ½ tsp. liquid.

Makes about 1¼ cups.

Mayonnaise variations are particularly easy when making your own. Add any of these to 1 cup of freshly made mayonnaise:

CAPER: ¼ cup minced sour pickles and ¼ cup chopped capers (press the moisture out of both), ½ tbsp. minced scallion and juice of ¼ lemon.

CURRY: ½ cup light cream, 2 tbsps. chopped chutney, 2 tbsps. curry powder (or to taste) mixed to a paste.

FINES HERBES: 1 tbsp. each of minced fresh chives, tarragon, parsley and chervil. (These are the traditional fines herbes, but quite literally any herbs can be used in your own combination and proportions.)

GREEN: ½ cup chopped cooked spinach, well drained; ½ tbsp. each of chopped parsley, tarragon and chives; ½ tsp. Dijon mustard.

GARLIC: ¼ tsp. garlic juice (or more to taste).

HORSERADISH: 1 tbsp. caviar and 1 tbsp. well-drained prepared horseradish.

LOUIS: ¼ cup heavy cream, whipped, ¼ cup chili sauce, 2 tbsps. each of minced green pepper and green onion and lemon juice.

PINK: ⅓ cup tomato purée, juice of 1 lemon and 1 tsp. grated lemon rind.

RAVIGOTE: 1 tbsp. each of minced capers, chives, sour pickle; thin with lemon juice and cream.

RÉMOULADE: 1 tbsp. each of minced chives, capers, dill pickle and parsley.

RUSSIAN: 3 tbsps. chili sauce and 1 tsp. each of minced pimiento and chives.

SHALLOT: ½ cup light cream, 1 tsp. brandy or Cognac, 4 tbsps. minced shallots, 4 tsps. lemon juice.

As you can see, you can mix almost anything with mayonnaise. Be sure to chill these variations for a couple of hours to thoroughly blend flavors.

TARTAR SAUCE

Mayonnaise is also an ingredient in a traditional tartar sauce, that ubiquitous accompaniment for seafood.

2 hard-cooked egg yolks	1 tsp. tarragon vinegar
salt and pepper	pinch of minced chives
1 cup olive oil	1 tsp. mayonnaise

Mash and pound the yolks to a paste. Add salt and pepper to taste. Pour in the olive oil in a constant thin stream. Pour slowly and beat with an electric mixer at low speed. Finish with vinegar and chives pounded with the mayonnaise.

PUFFY SAUCE

Sauces for broiled fish are normally added after cooking. However, there is a delicious exception that is quite impressive on fillets and steaks. This also uses mayonnaise.

¼ cup mayonnaise
1 tbsp. chopped drained pickle
1 tbsp. chopped parsley

dash of cayenne
1 egg white, beaten stiff

Combine all in a bowl and beat well. Spread evenly over almost cooked fillets. Reduce the heat, or lower the rack, and continue broiling for 3 to 5 minutes, until the sauce is puffed and golden brown.

ENOUGH for 6 to 8 individual fillets.

AÏOLI SAUCE

This close relative of mayonnaise is a strongly garlic-flavored cold sauce traditional in Provence. It is always served with *bourride*. There is no reason, however, why it should be restricted to that one dish so long as your family likes garlic.

4 to 8 garlic cloves
⅓ cup stale white bread crumbs
1 to 2 tbsps. white wine vinegar

¼ tsp. salt
2 egg yolks
1½ to 2 cups olive oil

Put garlic cloves through a press. Moisten the bread crumbs with vinegar and pound into a damp paste. Add the garlic and pound again into a smooth paste. Add the salt and egg yolks, pounding again until the paste is thick and smooth. Add the olive oil in minute amounts, pounding and stirring. When very thick and heavy, thin out with a few drops of additional vinegar. Continue adding the oil, by the spoonful, until the sauce is very thick and heavy—more so than mayonnaise. Can also be done (with care!) in a blender.

MAKES 3 cups.

COCKTAIL SAUCE FOR CLAMS AND OYSTERS

This bright dip is served almost automatically with clams and oysters. This can be as hot or as tame as you wish to make it. Here is a starting point.

3 tbsps. ketchup

3 tbsps. chili sauce

or 6 tbsps. ketchup and no chili sauce

1 tbsp. Worcestershire sauce

1 tbsp. prepared horseradish

2 good dashes of Tabasco

Mix well and chill to blend flavors.

CHINESE SWEET AND SOUR SAUCE

1 (15½-oz.) can pineapple chunks

⅛ cup sugar

¼ cup white vinegar

¼ cup diced celery

1½ tbsps. cornstarch

½ tbsp. soya

¼ cup sake

¼ cup diced scallions

Drain pineapple and reserve syrup. Add water to syrup to make ½ cup. Blend cornstarch and syrup to make a smooth paste. Stir in soya, sake and vinegar; cook over low heat, stirring constantly, until thickened and clear. Add the celery and scallions and simmer 5 minutes. Add pineapple chunks and simmer 2 minutes more.

MAKES about 2½ cups.

There are a few famous sauces based on seafood. They are most effective when served with poached fish steaks or fillets, but there's no reason why they can't also be served with sautéed fish. Some seafood-based sauces are used to enhance meat dishes, and others are delicious with pasta.

LOBSTER SAUCE

1 cup minced cooked lobster meat

2 cups béchamel sauce, hot

¼ cup heavy cream

¼ cup fish or chicken stock

2 tbsps. butter

salt and cayenne

3 to 4 tbsps. minced fresh dill

In a bowl, combine sauce, cream and stock. Beat in the lobster meat and butter until smooth. Or whirl it all in a blender. Heat without letting it boil; season to taste and mix well. Add dill and pour over dish to be sauced, or serve on the side.

MAKES 3½ cups.

KEYS CRAWFISH SAUCE FOR PASTA

Put cleaned crawfish tails (1 per serving) into a pressure cooker with ⅛ inch of olive oil and 1 or 2 tbsps. Key lime juice, 1 tbsp. minced fresh parsley, and 1 tsp. dried orégano. Cover pan, follow manufacturer's directions for your cooker and cook at 5 pounds pressure for 5 minutes.

ITALIAN MUSSEL SAUCE FOR PASTA

2 lbs. mussels
½ cup white wine
1 onion, chopped
1 carrot, chopped
¾ cup olive oil

2 garlic cloves, minced
3 tomatoes, peeled and chopped
salt and pepper
4 tbsps. chopped parsley

Steam the mussels with white wine, onion and carrot. Reserve mussel broth and the opened mussels still in shells. Heat oil and garlic; add tomatoes and simmer until thickened, about 20 minutes. Strain the mussel broth into tomato mixture; season with salt and pepper. Simmer while cooking pasta. Just before pasta is done, add mussels in shells to the sauce to heat through. Spoon over pasta and sprinkle with chopped parsley.

SERVES 4.

ITALIAN RED CLAM SAUCE FOR PASTA

24 small clams
1 to 2 tbsps. olive oil
1½ lbs. tomatoes, peeled and chopped

1 large onion, chopped
2 or 3 garlic cloves, chopped
handful of chopped fresh parsley

Put clams in a heavy pan over fairly high heat. Cover and steam and uncover as they begin to open; remove from shells. In the oil sauté the onion and garlic until softened but not browned. Add the tomatoes and cook, reducing somewhat. Add shelled clams and parsley and warm through. Pasta dressed with this sauce is not served with grated cheese.

NOTE: For this recipe use only small clams; don't cup up large ones as a substitute. This same recipe can be used for mussels.

SERVES 4.

ITALIAN WHITE CLAM SAUCE FOR PASTA

32 cherrystone clams
5 tbsps. olive oil

2 tbsps. minced Italian parsley
3 garlic cloves, minced

Shuck clams and reserve the juices. Chop clams coarsely. Heat oil and sauté garlic and parsley until garlic is golden. Stir in clam juice and chopped clams. Simmer without boiling for 3 minutes.

SERVES 4.

MEDITERRANEAN TUNA SAUCE

1 cup flaked cooked tuna
1 (2-oz.) can anchovy fillets, drained
    and mashed
1 cup olive oil, or ½ cup olive oil
    and ½ cup salad oil

¼ cup lemon juice
1 small jar capers, drained

Mash or blend the tuna and anchovies; blend in well the oil and lemon juice. Add capers. Let blend for 2 days. Serve cold with cooked veal or other meat.
    MAKES 2½ cups.

Variation:
When blending, add 2 raw eggs and 2 garlic cloves, crushed. Use as a cocktail dip or as a sauce for cold cooked fish the same day after blending. (Chill at least 3 hours.)

SALMON MAYONNAISE SAUCE

1 cup minced smoked salmon
¼ cup minced onion
¼ cup capers
1½ cups mayonnaise made with lemon
    juice

minced fresh dill
minced parsley

Blend salmon, onion and capers with mayonnaise. Add as much dill and parsley as you like. Let stand for at least 2 hours. For cold meats.
    MAKES 2½ cups.

There are some glamorous ways of serving fish that are basically easy and definitely palate pleasing. Aspic is impressive on a buffet table and cooling to the summer-heated eye and taste. It seals in the succulence of cold cooked food and offers many decorative possibilities. Aspic can be made in batches and kept refrigerated for up to 2 weeks or frozen for 1 month. Melt refrigerated or frozen aspic slowly over hot water before using.

BASIC FISH ASPIC

2 qts. fish stock
1 cup mixed chopped onion, carrot,
    celery and leek
    herb bouquet of bay leaf, parsley,
    celery leaves
1 cup dry white wine

1 tsp. peppercorns
1 tbsp. tomato paste
3 egg whites, beaten stiff
5 tbsps. unflavored gelatin
¼ cup brandy (optional)

Cook stock with chopped vegetables, herb bouquet, white wine and pepper-corns for 30 minutes. Strain and chill. If frozen at this point, it will keep several months. Combine melted stock with tomato paste, stiff egg whites and gelatin. Heat over a low heat, beating with a wire whisk until the liquid comes to a rolling boil and cooked egg whites rise to the surface. Remove from heat and let stand undisturbed for 15 minutes. Pour through a fine strainer lined with a fine cloth wrung out in ice water. (This extremely fine straining clarifies the final aspic.) At this point add the brandy, if desired.

Let the aspic cool until it is just at the point of setting; at that point coat your mold with some aspic. Let the mold chill until the coating is set. Add the main ingredients to the aspic and fill the mold. Chill until firm.

NOTE: Aspics can be frozen for a few weeks, the aspic stock several months. However, do *not* freeze a finished aspic made with previously frozen aspic.

FISH BALLS IN VARIOUS LANGUAGES

Cakes or patties, as we call them, croquettes or quenelles in French, or *cromesquis* in Russian—all made with finely minced and drained cooked ingredients bound in an extremely thick white sauce well seasoned to complement the basic ingredient. Variation occurs in the finishing; one is always fried; one can be either fried or oven baked; one is simmered in a poaching liquid. They all start with a thick sauce.

MOLDING SAUCE

1 tbsp. butter   2 tbsps. flour
½ cup milk

Melt butter over low heat; stir in flour and blend. Slowly add milk and seasonings (season very well) and cook slowly, stirring constantly, until very thick. Cool before adding the main ingredient (chopped, ground or puréed and very well drained) in the proportion of ½ cup sauce to 2 cups cooked fish.

CROMESQUIS

Form fish mixture into balls (small ones for hors d'oeuvre, larger for a main dish) and wrap each in a thin strip of ham. Chill. Make a fritter batter.

3 egg yolks	1 tbsp. melted butter
⅓ cup milk	½ tsp. salt
⅓ cup water	1 cup sifted flour
1 tbsp. lemon juice	2 egg whites, beaten stiff

Beat egg yolks with liquids and salt. Stir in the flour and fold in the whites just before using.

Dip the ham-wrapped balls into the batter. Deep-fry the cromesquis in oil heated to 375° until done, the crust well browned and the ball heated through to the center.

CROQUETTES

Spread fish mixture ¾ inch thick on a cookie sheet or flat plate. Chill well. Cut into shapes or form with the hands into pyramids, balls or cakes. Dip into lightly seasoned flour, then into beaten egg, then roll in seasoned bread crumbs. Chill well again. Deep-fry in fat heated to 375° for 2 to 4 minutes; or put on a greased cookie sheet and bake in a preheated 475° oven for 15 minutes.

QUENELLES

Best made with puréed ingredients. Combine the puréed fish with the sauce and beat to a smooth paste over a bowl of ice. Beat in a dash of Cognac and fold in 1 egg white, beaten stiff, to 2½ cups of fish mixture. Keep at all times over ice. The mix should have the consistency of well-whipped cream. Traditionally quenelles are shaped by being piped through a pastry bag in 1-inch strips, but they can be formed by shaping with 2 teaspoons briefly dipped into hot water. Gently drop the shaped pieces into a buttered cold skillet, leaving room between them for expansion. Gently pour on a boiling poaching liquid, preferably fish stock, to just cover the quenelles. Simmer uncovered for 8 to 10 minutes. These can be served cold as an hors d'oeuvre, or hot and plain as a first course, or with a sauce such as Newburg for a main dish.

For another quenelle recipe, see French Pike Quenelles.

FISH ROULADES

A roulade is an unusual way of serving preserved or precooked seafood, either for a light supper or as an appetizer. It is of course related to the jelly roll. The base for this version is a medium white sauce.

ROULADE BASE

2 cups medium white sauce, warmed   1 tbsp. sugar
4 eggs, separated

Remove sauce from the heat and add sugar and beaten egg yolks. Beat egg whites until stiff and fold in. Grease a jelly roll pan (10 by 15 inches) or cookie sheet. Line with wax paper and grease paper thoroughly. Dust paper with flour. Spread batter on the paper, and bake at 325° for 40 minutes, or until the top is golden. Turn out immediately on a fresh sheet of wax paper and peel off the paper that clings to the top. Spread surface with moistened filling and roll up like a jelly roll. Serve with a compatible sauce. The roulade can be reheated, briefly, over hot water, covered, and served with or without a sauce.

SEAFOODS IN BATTER

The batter into which bite-size pieces of fish or shellfish are dipped before deep-frying is another way of varying the flavor of the seafood. Use your own choice of herb and liquid.

BASIC FRYING BATTER

1 cup sifted flour	1 egg, slightly beaten
½ tsp. salt	1 cup liquid (water, flat beer or
½ to ¾ tsp. minced herb	milk)

Mix together the flour, salt and herb. Lightly beat the egg into the liquid; add to dry ingredients all at once and stir only until they are moistened. If the batter fails to cling to the seafood at first, dip food first into plain flour.

MAKES enough for 2 to 2½ lbs. seafood.

ITALIAN FRYING BATTER

½ cup flour	dash of white pepper
1 tsp. baking powder	2 tbsps. oil or melted butter
3 eggs, beaten	1 tbsp. sherry or brandy (optional)
½ tsp. salt	

Sift together flour and baking powder. Add beaten eggs, salt and pepper. Stir in the oil, and wine if used, and beat thoroughly. Dip bite-size pieces of seafood into batter. Fry in oil or fat heated to 375° until golden.

MAKES enough for 1 to 1½ lbs. seafood.

CHINESE TEMPURA BATTER

½ cup milk
¾ cup sifted flour
2 tbsps. cornstarch
1 tsp. baking powder

1 tsp. salt
2 tsps. oil, preferably peanut
2 eggs, lightly beaten

Add the milk, flour, cornstarch, baking powder, salt and oil to the lightly beaten eggs. Beat until smooth.

MAKES enough for 3 lbs. seafood.

FISH SOUFFLÉS

Soufflés are usually considered difficult. They don't have to be, and they are a delicious way of stretching leftover cooked seafood. Not only that, they can be assembled and frozen uncooked and kept for up to 3 months.

⅓ cup flaked cooked fish or minced cooked shellfish
1 tbsp. flour
¼ cup liquid (milk, or half fish stock and half milk)

1 tbsp. butter
1 large egg, separated
1 extra egg white
⅛ tsp. cream of tartar
salt

Blend flour with a small amount of the liquid, mixing well until it is lump-free. Heat remaining liquid with butter gently until the butter melts. Pour blended flour mixture all at once into hot liquid and stir constantly until sauce comes to a boil. Remove from heat. Beat the egg yolk slightly, add some of the hot sauce, and blend thoroughly until the yolk is warmed a bit. Stir the mixed yolk into remaining hot sauce. Beat the egg whites with cream of tartar and pinch of salt until peaks (whose tips droop a bit) form when the stopped beater is lifted from the bowl. Stir one quarter of the stiff whites into the sauce mix. Stir in the cooked seafood. Scoop the rest of the whites onto the top of the hot mix. Fold the whites into the sauce; use a soft spatula, and bring a bit of the sauce over the whites; this will help keep the soufflé from collapsing. Do this folding quickly and with a light touch. Scoop gently into an ovenproof dish, preferably straight-sided, that has been well buttered and dusted with grated cheese or flavored fine crumbs; fill soufflé dish no more than two thirds full./

If the soufflé is to be cooked immediately, first put a pan with enough water to come up at least half way on the baking dish into the lower third of the oven. Preheat oven to 350°. Regulate the heat so that the water doesn't quite simmer. Set the soufflé dish in the pan of water and bake for about 35 minutes. Soufflé is done when top is browned and risen and there is some slight shrinkage from the dish. The baked soufflé can be held in the oven, with the heat off, for a while. Serve in the dish in which it was cooked, or turn out onto a heated serving dish.

SERVES 1.

This basic recipe can be increased to make more servings. When increasing the other ingredients, use less than the multiple of cream of tartar, that is, 4 whole eggs and 4 egg whites with approximately ⅜ tsp. cream of tartar.

Freezing a Soufflé

Freeze the uncooked soufflé in its dish with the top covered with foil until frozen hard. After the soufflé is frozen, dip the dish into hot water for a few seconds to loosen it; slip out the soufflé and wrap in freezer paper or foil. When you want to cook the soufflé, prepare the same dish with butter and crumbs. Preheat the baking dish at the same time you preheat the oven, but do not defrost the soufflé itself. Bake at 350°, in the water bath, for about 50 minutes.

NOTE: It is not practical to freeze a soufflé containing more than 4 eggs, as it will not cook through properly.

SEAFOOD MOUSSE

A mousse is a light way to serve almost any kind of uncooked seafood since it uses a purée.

about 1¾ cups boned and skinned seafood	¾ cup flour
3 cups white-wine fish stock	2 whole eggs
½ cup water	2 extra egg whites
4 tbsps. butter	salt and pepper
1 tsp. salt	flavoring compatible to seafood
	½ to ⅔ cup chilled heavy cream

Boil the stock rapidly to reduce to 1½ cups; remove ½ cup and reserve. Continue to boil remainder and reduce to ½ cup. To this ½ cup, add water, butter and 1 tsp. salt. As soon as the butter is melted remove from the heat and add all the flour at once. Beat well to blend and continue to beat over medium heat for a minute or two until the mixture leaves the side of the pan. Remove from the heat. Make a depression in the mixture and add 1 whole egg. Beat vigorously to blend. Repeat with the second egg and each egg white separately. Let cool or chill.

Purée the seafood in a grinder or blender to make 1½ cups using reserved stock. Beat well with 1½ cups of first mixture until the mousse mixture has enough body to hold shape. Beat in the flavorings of your choice and beat in the cream, a spoonful at a time, being sure the mixture continues to hold its shape. Spoon into a greased 4-cup mold, or individual molds, to within ¼ inch of the edge. If the mousse is prepared ahead, it can wait refrigerated for several hours if covered with a sheet of buttered wax paper./Set the mold in a pan of boiling water and pour enough additional boiling water around the mold to come up two thirds of the way up the sides. Put in lower third of a preheated 375° oven. Bake for about 1 hour, or until the mousse swells a bit around the top of the mold. Pour off accumulated liquid before unmolding onto a hot plate. Serve with an appropriate hot sauce.

SERVES 4 to 6.

FISH IN PASTRY CONTAINERS

CRÊPES

Crêpes are the French version of the American pancake. They can be used for everything from appetizers to desserts. They are not only easy to make, but can be frozen for some weeks. Freeze them individually on a cookie sheet; when they are well frozen, stack them in a plastic bag; handle gently so as not to snap them into bits. When you are ready to use them, and it takes only minutes to defrost them if they are frozen and stored this way, they are handy casings for almost anything. Usually after filling they are topped with a sauce of some kind and thoroughly heated in a 350° oven.

Batter for Crêpes

3 large eggs
¾ cup unsifted flour

¼ tsp. salt
1 cup milk

Beat the eggs until light. Add remaining ingredients and beat smooth. Let stand for 1 hour, covered but not refrigerated, before cooking. Heat a heavy skillet until water drops jump. Lightly grease the skillet with butter; add enough batter to barely cover the bottom; quickly rotate the skillet to spread batter into a thin layer. When browned, turn and cook the other side. The whole cooking takes not much more than 1 minute.

MAKES about 12 (8-inch) crêpes, 16 (6-inch) crêpes, or 24 (4-inch) crêpes for hors d'oeuvres.

CREAM PUFFS

Cream puffs, which are equally impressive containers for sauced small bites of seafood, are almost as easily made as crêpes and also can be kept frozen for several weeks.

1 cup water	1 cup sifted flour
⅛ tsp. salt	4 eggs
½ cup bland cooking oil	

Heat the water to boiling; add salt and oil and bring again to a boil. Reduce heat as low as possible and add flour all at once. Stir hard until a ball forms. Remove from the heat and add the eggs, one at a time, beating very well after each. Beat until the mix is very thick and shiny and "cracks" from the spoon. Shape by teaspoon for appetizers, tablespoon for entrées, separating well on a cookie sheet. Bake in a preheated 450° oven for 20 minutes; reduce temperature to 350° for an additional 20 minutes.

MAKES 48 appetizers, 12 main courses.

PIECRUST

Piecrust, your own favorite home recipe, a mix, or prepared shell from the market, is also handy for attractively packaging these sauced bites. Bake the filled crust in tart pans, or fold into dough packets for individual servings, or use a full-size pie pan, with or without a top crust. If you do not use a top crust, be sure there's enough sauce so that the pie doesn't dry out. If you use a top crust, slash it so that steam can escape. Bake only as long as you normally do to insure the crust is done.

French pie and tart pastry, which is richer than ours, is more of a bother but is worth the effort. Both uncooked dough and baked shells can be frozen.

FRENCH PIE AND TART PASTRY (PÂTÉ BRISÉE)

2 cups instant flour
½ cup butter, in ¼-inch pieces, chilled
3 tbsps. hydrogenated vegetable shortening, in ¼-inch chips, chilled

1 egg
⅓ cup ice water
pinch of sugar
1 tsp. salt

Blend flour, butter and shortening with a pastry blender, or with an electric mixer at medium speed, until particles of fat reach the size of very coarse meal. Beat egg, water, sugar and salt to blend, and pour into flour mixture. Mix quickly to form a rough mass, or *just* until the beaters clog. Turn onto a board and press into a mound. Taking 2 tbsps. at a time, smear the dough flat with the heel of your hand for final blending. Scrape all the bits into a ball, dust lightly with flour, and wrap in wax paper to chill for at least 2 hours. (Dough can now be frozen, if you wish.) Roll out dough ³⁄₁₆-inch thick.

To Prebake Tarts or Pie Shells
Fit part of the dough into a special tart pan, or a cake pan with a removable bottom, or pat over the greased underside of a pan of any shape that doesn't have a removable bottom. Trim edges of dough. If the dough is *in* a pan, prick the bottom at ¼-inch intervals, line with greased foil, and fill with dried beans to keep the dough flat. If dough is arranged *over* the bottom of a pan, prick it in the same way. Refrigerate for 1 hour. Bake at 425° for 4 to 6 minutes, or until the shell is barely colored. Remove the foil and beans, if you've used them. (Shells can be frozen at this point, if you wish.) Then finish baking until the pastry is crisp and golden, 10 to 15 minutes.

If the tart is to be filled before the baking is completed, let the shell cool after removing foil and beans. Then fill with prepared filling and finish baking.

Pies with 2 crusts are filled while the dough is still unbaked, but after the lower crust in the pan and the rolled dough for the top are chilled in the refrigerator.

MAKES 1 8- to 10-inch tart shell or equivalent.

SEAFOOD QUICHE

Bake the tart shell up to the point where the foil and beans are removed. Chill. Make the filling. Measure enough chopped cooked seafood to equal two thirds of the volume of the tart pan (for a 4-cup tart shell, measure 2⅔ cups). Mix seafood with barely enough liquid or light sauce to moisten. Spread in the cooled shell. Top with enough custard to fill the shell to within ⅛ inch of the rim. (Make custard with 1 cup milk to 1 egg, with appropriate seasonings, or in those proportions for tarts of various sizes.) Dot top with chips of butter. Bake on a greased cookie sheet at 375° for 25 to 30 minutes, or until custard tests done. Serve hot, warm or cold. A 9-inch quiche will make about 6 servings, or more if cut into tiny pieces for appetizers.

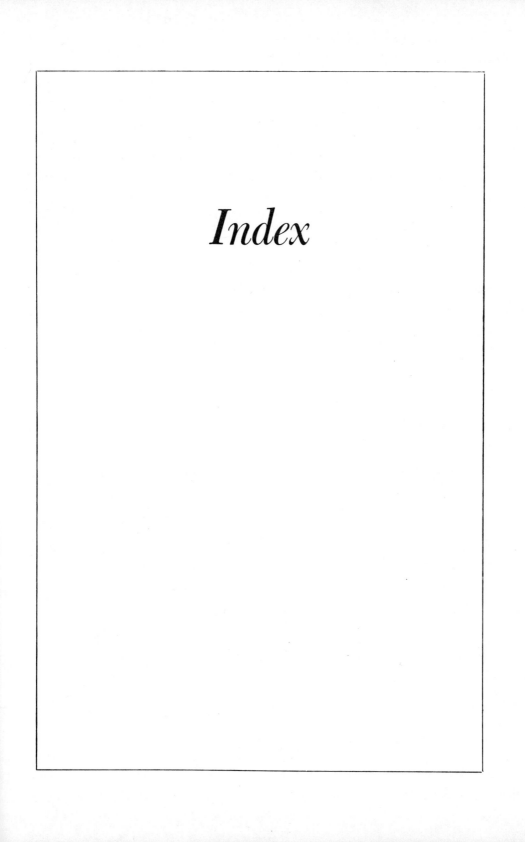

Index

Following in alphabetical order are many of the names of fishes to be found in North American fresh and salt water. The only names capitalized (even though a proper name) and with page references are those from the American Fisheries Society's *List of Common and Scientific Names of Fishes from the United States and Canada,* Special Publication No. 6 of 1970. The same capitalization system is used for subspecies following the general species headings. All other names are cross-referenced to these preferred names.

In some cases a preferred name is incorrectly applied to another species, in which case both names are capitalized in an entry and connected by "or." "Or" is also used to link the various preferred species to which a particular colloquial name is applied, regardless of the locales in which it may be used. In the case of these listings, it is undoubtedly preferable to have a positive identification of your fish.

Some freshwater fishes are called by the same name (at least locally) as some saltwater species: in this case I have identified the source by *fw* for fresh water, *sw* for salt water, hoping to lessen the difficulty of identification. Freshwater basses are abbreviated in much the same manner: *lm* for Largemouth, *sm* for Smallmouth.

In parentheses following the capitalized entries is the page span for the whole section in which appropriate recipes will be found. Also in these parentheses are my personal opinions as to edibility: pr for poor, fr for fair, gd for good, ex for excellent. Below the species listing are recipes which particularly refer to the species.

Please note that not all subspecies of some of the fishes are to be found in the same basic category. When this occurs, page references follow the specific subspecies listing. The other subspecies, unless also so noted, fall in the same category as the general heading.

Fishes which are on the International Game Fish Association record list are denoted by an asterisk; those on the International Spin Fishing Association record list with #.

Note: Many species, even though edible in some areas, may be non-edible in others, or at certain times of the year. If you are new to an area, always check locally as to edibility.

abadejo—Grouper
Abalone (214–50)
   how to prepare, 214
   California, steaks, 235
   West Coast, cream soup, 222
   West Coast, pot roast, 235
acara aya—Snapper, red
ahi—Tuna
air drying, 43–44
aguja—Needlefish
alabato—Halibut
albacora—Swordfish
Albacore*# (84–114, ex)
albacore, false—Tunny, Little
alilonghi—Albacore
allison—Tuna, Yellowfin
allmouth—Goosefish
amberfish—Yellowtail
Amberjack*# (198–201, pr)
ampla—Marlin, Blue
Anchovy (148–63, pr except brined)
angler—Goosefish
Argentine (148–63, fr panfish or pickle)
aspic, basic fish, 362
atun—Tuna

bacalao—Cod
bacalo—Grouper
bait stealer—Pinfish
baking, preparing for, 21–23
balloon fish—Puffer, Northern
banana fish—Bonefish or Ladyfish
barb—Kingfish, Southern
Barracuda, warning, 10 (51–83, fr) Great,*# Pacific#
   Bolivian baked fillets, 76
barracuda, ocean—Wahoo
Barrelfish (84–114, fr)
barrilete—Bonito
Bass (*fw*) (51–83, fr to ex) Largemouth,# Smallmouth.# black—*sm* or *lm*, Spotted or Redeye or Rock; blue-green see Sunfish or Pumkinseed; big-mouth—*lm;* brassy—Yellow; bronze-backer—*sm;* buffalo see Warmouth; calico see Crappie; green—*lm;* kentucky—Spotted; lake—Rock; oswego—*sm;* Redeye or Rock; Rock or see Warmouth; silver—White; Spotted; Striped or White or Yellow; Suwannee; swego—*sm;* sunfish—Rock; White—*sm* or Rock; yellow—*lm* or *sm*